This publication was evaluated by the ENCATC Research Award Jury

Jury President
Gerald Lidstone, ENCATC President, Goldsmiths, University of London, United Kingdom

Jury Members
Elena Borin, Link Campus University, Italy

Dan Green, H. John Heinz III College of Public Policy and Management at Carnegie Mellon University, United States

Annika Hampel, Max Planck Institute for the Study of Crime, Security and Law, Germany

Michal Lázňovský, Academy of Performing Arts in Prague, Theatre Faculty, Czech Republic

Richard Maloney, New York University, United States

Jaime Alberto Ruiz Gutiérrez, Universidad de los Andes at Bogota, Colombia

Annick Schramme, University of Antwerp, Belgium / Antwerp Management School, Belgium

Li-Jung Wang, Taiwan Association of Cultural Policy Studies (TACPS)

About ENCATC

ENCATC is the leading European network on cultural management and policy. It is a membership NGO gathering over 100 higher education institutions and cultural organisations in over 40 countries. ENCATC was created in 1992 to encourage the exchange of knowledge, methodologies, experiences, comparative research and regular assessment of the sector's training needs in the broad field of cultural management from a European point of view through a wide range of working groups, projects, activities and events. ENCATC holds the status of an NGO in official partnership with UNESCO, of observer to the Steering Committee for Culture of the Council of Europe, and is co-funded by the Creative Europe programme of the European Union.

About the ENCATC Research Award

The ENCATC Research Award on Cultural Policy and Cultural Management was launched in 2014 by the European network on cultural management and policy, ENCATC, to reward the best recently published PhD thesis presented by a young researcher.

This prestigious recognition aims to stimulate academic research in the field of cultural policy and cultural management with an emphasis on its applied implications. The ENCATC Award also has the ambition to contribute to the process of creating a network of scholars who are competent in doing comparative research projects in cultural policy and cultural management.

The ENCATC Research Award is granted each year to a recently published PhD thesis exploring, through comparative and cross-cultural research, issues at stake and taking a step from evaluative (descriptive) to comparative applied research. In addition, this Award is rewarded to a PhD thesis that can inform policymaking and benefit practitioners active in the broad field of culture.

Series Titles by ENCATC Members

N° 7 – Cécile Doustaly (Ed.), Heritage, Cities and Sustainable Development. Interdisciplinary Approaches and International Case Studies, 2019.

Series titles by ENCATC Research Award Winners

N° 8 – Biljana Tanurovska-Kjulavkovski, Modelling Cultural and Art Institutions, 2021.

N° 6 – Alba Zamarbide Urdaniz, Buffers beyond Boundaries. Bridging theory and practice in the management of historical territories, 2019.

N° 5 – Rebecca Amsellem, Museums go International. New strategies, new business models, 2019.

N° 4 – Elena Borin, Public-Private Partnership in the Cultural Sector. A Comparative Analysis of European Models, 2017.

N° 3 – Annika Hampel, Fair Cooperation. A New Paradigm for Cultural Diplomacy and Arts Management, 2017.

N° 2 – Alessia Usai, The Creative City. Cultural Politics and Urban Regeneration between Conservation and Development, 2016.

N° 1 – Elodie Bordat-Chauvin, When Cultural Policies Change. Comparing Mexico and Argentina, 2015.

Social Innovation, Social Enterprises and the Cultural Economy

Faced with a depleted planet and a series of connected crises, socially minded agents and entities within the world of culture and the arts are reacting from within. With insights from sociology, economics and cultural management and policy, this book aims to chronicle the journey of SMart – a cultural and artistic social enterprise now present in eight European countries – in order to illustrate such organisation's efforts to achieve its potential for social innovation and transformation. Tackling the endemic precariousness and intermittency of work through innovative arrangements for cultural workers and artists has been central to these efforts. In many cases, however, this activism not only had a direct impact at the level of individual and collective labour but also has transformed the ways culture is 'governed'.

Readers of this book will better understand the connection between social innovation and culture and the arts; gain awareness of the trends and transformations within the field of culture and cultural work and their connection with institutional arrangements; and critically engage with the processes, challenges and benefits of scaling up and diffusing social innovation.

The debates presented will be of relevance to scholars and students across disciplines, policymakers at both EU and national levels, practitioners and social activists.

Rocío Nogales Muriel is Director of the EMES International Research Network (Belgium/Spain) and Adjunct Professor at the University of Zaragoza (Spain).

ENCATC Advances in Cultural Management and Policy

ENCATC has recognized that education in the fields of cultural management and cultural policy cannot and should not be separated from on-the-ground research. Following this stipulation, since its creation, ENCATC has always been very active in pursuing, publishing, presenting, and disseminating research in the fields of cultural management and cultural policy to improve and build upon understanding of cultural management and cultural policy issues. In line with the above-mentioned approach, ENCATC established a series of book publications by research award winners and its members.

The series exists to foster critical debate, publish original cultural management and cultural policy research, and facilitate discussion about cultural management and cultural policy among researchers, educators, scholars, policy makers, and cultural managers. It is also intended to serve as reference material for educators and to support lifelong learning for policymakers and practitioners.

Book Series Publishing Partner
ENCATC European network on cultural management and policy
1, Avenue Maurice
B-1050 Brussels
Belgium
Tel: 0032.2.201.29.12
info@encatc.org; www.encatc.org

Books in the series include:

Social Innovation, Social Enterprises and the Cultural Economy
Cultural and Artistic Social Enterprises in Practice
Rocío Nogales Muriel

Social Innovation, Social Enterprises and the Cultural Economy

Cultural and Artistic Social Enterprises in Practice

Rocío Nogales Muriel

Routledge
Taylor & Francis Group
LONDON AND NEW YORK

eNCATC
The European network on cultural management and policy
30
SINCE 1992
ANNIVERSARY

First published 2023
by Routledge
4 Park Square, Milton Park, Abingdon, Oxon OX14 4RN

and by Routledge
605 Third Avenue, New York, NY 10158

Routledge is an imprint of the Taylor & Francis Group, an informa business

British Library Cataloguing-in-Publication Data
A catalogue record for this book is available from the British Library

ISBN: 978-1-032-37829-9 (hbk)
ISBN: 978-1-032-37831-2 (pbk)
ISBN: 978-1-003-34214-4 (ebk)

DOI: 10.4324/9781003342144

Typeset in Sabon
by Newgen Publishing UK

This publication has been peer-reviewed.

The European Commission support for the production of this publication does not constitute an endorsement of the contents which reflects the views only of the authors, and the Commission cannot be held responsible for any use which may be made of the information contained therein.

Contents

Foreword

The work presented here deals with a topic of notable social significance: how innovation proposed by a social enterprise and from a solidarity economy logic can contribute to social (and, in a certain way, economic) transformation. That is, the core of this book is to study whether a specific subset of social enterprises active in the field of culture and the arts could contribute to the intricate economic, environmental, political and cultural transitions capable of providing transversal solutions.

This book is an adaptation of the doctoral thesis of Rocío Nogales Muriel, carried out within the CECUPS research centre of the University of Barcelona, under the supervision of Professor Teresa Montagut. The author won the 7th ENCATC Research Award in 2020, which is the most important international recognition for excellence in cultural policy and cultural management research.

The work reviews – in a critical and pedagogical way – the different conceptual approaches developed by the literature on the subject, incorporating a comparative view based on three case studies to contrast the different hypotheses raised. It analyses the adaptation of the same social innovation strategy in three European countries with different institutional, social, political and economic characteristics and contexts: Austria, Hungary and Spain. This makes it possible to evaluate both those aspects in which social innovation is adapted to the demands of each of these national contexts, and those others where the sector, its organisations and professionals are organised following similar parameters of social transformation.

The selection of the field of study – the world of arts and culture – is particularly relevant given its singularity in terms of social value, structuring of its value chains and institutional organisation. The forms of organisation of work in cultural production and distribution follow patterns that are uncommon to those of other economic sectors. Only in some cultural domains with a greater presence of public employers (museums, libraries, archives or municipal cultural services) or with medium-sized companies (radio/television, audio-visual, symphony orchestras) is the ratio of employees close to the average proportion of the economy, but in the rest of the cultural sector, not only is the percentage of freelance independent professionals particularly high, often linked to temporary projects, but it is also dominated by small (and very small) companies and organisations.

Likewise, the incentive and remuneration system does not follow the conventional guidelines of an alleged economic 'rationality'. In order to materialise the creative project, most artists and cultural professionals accept lower remuneration than other professionals with similar educational levels. The level of self-exploitation is also not comparable to that in other sectors, since it not only occurs in the initial phases of seeking professional recognition but often continues throughout the professional career, particularly among those who do not achieve status at the top of the podium. On the other hand, the high intensity and short-term nature of many contracts and projects, with frequent periods without activity, generate notable imbalances in the social contribution systems. And all this occurs without considering the long periods of conceptualisation and pre-production of projects that are difficult to incorporate into limited budgets due to the difficulty of making the projects viable.

In this context of fragility, the search for innovative social solutions that will allow risk-sharing and reduce management and transaction costs is seen as an increasingly broad need. The development of the SMart cooperative, initially in Belgium and later spreading to various European countries, is a particularly appropriate response to many of these challenges. However, the European reality is believed to be much more heterogeneous than from other continents, since both the models of state support and intervention in culture and the development of the cultural system itself have followed different paths. In this sense, the three case studies presented – Austria, Hungary and Spain – allow the author to analyse the different levels of adaptation of the same kind of social innovation strategy. The selection of countries has been made based on evaluating the typology of welfare models, civil society and social enterprise patterns and the variations in terms of development of the social and solidarity economy and the evolution and shape of the cultural system.

A study such as the one written by Rocío Nogales Muriel could not end without a final chapter that includes a set of recommendations that are particularly useful for policymakers, umbrella organisations and cultural operators themselves. Thus, I recommend its reading to all those interested in the analysis of the forms of cultural organisation and the mechanisms of the social and solidarity economy to innovate and provide fairer and more supportive models for solving problems.

Lluís Bonet
Professor of Applied Economy, University of Barcelona

Acknowledgements

This volume is the result of a doctoral path completed at the University of Barcelona, ending with the thesis titled 'Social Transformation and Social Innovation in the Field of Culture: The Case of the SMart Model and Its Adaptation across Europe'.[1] Three years after its completion, the European network on cultural management and policy (ENCATC) granted it the Research Award and included it in the ENCATC Book Series on Cultural Management and Cultural Policy Education, published by Routledge. All my appreciation and gratitude go first to my dear colleagues at ENCATC, who took the time to read my work and supported it in such a magnificent way.

I am thrilled to follow the steps of my predecessors, particularly Dr. Biljana Tanurovska-Kjulavkovski, whose contributions explored the emerging institutions of culture and art that operate as 'agencies of action', situated within civil society culture or within the independent cultural scene to promote a bottom-up approach. Indeed, these new types of institutionality also constitute the core of my work, particularly with regard to the material conditions of artists and creators and their potential contribution to the eco-social crisis we are facing. In this sense, this book aims to nurture an approach to arts and culture that is critical and constructive and, at the same time, questions the status quo that serves a minority of creators and 'audiences'; it detects and raises the visibility of the (informal and institutionalised) grassroots innovations developed by agents themselves; it studies their development and dares to make concrete proposals to create an institutional pluralism that guarantees cultural rights; and contributes to the well-being of all, including the planet.

Undertaking a path of creative enquiry entails plenty of unknowns to be tackled, very often amidst great solitude. This is the case for scholars and poets, also for musicians, painters and actors. In my case, I was blessed to count on the support of a community of peers; colleagues (particularly from the EMES International Research Network); a wonderful thesis director, Professor Teresa Montagut; and family and friends who have encouraged me to continue: this book would not have been a reality without them.

Time provides an excellent perspective to see the ideal improvements of a contribution like this one. Some of them are related to the methodology, and others to the capacity of bringing out the results to the relevant audiences. Regarding the former, the potential for further qualitative and quantitative analyses is much larger than what is reflected in this volume. Moreover, should the occasion arise, members should be incorporated into the research process as a way to include their perceptions in the conclusions. Regarding the latter, there is the perceived need to increase the level of transfer from the academic realm to the social one, with special emphasis on dissemination beyond the specialised cultural sphere. Unfortunately, this is something that demands a phenomenal quantity of resources that are not always at hand, together with the support of other agents capable of embracing the recommendations and bringing them to the right level of political relevance. Having said this, the current version of the thesis has been revised to address some of the comments made during the final phases of the writing and defence process; the contents have also been slightly updated when possible.

My deepest gratitude goes to Professor Tracey Coule for her reading and feedback, as well as to Dr. Kai Roland Green for the detailed and careful proofreading of the final manuscript. I am grateful to the Routledge team – Terry Clague and Naomi Round Cahalin – as well as to Isabel Verdet from ENCATC for their guidance and support throughout the publication process. A great thanks goes to Professor Lluís Bonet and Susanne Westhausen for their amazing foreword and afterword, respectively. Thanks to my family and my partner for their care and support through the most difficult times, but mostly for the moments of joy they are able to create and share with me everyday.

This award comes with a combination of honour and responsibility for me, both for the people involved and for the relevance my contribution may have. From that point of view, and as a community culture activist, I had to redefine my relationship with my 'object of study'. As important as academic contributions are, it is no longer enough to cite, contribute to the scientific discussion and accumulate mentions and publications. The moment we are going through within our communities obliges us to position ourselves as citizens as well. Indeed, we are to speak loud and clear but also to accept dialogue and the evolution of our views and standpoints as a natural way of reflecting what we have learned in the way. The compass leading the road ahead should point towards a better life for all beings and a planet that is deeply cared for, as each of us care for our home.

Note

1 The PhD research was conducted between 2013 and 2017. The period covered in the field work ended in 2015, but some additional material is included as a way to update the current status of the SMarteu project and that the three national cases were studied in detail until the beginning of 2020, which coincides with the start of the Covid-19 pandemic.

Introduction

This volume aims to explore the potential of social enterprises to bring about social transformation in the field of culture and the arts, thereby contributing to social innovation against the global backdrop of the eco-social transitions (Matthies, 2017). Faced with a depleted planet and interlinked crises, various agents and entities in the world of culture and the arts are reacting from within. One of these efforts revolves around innovative work arrangements for cultural workers and artists to fight against endemic precariousness and intermittency. In many cases, this activism has overspilled the labour area to demand cultural rights from entirely new ways of governing culture.

The way in which culture is present across societies is connected to how other areas of human action evolve in each of these societies. In the public sphere, culture is connected to economic and political events as well as to notions about the 'collective', while in the private realm, culture is intrinsically linked to practices of individual subjects. When speaking about Europe, the notion of the public sector underwent a profound transformation with the welfare state reforms of the 1970s and the 1990s, which contributed to the consolidation of neoliberal policies across Europe (Gilbert, 2003; Fraser, 2013). Private initiative and responsibility became the basis for economic growth, with the state having a role to ensure an equally enabling environment for private action. Culture being one of the central areas of action of welfare states, these transformations had a direct impact on culture and the arts across Europe. Cultural workers and artists traditionally used to work under precarious labour arrangements, having to face shrinking budgets and antagonistic discourses about the true meaning and value of culture and the arts. The financial and economic crisis of the late 2000s was the logical materialisation of these new policies and ideas about the role of and interaction between the public and the private spheres. This, coupled with changing attitudes towards the depletion of natural resources, which is contributing to an accelerated destruction of the planet, places our societies at crossroads that requires immediate action.

New values and practices are emerging everywhere in the face of the current cultural crisis, driven by actors and groups to whom new technologies

DOI: 10.4324/9781003342144-1

have offered an opportunity to express themselves as never before, as is the case of 'ethical hackers' (Castells et al., 2012: 13). Indeed, there are many models for change in progress that question the circle of despair that results from the perceived lack of a future and paralysis of action, which translates into life and social uncertainty and more despotic and violent authoritarianism (Morin, 2011; Garcés, 2017). Building on the work of previous social movements and new institutional arrangements, new citizen-led initiatives are (re)appearing that are questioning and offering an alternative to previous socioeconomic-political orders and systems (Nogales Muriel, 2022). They remain undetected by the vast majority, but they continue to thrive, away from media exposure and general public attention.

The solidarity economy, enlightened by emancipatory experiences in Latin America and its quest for economic democracy as a prerequisite of any kind of political democracy, constitutes one of the areas of practice and research that has gained a new centrality in the context of interlinked crises (Coraggio, 2011; Fraser, 2013; Hillenkamp and Laville, 2013; Laville et al., 2016). The social economy, which developed hand in hand with solidarity economy in Europe, has witnessed an increase in economic weight and recognition by political institutions across European member states and at the international level.[1] Such increases, however, have not come without tensions caused by an over-corporatisation of some of its most representative forms (e.g. multinational cooperatives), and therefore the loss of the real participatory dimension to organisations centred on ensuring their financial sustainability (whether from the market or the public sector) or the focus on the interest of members as opposed to the general interest (single-stakeholder organisations).

At the epicentre of these tensions, social enterprises emerged across Europe around four decades ago (Borzaga and Defourny, 2001). Embedded in the social and solidarity economy (or the third sector, according to national idiosyncrasies), the transformational potential of social enterprises was soon recognised by disadvantaged groups and public administrations (Defourny and Nyssens, 2010). More recently, groups of citizens working for the general interest across various activity areas or within transition-enabling initiatives have also embraced this transformational potential. Social enterprises stand at the crossroads of markets, civil society and the public sector, placing them in a critical position: depending on the logic, actors and contexts at play, social enterprises can develop into institutional arrangements that ensure to varying degrees the general interest through their social mission and sustainability (via the real participation of all their stakeholders) and the carrying out of economic activities that are fully consistent with their missions (EC, 2020). It is within this type of sustainability that social transformation can be located despite the risk of becoming a tool for the dismantling of the welfare state through the surrender of public service provisions (Hulgård, 2011).

The underlying assumption of this research is that social enterprises rooted in the principles and values of social and solidarity economy provide a context whereby the logics of competition and collaboration intrinsic to social innovation processes can coexist and contribute to systemic social transformation. Social enterprises achieve this through the mobilisation of bottom-up intelligence and social creativity of their actors who together *bricolage* intelligent solutions. These solutions include tapping on resources of a different nature (i.e. stemming from the market, reciprocity and redistribution), encouraging multi-stakeholder governance or taking advantage of top-down support offered by traditional institutions. In other words, some social enterprises can be considered as adaptive, self-organising systems that are able to cope with drastically changing contexts (Defourny and Nyssens, 2021).

In addition to their social mission, social enterprises have been pioneering in some areas of activity which offer not only innovative products and services but also a new way of governing the relationship with stakeholders – in many cases different types of stakeholders. To give an example, in the 1990s, Belgian social enterprises led the recycling and reuse industry as well as the development of fair trade (Huybrechts, 2016), while in the 2000s, social enterprises across Europe were leading a paradigm change in the production and governance of community-led renewable energies (Huybrechts and Haugh, 2018). Culture and the arts are emerging as one of the new areas of activity where the social and solidarity economy, and particularly social enterprises, is bringing to light a transformative potential nested in communities that remained hidden or ignored (Nogales Muriel, 2019; Caruana and Nogales Muriel, 2020).

Cultural and Artistic Social Enterprises (CASE), a specific subset of social enterprises in the field of culture and the arts, appear to be a promising institutional arrangement and constitute the core of this volume. I propose the term 'Cultural and Artistic Social Enterprise' or its acronym – CASE – to refer to social enterprises that are active in the field of culture and the arts. On the one hand, the reason for proposing a new term is based on the relevance of culture for social enterprises. As explained throughout this book, culture and the arts constitute an activity field that is quintessential to the general-interest goal pursued by social enterprises: firstly, culture is considered to have a meritorious dimension and, secondly, social enterprises are natural providers of this kind of goods and services (Tortia and Borzaga, 2020).[2] On the other hand, it may be useful to have a specific expression to refer to social enterprises which, as a result of their presence in concrete activity fields, may be characterised by unique traits (in addition to the general traits shared by all social enterprises).[3]

This volume analyzes the SMart model, which in the form of CASE aims to ensure the administrative and legal coverage of cultural and creative workers during periods of not only professional activity but also unemployment. The initial analysis focuses on how SMart achieved its mission before studying how it expanded its model from Belgium to other geographic regions. In addition to the core administrative services, innovative services for artists and creative professionals continued to be developed, including political lobbying related to labour rights and social protection and a European platform for artists' mobility. Initially created as a Belgian association in 1998, it has grown exponentially and expanded to 40 cities in nine European countries, gathering over 95,000 members working under a common, national umbrella cooperative.[4]

The replication of such a successful model brought about profound transformations, both within the organisation and into the field of culture and the arts. A central challenge in the process was the empowerment and inclusion of the actors involved, aiming to increase the emergence of creative solutions to help the organisation adapt itself to new contexts and conditions.

During a time characterised by 'transitions', this volume sets out to explore how innovative institutional arrangements such as social enterprises are being developed by the cultural and artistic sector (Nogales Muriel, 2023). Their embeddedness in the social and solidarity economy places these contributions in a wider framework of social transformation with the potential to contribute to other transition areas (food, energy, housing, mobility, etc.). In this sense, they become allies of the many social agents that are pressing with immediacy to address and reverse, to the degree possible, some of the trends at play in our societies that put our sustainability and well-being at risk.

Bottom-up and collective citizen movements constitute the most common mode of the creation of social enterprises in Europe (EC, 2014). Moreover, this bottom-up impulse represents one of the ways to ensure that the actors concerned achieve the necessary economic emancipation as a precondition for reaching political emancipation. This emphasis on the emancipatory potential of social enterprises is reflected in the focus of social enterprise research, which moved from the entrepreneurial and managerial aspect of this institutional arrangement to its socially transformative potential. Indeed, social enterprises are considered here as effective institutional mechanisms whereby citizens can articulate their aspirations to transform society following the collective interest and the common good.

Likewise, culture and the arts represent the battlefield where some issues related to the contemporary way of being in the world are enacted (e.g. life and work precariousness). Simultaneously, it also constitutes the remaining territory where new possibilities for emergent systems can be imagined. In this regard, culture and the arts share with the social and solidarity economy the very impulse of conceiving, articulating and carrying out alternative ways of functioning in the world. Social and solidarity economy together with culture and the arts are likely to result in concrete practices that open up to a self-improving process of cooperation, innovation and political action with the ultimate effect of producing positive social transformation. This process is summarised visually in Figure 0.1.

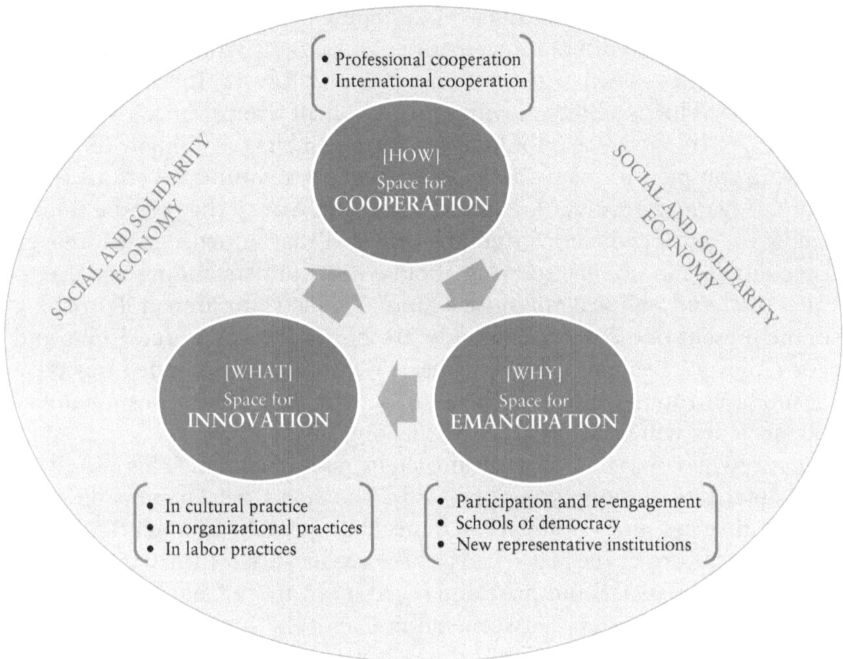

Figure 0.1 Spaces for social transformation opened by CASE.

Culture and the arts and CASE have the potential of being a vector for change of social transformation. I locate the innovative, transformative experience of SMart in the emancipatory social innovation tradition, combining it with an emergent systems approach based on an ecological conception of society, its actors and interactions. Considered as an emergent system, its adaptive capacity is of paramount importance to its own survival but also, most importantly, to the achievement of its self-assigned goals. In this context, the SMart case, both at the level of its original organisational development (via SMartbe) and its geographic expansion (via its adaptation to nine different national contexts), provides a unique example of adaptive strategies and processes.

The present research was undertaken with full awareness that the creation of new paradigms in economic, social and political behaviours will involve the revision of how we understand science. In this sense, the research is located in the emergent systems approach whereby science itself needs to be re-embedded into the processes that it studies. What is at stake is moving from 'academic' to 'post-academic' science that 'values above all intellectual qualities such as curiosity, creativity, and knowledge, and does so for the sake of the public rather than the corporate good' (Nordmann et al., 2011: 1).

Moving towards a 'post-normal' science involves extending the disciplinary knowledge of 'normal science' to cope with a complex world, with real actors equipped with muting identities and subjectivities plus the irreducible uncertainties ahead of them (Funtowicz and Ravetz, 1993; Nordmann et al., 2011). This is about moving beyond science for science's sake to a complex type of science that looks beyond itself and has as ultimate objective of solving complex problems in society via the activation of various types of knowledge and epistemologies, articulated in a way that can be understood by the actors who constitute the origin of that knowledge. Moreover, science should aim not just to bring about correct understanding but also to create social and political conditions more conducive to human flourishing than the present ones, as articulated by the critical theory of the 1960s and 1970s (Adorno, Benjamin, Horkheimer). Without this expanded objective to ensure a virtuous connection between science and society, sustainability of our societies will be jeopardised in the long run.

The present volume is divided into eight main chapters. This introductory chapter sets the context for the study. The next three chapters describe the main theories and notions that frame the research. Chapter 1 sets the contexts of culture at the crossroads of the twenty-first-century transitions. Chapter 2 covers social enterprise and social innovation; Chapter 3 explores the intricate relationship between culture and the arts; and Chapter 4 describes how social innovation diffuses, with an emphasis on the adaptation and replication of social enterprises.

Chapter 5 dives into the *source* or *mother* social enterprise at the heart of the scaling-up process under study – SMartbe. It also summarises the main stages involved in the launch of the European platform – SMarteu – by gathering the various national SMart offices. The chapter ends with an evaluation of the scaling-up strategy based on a statistical analysis of the data.

Chapter 6 opens with the set of criteria applied to select the three country cases (Austria, Spain and Hungary) and is then divided into the contextual general analysis and the description of the national SMart implementation efforts. An institutional framework analysis on the three countries is conducted to describe the development of civil society, the third sector and social enterprise as well as the cultural field. Chapter 7 analyses the national organisations that have implemented the SMart model in the three select countries – SMartat (Austria), SMartib (Spain) and SMarthu (Hungary). Each national SMart experience is described at length, emphasising its history, the functioning and services offered, and the lessons learned and prospects for the future. Each country's analysis ends with some conclusions about the context and repercussions for the launch of SMart.

Chapter 8 gathers the main conclusions of the study, particularly the specific lessons learned about the SMart model. Then, some recommendations follow for both policymakers and practitioners. Lastly, a discussion about limitations of the research and possible contributions is offered along with suggestions for some valuable avenues for future contributions to the academic discussion.

Notes

1 The EU Social Economy Action Plan was adopted by the European Commission in December 2021. This Action Plan puts forward concrete measures to help mobilise the full potential of the social economy, building on the results of the 2011 Social Business Initiative and the 2016 Start-Up and Scale-Up Initiative (https://ec.europa.eu/social/main.jsp?catId=1537&langId=en). At the international level, the UN created in 2013 a special inter-agency task force devoted to the social and solidarity economy that also includes non-UN observer members (https://unsse.org). A UN resolution on the social and solidarity economy is expected to be approved in the current of 2023.

2 Meritorious (or merit goods) are those in the best interest of the population but that cannot be provided following a private exchange logic as users and beneficiaries are not in a position to pay for them. Culture, education and health services are classic examples of merit goods as it concerns asymmetric information and issues of equality or equity.

3 In this sense, I followed the naming trend of social enterprises active in specific socially innovative fields, such as *WISE* ('Work Integration Social Enterprise') (Nyssens, 2006) or *REScoop* ('Renewable Energy Sources Cooperatives') (www.rescoop.eu).

4 The research included in this volume covers the time period of 1998 until December 2015, which necessarily involves leaving a vibrant developmental period outside of the analysis of the consolidation of the SMart model. Given the profound impact of the Covid-19 pandemic in culture and the arts, it is worth reminding oneself that such impact falls out of the timeframe of this volume, which explains the lack of reference to it. Please see in Chapter 8 the section entitled 'Methodological Proposals for Future Research'.

References

Borzaga, C. and Defourny, J. (eds) (2001) *The Emergence of Social Enterprise*, London: Routledge.

Caruana, V. and Nogales Muriel, R. (2020) Unlocking the Transformative Potential of Culture and the Arts through Social Enterprise, Empower-SE Stakeholder Brief No. 5. Liege: EMES/COST. Available at https://bit.ly/2KR9n2S.

Castells, M., Caraca, J. and Cardoso, G. (eds) (2012) *Aftermath: The Cultures of the Economic Crisis*, Oxford: Oxford University Press.

Coraggio, J. L. (2011) *Economía social y solidaria. El trabajo antes que el capital*, Quito: Abya Yala.

Defourny, J. and Nyssens, M. (2010) Conceptions of Social Enterprise and Social Entrepreneurship in Europe and the United States: Convergences and Divergences, *Journal of Social Entrepreneurship*, Vol. 1 (1), pp. 32–53.

Defourny, J. and Nyssens, M. (2021) *Social Enterprise in Western Europe: Theory, Models and Practice*, London: Routledge.

European Commission (EC) (2014) *Mapping study of social enterprises and their ecosystem in Europe*. Brussels: European Commission.

European Commission (EC) (2020) *Social Enterprises and Their Ecosystems in Europe. Comparative Synthesis Report*, Luxembourg: Publications Office of the European Union. Available at https://europa.eu/!Qq64ny [accessed 15 November 2021].

Fraser, N. (2013) Marchandisation, protection sociale, émancipation : vers une conception néo-polanyienne de la crise capitaliste. En I. Hillenkamp, J.-L. Laville (dir.) *Socioéconomie et démocratie. L'actualité de Karl Polanyi*, Toulouse, Erès, pp. 39–63 .

Funtowicz, S. O. and Ravetz, J. R. (1993) The Emergence of Post-Normal Science. In R. Schomberg (von) (ed.), *Science, Politics, and Morality: Scientific Uncertainty and Decision Making*, 85–123, Dordrecht: Kluwer.

Garcés, M. (2017) *Nueva ilustración radical*, Madrid: Anagrama.

Gilbert, N. (2003) *Transformation of the Welfare State: The Silent Surrender of Public Responsibility*, Oxford: Oxford University Press.

Hillenkamp, I. and Laville, J.-L. (eds) (2013) *Socioéconomie et démocratie. Actualité de Karl Polanyi*, Paris: ERES.

Hulgård, L. (2011) Social Economy and Social Enterprise: An Emerging Alternative to Mainstream Market Economy? *China Journal of Social Work*, Vol 4 (3), pp. 201–215.

Huybrechts, B. (2016) *Fair Trade Organizations and Social Enterprise. Social Innovation through Hybrid Organization Models*, New York: Routledge.

Huybrechts, B. and Haugh, H. (2018) The Roles of Networks in Institutionalizing New Hybrid Organizational Forms: Insights from the European Renewable Energy Cooperative Network, *Organization Studies*, Vol. 39, pp. 1085–1108.

Laville, J. L., Hillenkamp, I., Eynaud, P., Coraggio, J. L., Ferrarini, A., de França Filho, G. C., Gaiger, L. I., Kitajima, K., Lemaître, A., Sadik, Y., Veronese, M. and Wanderley, F. (2016) Théorie de l'entreprise sociale et pluralisme: L'entreprise sociale de type solidaire (Theory of Social Enterprise and Pluralism: Solidarity-Type Social Enterprise), *Revue Interventions économiques*, Vol. 54, pp. 1–16.

Matthies, A.-L. (2017) The Conceptualisation of Ecosocial Transition. In A.-L. Matthies and K. Närhi (eds), *The Ecosocial Transition of Societies: The Contribution of Social Work and Social Policy*, London: Routledge, pp. 17–35.

Morin, E. (2011) *La Vía. Para el futuro de la humanidad*, Barcelona, Paidós Ibérica.

Nogales Muriel, R. (2019) Comunes y nuevas institucionalidades en el arte y la cultura: ¿hacia una soberanía y democracia cultural? (The Commons and New Institutionality in the Arts and Culture: Toward a Cultural Sovereignty and Democracy?), RIESISE, *Revista Iberoamericana de Economía Solidaria e Innovación Socioecológica*, Vol. 2, pp. 77–102.

Nogales Muriel, R. (2023) Regaining Our Imagination to Face Up and Resist Reality: Lessons from Ecofeminism, the Commons, and the Social and Solidarity Economy for Culture and the Arts in a Transition Context. In R. Mirabella, T. Coule and A. Eikenberry (eds), *Handbook of Critical Perspectives on Nonprofit Organizing and Voluntary Action: Concepts, Applications and Future Directions*, Cheltenham: Edward Elgar.

Nordmann, A., Radder, H. and Schiemann, G. (2011) *Science after the End of Science? An Introduction to the 'Epochal Break Thesis'*, Pittsburgh, PA: University of Pittsburgh Press. Available at www.upress.pitt.edu/htmlSourceFiles/pdfs/9780822961635exr.pdf [accessed 15 November 2021].

Nyssens, M. (ed.) (2006) *Social Enterprise. At the Crossroads of Market, Public Policies and Civil Society*, London: Routledge.

Tortia, E. and Borzaga, C. (2020) Social Enterprises and Welfare Systems. The Role of Multi-Stakeholder Governance and Price Discrimination, *Journal of Entrepreneurial and Organizational Diversity*, Vol. 9 (2), pp. 23–44.

1 Culture at the Crossroads of the Twenty-First-Century Transitions

1.1 Setting the Context: Evolutionary Trends in the Labour and Cultural Spheres

Five general trends related to deep transformations currently in progress are relevant to the focus of this volume. The first one relates to the transformation of labour from stable to precarious (including labour subjectivities on the part of workers). Neoliberal policies have exacerbated three mutations already in play:

- The crumbling of the *wage society*, which makes it impossible to use 'the criteria and categories with which labour's relationship with value was calculated, [when] its accountability now appears totally inadequate' (Turrini and Chicchi, 2013: 2). This inadequacy has turned work into an 'immeasurable activity'.
- The consolidation of a *knowledge society* framework, where work expresses itself as an activity of general intellect 'that is generated in informal spaces of social cooperation outside the traditional property frame of the capitalist society' (Turrini and Chicchi, 2013: 2).
- The identification between life and capitalism, resulting in the 'bio-economic accumulation paradigm' in the current global era, which causes generalised insecurity and uncertainty beyond the sphere of work without social and/or institutional mediation (López Petit, 2009; Turrini and Chicchi, 2013).

The combination of these three transformations has resulted in a transversal trend of labour precariousness and the emergence of arrangements based on 'flexicurity' – combining the increased demand for flexibility by employers with workers' need for certain levels of labour and social security (Nanteuil (de), 2005). Although this precariousness was already something present in the field of culture and the arts, public budget cuts have caused an interlinked destruction of the institutions and ecosystems where artists had traditionally thrived (albeit precariously in the case of the vast majority)

DOI: 10.4324/9781003342144-2

(ENCC, 2021). This situation has contributed to increasing the insecurity of cultural workers and artists.

The triumph of the entrepreneurial mantra – a second trend identified as background of the present study – has also reached the cultural and artistic sector in the form of a drive towards entrepreneurship (Rowan, 2010). Unfortunately, the meeting of a culture of entrepreneurship with culture and the arts has resulted in further insecurity for workers as well as additional negative consequences, such as the self-exploitation of workers based on values such as passion, commitment and vision (Zafra, 2017).

The commodification of culture and the arts and its progressive melting into the economic flow of mass consumption has a long-standing tradition (Adorno and Horkheimer, 1944; Adorno, 1991; Harvey, 1989), so one can hardly say that it is a new trend. What represents a new trend – and the third background trend of this study – is the exacerbation of this commodification by the understanding of recent cultural production as a mass spectacle, targeted to a mass media market under the guidance of major corporations undergoing progressive merging processes (Gotham and Krier, 2008; Muñoz López, 2007).

The fourth trend is the gradual mutation or disappearance of traditional cultural institutions. Indeed, the enlargement of the concept of 'specialised cultural sphere' has brought about the incorporation of a broad spectrum of activities and new actors (the public, civil society and private companies) and a weakening of the ties to the classical arts (Rodríguez-Morató, 2012). A fascinating aspect from research standpoint is how this mutation is taking place, particularly the emerging cultural and artistic practices that are being generated from civil society or within the independent cultural scene (Tanurovska-Kjulavkovski, 2021). Such transformation is evident both in major, flagship public organisations and more grassroots initiatives: even though they are affected by the decrease in public budget, they are finding ways to stay afloat via the activation of new resources and the consolidation of their relevance to a post-crisis society (REACC, 2021).

The role of new technologies in the development of bottom-up and networked initiatives, and the increasing disaffection of citizens with politics and the way 'the public' is being governed, constitutes the last trends of this analysis.

The cultural and creative sectors have been directly impacted by this convoluted context and the endemic precariousness that has come to be associated with them. Contracts in general, let alone long-term contracts, are increasingly rare, and making a decent living out of a creative or cultural job constitutes an exception. Project-based or work-for-hire contracts abound; however, they overlook not only previous experience or training but also the preparation required to produce a high-quality cultural event or output, such as rehearsals or travel. Also, very often, contracts are oral and thus remain in the informal domain, forcing many of these activities to remain in the informal economy. An additional disadvantage is the absence of opportunities usually available to employees, such as social benefits and coverage, training and occupational risk prevention courses. This complex situation is more damaging in countries where there is not a tradition of ensuring the social benefits of these workers via the legal status of artists. Overall, the field has become so precarious that it is challenging to engage in any policy or strategic discussion around culture and the arts.

1.2 Recent Transformations within the Field of Culture and Cultural Work

Four phenomena at play within the cultural sector are particularly relevant for this discussion: firstly, the transformation of artists and cultural workers into the epitome of the 'new professionals'; secondly, the emergence of new institutional arrangements (social enterprises) within the cultural and creative sectors; thirdly, the defining traits of new transformative collective entrepreneurial endeavours under the umbrella of what is known as the social and solidarity economy; and fourthly, the incorporation of culture into the transition discourse. These four lines constitute the research backbone of this volume and are succinctly explained below.

1.2.1 Artists and Cultural Workers as Epitomes of the 'New Professionals'

Even though the current employment situation of cultural workers and artists has contributed to increasing their insecurity, an important paradox is at work. Creativity, flexibility, vision, drive and autonomy, which were considered endemic traits of workers in the cultural and creative sector, have nowadays joined the list of 'universal desirable attributes' across activity fields (Ruido and Rowan, 2007; Turrini and Chicchi, 2013).

The typical profile of creative professionals working on a project basis is that of 'flexible, multi-skilled and independent individuals with good communication skills. They have dared to take risks and know where to find useful sources of information. They have extensive contact lists, are well established within networks, and show themselves to be capable of employing other artists and of bringing people from varying backgrounds together' (SMartbe, 2012).

The endemic precariousness of artists and cultural workers has prompted reactions both from the sector itself and from public administrations. An important strand is the transformation in public cultural agencies and the increase in cultural participation of various audiences, which have facilitated the building of bridges between culture and the social and solidarity economy.

1.2.2 The Emergence of New Institutional Arrangements for Culture: Social Enterprises

Although many collective endeavours stemming from culture remain in the realm of the informal economy, some are set up as organisations. Social enterprise, a new institutional arrangement considered as a vehicle for social innovation, has slowly begun to emerge in the field of culture. This context offers a unique test-bed to study how the new 'culture society' (Rodríguez Morató, 2012) has brought about new institutions, actors and dynamics (e.g. the new centrality of culture in society and a process of dedifferentiation of human spheres of action) to provide a response to the modified cultural demands of citizens.

Social enterprises have existed in Europe for over four decades, and their natural environment from which they emerge was the social and solidarity economy. Despite the numerous efforts to define social enterprise, there is not a shared definition in Europe: some approaches link them to the social and solidarity economy in direct connection with a transformational aim, while others consider them as new ways of doing businesses that tackle neglected societal challenges in a more efficient way.

However, most actors do share a basic understanding of the three core traits of social enterprises: the existence of a social mission aimed towards society's general interest, a sustained economic activity and a participatory mode of governance. This social mission translates into the achievement of a social transformation that contributes to the well-being of a wider social group or society at large. In the case of Europe, the main impulse behind the creation of a social enterprise has been citizens following a process of bottom-up recognition of shared needs and identification of possible solutions.

1.2.3 Transformative Collective Entrepreneurial Endeavours: The Social and Solidarity Economy

The social and solidarity economy has existed in Europe for centuries, but its existence as a relevant historical development has remained concealed in the past half century, mainly due to clashing political agendas (Laville and Amaro, 2016). At a moment when several conditions are rendering visible the contributions of the social and solidarity economy to the well-being of European societies, there is an urgency to reframe the way in which social enterprises and the social and solidarity economy interact. Regarding social enterprises, a note of caution should be added about the risk of instrumentalisation by some traditional institutions, such as the strong isomorphic trends in public policies providing core financing for their functioning, or the strong Anglo-Saxon influence in some approaches to social enterprise, which nevertheless cannot be ignored given the interconnected nature of socioeconomic exchanges in our society. Regarding the traditional social economy, the extremely uneven development across countries has led to over-institutionalisation in some countries (Spain or France) and complete unawareness of the notion in others (Germany or Finland). While, in principle, support from institutions is something desirable, it can also lead to corporatist behaviours that prevent new dynamics and players from entering the playing field. Indeed, this was the case with the social and solidarity economy: the combination of both terms (*social* and *solidarity*) under a single label is something relatively recent that can be traced historically, mainly in the socioeconomic history of France and Spain.

The urge for this reframing stems also from the fact that the wider social and solidarity economy represents the larger cultural context in which social enterprises can fulfil their transforming potential. Such an approach helps to explain how the notions of 'social enterprises' and the larger 'social and solidarity economy' are connected. By focusing on complementarities rather than on divergent traits, the quarrels over definitions and borders that have characterised the interactions among some *families* of the social economy (cooperatives, associations, mutual societies and foundations), and between the social economy and the solidarity economy – or even the third sector – in the last decades in Europe, can be left behind (Nogales Muriel and Nyssens, 2023).

1.2.4 The Incorporation of Culture into the Transition Discourse

No reflection about social transformation and sustainability can be made without connecting it to the wider issue of the economic and environmental transitions (including energy and food transitions). These multiple transitions are not detached phenomena, but rather connected strategies that have been severed from each other, limiting their systemic reach and ability to implement transversal alternatives. In this context, the questioning of emerging types of institutions and actors (such as social enterprises) should be connected to the ability to acknowledge and facilitate this intricate array of multiple coexisting transitions. These are 'unpostponable transitions' that cannot be postponed and that require inter alia a new set of institutional arrangements (Calle, 2013).

The sustainability and transformation discourse entered the realm of culture and the arts with a slight delay, if compared with areas such as energy and food. The potential of culture and the arts to transform societies began to be tapped in policymaking around the 1980s in Europe, the US and Australia (Duelund, 2003). The approach was an 'instrumental cultural policy' focusing on funding 'flagship' cultural institutions and initiatives, as well as creating jobs and contributing to national GDP (Belfiore, 2002). This instrumentalisation of the delivery of culture by local, national and European public bodies undoubtedly benefited some cultural organisations and even contributed to connecting culture to other policy areas such as social and labour policies (Pascual i Ruiz, 1998). However, 'art for art's sake', or the intrinsic value of culture as a concrete embodiment of proposals stemming from citizens, was put aside (Lindeborg and Lindkvist, 2013). More recently, the term 'creative industries' was coined, and the UK hailed it shortly before approving the construction of the £789M 'Millennium Dome'. It was presented as a site for national pride and celebration, but turned out to be a failure (Grodach and Silver, 2013).

One of the results of this instrumentalisation was a 'toolkit approach' to impact the assessment of culture and the arts that 'has tended to privilege quantitative approaches borrowed from the disciplines of economics and auditing' (Belfiore and Bennett, 2010: 5). The present research suggests that the perceived urgency of the various unpostponable transitions has called upon existing and emerging cultural actors and institutions to occupy a more central role in facilitating these transitions, although there is confusion about how exactly culture and the arts can make a meaningful contribution. In addition, the risks of instrumentalisation and banalisation remain very high.

Currently, culture and the arts are evoked in everyday practice and literature from diametrically opposing views that range from the 'commodifying' conception of culture as spectacle in a global market, detached from territories and any specific cultural background, to the 'emancipatory' view, whereby the process of collectively creating culture expresses collectively imagined and plausible alternatives that suit the majority of citizens while addressing pressing challenges related to the transitions. Against the dominant dystopian discourse, liveable futures demand 'ecotopias' capable of seducing and moving to concrete action (Fernández Casadevante, 2020). I propose a 'cultural transition', which takes into account the place and role of culture and the arts in changing society, to be tackled transversally. That social enterprises set up by artists and creators pursuing a cultural/artistic mission are beginning to be more visible and numerous is a promising start. Now, the question is whether (and how) Cultural and Artistic Social Enterprise (CASE) takes into account the other unpostponable transitions our society is currently also facing.

1.3 SMart and Its Presence across Europe

An interesting strategy to tackle such pressing problems was the core case of this study, SMart – an organisation that exists to reinforce the autonomy of artists as well as cultural and creative professionals. Although the organisation was not directly aimed at producing art, it eventually contributed to cultural and artistic production by supporting creators. Indeed, this member-based association has the ultimate goal of ending precariousness, first in the cultural and the arts sector and more recently in other labour activity sectors characterised by endemic precariousness. Indeed, today, academics from various disciplines and policymakers consider SMart a reference for the fight against precariousness at the international level (Díaz Molina et al, 2019; Iglesias-Onofrio and del Moral-Espín, 2023).

In 1998, a music band manager (Pierre Burnotte) and an industrial engineer (Julek Jurowicz) teamed up to provide a practical support to professionals of culture and the arts as well as other 'creative workers' who mostly work intermittently and on a project basis. They identified a growing demand from cultural workers facing difficulties vis-à-vis the administrative aspects of their status and activities. They founded SMartbe, which included a group of non-for-profit organisations under Belgian law. SMartbe rapidly met a significant success, in terms of both membership size (173 employees, 50,000 members and a turnover of €130 million by 2012) and the recognition of the 'SMart model' by labour and culture public administrations and private actors.

The basic ideals underpinning the SMart model are mutualisation and a non-profit nature, which also included the pooling of income and reinvestment of any economic surplus in the organisation; it is a democratic structure where every member has a voice and access to the tools to make projects of cultural creative professionals come to fruition.

By initially providing indirect support to artistic production, SMart was able to gather a community of otherwise unconnected peers. By sharing losses and benefits in a solidarity-based manner, they minimised individual risks. By doing things in a participatory way, they co-created goals and strategies to help them reduce mission drift, irrelevance and lack of commitment. Wyzomirski and Cherbo (2003: 196) defined this type of support institution as 'organisations that provide services and support for individuals, groups and institutions engaged in the arts and culture' and which have traditionally taken the form of federations and other professional organisations.

SMart gave priority to addressing the operational aspects of the services offered, which in turn resulted in artists and creative workers having the time and peace of mind to do their job. By making administrative and financial tools available to members for the exercise of their professional activities and ensuring communication among them, opportunities for new creative activities emerged. By forming an archipelago where once there were only islands, a critical mass was reached. In turn, this critical mass allowed the identification of critical needs for the sector (and sub-sectors) and the formulation of strategies required to address them. Putting risks and benefits in common and absenting from a profit-maximising aim constitute the two pillars over which SMart developed its core services. Nurtured by the values that social and solidarity economy treasures, a socioprofessional association emerged with the goal of ensuring the representation of their members, not only in a symbolic way but also down to the last detail, including making decisions regarding the way generated resources are to be invested and framing of strategic directions of the organisation. External support was ensured in the form of a specific legal framework for the artistic sector, along with financing and academic support.

On the basis of this proven concept and the close relationship with other European actors in the field of culture and the arts, the idea of geographically expanding beyond Belgium appeared as early as 2004. From that moment on, a double move was set in motion: on the one hand, the opening of national SMart offices and the setting up of an informal European platform, whose transitioning into a formal organisation is still to be seen; on the other hand, the internal process of transformation of the social enterprise SMartbe (mother organisation) to the new responsibilities that being the leader of such an ambitious agenda required.

However, this process was (and continues to be) a complex and challenging one. Its main difficulties are illustrated in the various adaptation processes the model went through as a result of the geographic expansion that began as early as 2006. In ten years, SMart had to overcome the organisational challenges of its expansion while keeping its 'mother' organisation solid and ensuring participative governance. Recognising the local level and its idiosyncrasies, encouraging exchange and constructive criticism among actors, allowing for failure, enhancing participation and having enough time for going through processes without being rushed are concretising the vision of SMarteu.

The SMart model constitutes the first socially innovative initiative emanating from the social and solidarity economy in the field of culture that has scaled up across Europe with a view to expanding its social impact. This adaptation and replication has reached different degrees of implementation across the nine countries where the model has been exported to. The richness of experiences that accumulate in this process provides a source of lessons regarding the innovation paradigm applied to culture and the arts and how CASEs are able to (co-)construct new spaces for social transformation in the cultural field at local, national and European levels.

SMart is active in the field of culture and rooted in the social economy (with the sharing of risks and benefits and its not-for-profit aim) as well as the solidarity economy (through cultural workers' and artists' economic and political emancipation). Considering the critical moment of transformation of both areas (social and solidarity economy and culture), the relative effective and symbolic power they can deploy in processes like geographic expansion can determine the success or failure of the initiative. Our research concluded that the SMart model harnesses and promotes the creation of spaces for cooperation (including international cooperation), innovation (with a proven business model), emancipation (both economic and political with the backing of a critical mass of actors and key alliances) and criticism of the approach to culture as a commodity in the global market. Together, these four areas can be considered emancipatory social innovation, leading to social transformation in the field of culture on the European scale, making SMart one of the most meaningful (and rarest) examples of how this transformation can take place transnationally.

References

Adorno, T. W. (1991) *The Culture Industry: Selected Essays on Mass Culture*, London: Routledge.

Adorno, T. W. and Horkheimer, M. ([1944] 2002) *Dialectic of Enlightenment*, Stanford, CA: Stanford University Press.

Belfiore, E. (2002) Art as a Means of Alleviating Social Exclusion: Does It Really Work? A Critique of Instrumental Cultural Policies and Social Impact Studies in the UK. *International Journal of Cultural Policy*, Vol. 8 (1), pp. 91–106.

Belfiore, E. and Bennett, O. (2010) Beyond the 'Toolkit Approach': Arts Impact Evaluation Research and the Realities of Cultural Policy-Making, *Journal for Cultural Research*, Vol. 14 (2), pp. 121–142.

Calle, A. (2013) *La transición inaplazable. Salir de la crisis desde los nuevos sujetos políticos*, Barcelona: Icaria.

Díaz Molina, S., Martínez Vicente, E., Valiente, M.-C. and Saldivar, J. (2019) Blockchain for Empowering the Artistic Culture: The Case of Smart. Available at https://p2pmodels.eu/smart/ [accessed 25 November 2021].

Duelund, P. (ed.) (2003) *The Nordic Cultural Model*, Copenhagen: Nordic Cultural Institute.

European Commission (EC)(2014) *Mapping Study of Social Enterprises and Their Ecosystem in Europe*, Brussels: European Commission.

European Network of Cultural Centres (ENCC) (2021) *Invisible Damage: Cultural Centres across Europe Warn against Severe Long-Term Effects on the Foundations of Socio-Cultural Work*, Brussels: ENCC. Available at https://encc.eu/sites/default/files/2021-09/encc_report_invisible_damage.pdf [accessed 21 February 2022].

Fernández Casadevante 'Kois' (2020) Apología de la utopía (Apology of the Utopia), *CTX Contexto y Acción*, 24 August. Available at https://ctxt.es/es/20200801/Firmas/33157/ecologismo-utopia-relatos-casadevante-kois.htm [accessed 15 January 2022].

Funtowicz, S. O. and Ravetz, J. R. (1993) The Emergence of Post-Normal Science. In R. Schomberg (von) (ed.), *Science, Politics, and Morality: Scientific Uncertainty and Decision Making*, 85–123, Dordrecht: Kluwer.

Gotham, K. F. and Krier, D. A. (2008) From the Culture Industry to the Society of Spectacle: Critical Theory and the Situationist International. *Current Perspectives in Social Theory*, Vol. 25, pp. 155–192.

Grodach, C. and Silver, D. (2013) *The Politics of Urban Cultural Policy: Global Perspectives*, London: Routledge.

Harvey D. (1989) *The Condition of Postmodernity*, Oxford: Basil Blackwell.

Iglesias-Onofrio, M. and del Moral-Espín, L. (2023) Smart Ibérica Business Impulse Cooperative: 'Not Just a Means of Invoicing for Your Work'. In S. Pérez de Guzmán, M. Iglesias-Onofrio and I. Pais (eds), *Contingent Workers' Voice in Southern Europe*, pp. 75–94, Cheltenham: Edward Elgar Publishing.

Laville, J. L. and Amaro, R. (2016) *Social Innovation in Europe: What Relation with Solidarity Economy? Towards a Plural European Vision of Social Innovation*. Available at www.socioeco.org/bdf_fiche-document-4518_en.html [accessed 11 February 2022].

Lindeborg, L. and Lindkvist, L. (eds) (2013) *The Value of Arts and Culture for Regional. Development. A Scandinavian Perspective*, London: Routledge.

López Petit, S. (2009) *La movilización global. Breve tratado para atacar la realidad*, Madrid: Traficantes de Sueños.

Muñoz López, B. (2007) 'De las industrias culturales a los circuitos culturales la metamorfosis de un proceso ideológico' [From cultural industries to cultural circuits: the metamorphosis of an ideological process], *Sociedad y utopía: Revista de ciencias sociales*, No 29, 19–36.

Nanteuil (de), M. (2005) La flexibilité est-elle un choix rationnel? In M. Nanteuil (de) and A. El Akremi (eds), *La Société flexible. Travail, emploi, organisation en débat*, 51–78, Ramonville: ERES.

Nogales Muriel, R. and Nyssens, M. (2023) Empowering Knowledge and Training in Higher Education to Leverage Social Economy Action on Societal Challenges. In Krlev, G., Pasi, G., Wruk, D., Bernhard, M. (eds.) *Social Economy in Science – Transforming the Economy & Making Society More Resilient.* Oxford: Oxford University Press (forthcoming).

Nordmann, A., Radder, H. and Schiemann, G. (2011) *Science after the End of Science? An Introduction to the 'Epochal Break Thesis'*, Pittsburgh, PA: University of Pittsburgh Press. Available at www.upress.pitt.edu/htmlSourceFiles/pdfs/9780822961635exr.pdf [accessed 30 January 2016].

Pascual i Ruiz, J. (1998) *EMPIRIC: Third System, Culture, Employment*, Brussels: European Commission/Interarts.

Red de Espacios y Agentes de Cultura Comunitaria (REACC) (2022) *Delineando horizontes comunes para el arte y la vida en España: Resultados del primer estudio de la Red de Espacios y Agentes de la Cultura Comunitaria.* Available at https://reacc.org/primerinformediagnostico/ [accessed 21 February 2022].

Rodríguez Morató, A. (2012) The Culture Society: A Heuristic for Analyzing Cultural Change in the Global Age. In A. Sales (ed.), *Sociology Today: Social Transformations in a Globalizing World*, pp. 316–336, London: Sage.

Rowan, J. (2010) *Emprendizajes en cultura. Discursos, instituciones y contradicciones de la empresarialidad cultural*, Madrid: Traficantes de Sueños.

Ruido, M. and Rowan, J. (2007) In the Mood for Work. ¿Puede la representación alterar los procesos de valorización del trabajo cultural? In *Producta50: una introducción a alguna de las relaciones que se dan entre la cultura y la economía*, Barcelone: Yproductions. Available at www.workand-words.net/es/texts/view/500 [accessed 12 May 2022].

SMartbe (2012) *Developing Your Artistic Projects. The example of SMartbe Activities.* Available at www.smart-eu.org/media/uploads/2013/04/SMart-Activities-ENG.pdf [accessed 30 January 2016].

Tanurovska-Kjulavkovski, B. (2021) *Modelling Cultural and Art Institutions*, Brussels: Peter Lang Verlag.

Turrini, M. and Chicchi, F. (2013) Precarious Subjectivities Are Not for Sale: The Loss of the Measurability of Labour for Performing Arts Workers, *Global Discourse*, Vol. 3 (3&4), pp. 507–521.

Wyzomirski, M. J. and Cherbo, J. M. (2003) Understanding the Associational Infrastructure of the Arts and Culture. In V. B. Morris and D. B. Pankratz (eds), *The Arts in a New Millennium: Research and the Arts Sector*, 191–208, Westport, CT: Praeger.

Zafra, R. (2017) *El entusiasmo. Precariedad y trabajo creativo en la era digital* [Enthusiam. Precariousness and creative labour in the digital era], Barcelona: Anagrama.

2 Social Enterprise as a Vehicle for Social Innovation in Culture

2.1 Preliminary Concepts

Before entering into a discussion on social enterprises as a possible vehicle for social innovation in the field of culture and the arts, it is worth explaining what I understand by *social value* and *social transformation*. These terms are used sometimes interchangeably with *social innovation* itself, whereas in the present research they are not equivalent.

2.1.1 *Social Value*

The creation of 'social value', understood as a positive achievement for society overall, has been identified as the main objective of social enterprises (Lautermann, 2013). However, there are different ways of defining 'social value' depending on how 'value' is understood.

The notion of value has interested sociologists such as Max Weber and Emile Durkheim and economists such as Karl Marx and Vilfredo Pareto for a long time. However, after World War II, economists focused on the notion of *value* (singular), while sociologists (and anthropologists) focused on the world of *values* (plural). Bassi (2012) states that this separation rested on the assumption that there was both a unique (objective) dimension of value that measured the economic (monetary) value of goods and services and a subjective dimension of value based on judgements. The objective dimension was the area of study of economists, while the other side – 'the messy world of values where different points of view about what is good or bad are confronting themselves' (Bassi, 2012: 4) – constituted the study area of sociologists and economists. The economic approach to value has been predominant until the 2000s, focusing the discussion on the intrinsic (use value) versus the exchange (market value) values of goods and services.

T. Parsons' (1951) 'four functions scheme' was used to understand the four types of quantitative and qualitative increments in value ('added value') that social enterprises can produce: economic, political, social and cultural. In this framework, the specific contribution of social enterprises would be the production of a sense of responsibility towards the public, a number of

DOI: 10.4324/9781003342144-3

goods and services (the majority of them being of a relational, collective or meritorious nature) for organisations and territories and, in the end, a robust amount of social capital at all levels of social systems. Therefore, the main difference in the social value produced by social enterprises is not so much in 'what is produced but rather mainly in how to produce and above all with and for whom they produce' (Bassi, 2012: 7).

Social value will also be used in the current research as developing a 'social value proposition' in the sense that what a social enterprise offers 'needs to be of economic value to the people that it wants to attract' (Scholz, 2015: 18). That organisations with both a social aim and carrying out an economic activity sometimes fail to clearly articulate their social value proposition constitutes an obstacle to the creation of social value.

Lastly, the term *social impact* is associated with how the creation of social value is measured over time and focuses on outputs (short term, measurable) and outcomes (medium and long term and more complex to quantify). The profusion of performance-driven financing (both public and private) has resulted in an overuse of the term 'social impact', which is sometimes wrongly used interchangeably with 'social value'.

2.1.2 Social Transformation

Classical sociology has defined social transformation as large-scale changes such as revolutions, colonialism or long-term economic development, but more recently it has also been applied to the modifications that alter the inertia of organisations. Indeed, change can be brought about, as sociology has shown us, via social movements, political action, individual and network action and so on. The introduction of bottom-up instead of top-down transformations represented a unique turning point to widen our understanding of social transformation (Subirats, 2005).

For the present study, I locate social transformation in the wider context of multidimensional transitions we are facing today. Indeed, I distinguish among four transitions (economic, environmental, social and cultural) currently at play that include other deep transformations.

Sense-making and new participation structures constitute two key pillars for implementing transformation: the former provides meaning and includes a sense of vision, the discourses used to articulate it as well as ethical and emotional motivations, while the latter provides the concrete platforms (both physical and virtual) whereby collective action is organised and goods and services produced (Calle et al., 2013).

In addition to the larger transitional context of social transformation and its pillars, I focus on the 'process dimension' of social transformation: social transformation should not be conceived of as an outcome insofar as social and economic transformation should be combined with political and democratic innovation (Subirats, 2005). The new social enterprise breed that social cooperatives embody, which can be located in the social and solidarity economy, thrive on bringing about and maintaining this social transformation.

2.1.3 Social Innovation

Social innovation is widely understood as new solutions to existing social problems, usually in the form of services, products or new institutional arrangements (BEPA, 2010; Evers et al., 2014; Moulaert et al., 2014). An aspect that seems to generate agreement is the potential for replication in order to achieve any relevant social impact; therefore, social innovation replication has attracted a lot of scholarly attention. However, it is worth noting that the majority of research conducted on social innovation stems from the knowledge gathered from purely market-based firms and focuses on interventions (e.g. programmes, projects, actions, etc.) which limit the transformative potential of the studied social innovation (Osburg, 2013). Indeed, the tools developed for the traditional market are not transposable to the social field, mostly because they fail to recognise some of the essential traits at work in the social and solidarity economy, including the existence of different economic logics (redistribution and reciprocity as opposed to market exchange), the embeddedness in local contexts or the presence of participation mechanisms that allow internal and external stakeholders to play pivotal roles (Mendell and Alain, 2015).

Moreover, as some critics have noted, a significant part of the story of social innovation has been systematically ignored, particularly its connection to a tradition of solidarity-based movements (Laville and Amaro, 2016). This oversight has resulted in a biased notion of social innovation in the policies and discourses at play in the public space today in Europe. Interestingly enough, the actors of these forgotten European social innovation traditions were mostly the proto forms of social economy organisations that relied on solidarity principles during the nineteenth century. In short, the fatal combination of these two elements (ill-suited analytical tools and the invisibility of a part of the social innovation tradition) requires that the history of social innovation be retraced in the context of social and solidarity economy and reformulated inter alia through social enterprises that are active in the field of culture and the arts.

2.2 The Varied Landscape of Social Enterprise

In general, the dominant disciplines in the study of social enterprises have been economics and business studies. In the last decade, researchers in these fields have been very effective at explaining the economic rationale behind social enterprises (Zamagni, 2012) and the characteristics, dynamics and strategies of these organisations in an uncertain and resource-limited environment. In addition, the arrival of the 2008 financial and economic crisis and the turn towards austerity contributed to the advent of a more financial approach to social enterprise research, as illustrated by the vast body of literature on 'social' and 'impact investment'. Political science research – mostly in Europe – has also concerned itself with the study of the emergence and development of social enterprises, given the close contact these organisations have with European public administrations at all levels. Sociology has been instrumental in our understanding of specific issues such as social capital.

The series of theories gathered under neo-institutionalism (resource dependence theory, agency theory, stakeholder theory, etc.) were instrumental in incorporating a sociological dimension into institutional theory. This approach allowed the study of organisations in order to understand how they act and interact with each other and with other actors in the environment. The same approach was rapidly brought into the emerging social enterprise research field, resulting in the development of ad hoc approaches such as 'hybridisation' and the 'multi-stakeholder' approach (Battilana and Lee, 2014; Borzaga and Depedri, 2015; Doherty, Haugh and Lyon, 2014; Novkovic, 2019). Yet, an additional development around institutions and their transformation would be crucial for a study like the present one to take place: new institutionality. Taking as a departing point the progressive retrenchment of the welfare state, the deactivation of traditional institutions and the disaffection of citizens, this stream explores the emergence of new institutionalising dynamics and actors that appear in response to the inability of existing institutions to ensure the well-being of most members of society. Additional streams of sociological research of relevance to this inquiry are ecological theory and theory on emergent systems.

So far, social enterprise research has drawn heavily on management and political science approaches. In this context, sociology and particularly its new interdisciplinary approaches (such as ecological theory) constitute an interesting perspective from which to question the potential and limits of social enterprises as new working institutional arrangements. Moreover, the present study introduces social processes at work that aim to bring social institutions, structures and dynamics to light.

In this context, the development of the abovementioned innovative approaches and the comeback of social movement theory point to the need for additional explanatory devices to understand the 'social' dimension captured by social enterprise. Social enterprises could be considered as an organisational breed emerging from the convoluted economic and social environment of the turn of the twenty-first century, spanning from the 1980s to the 2020s. In these 40 or so years, a series of concatenated crises (not only economic or financial) and transformations has created a new set of reference points for any kind of social activity and thus the need to revisit the discipline-based tools available for research. Social enterprises may be considered as a very specific way in which such convolution has crystallised.

From a broad sociology standpoint, there is a need to revisit the presence and weight of social structures and social interactions at play in social enterprises, given the tension between the social mission and the economic goal. Moreover, the intricate array of transitions (social, economic, environmental and cultural) crossing this research calls for a reformulation of notions like 'boundaries', 'facilitation' and 'translation'.

As is the case with most social phenomena, the compartmentalisation of knowledge into disciplines falls short of the need for multidimensionality required to approach this knowledge. In addition, bringing forward new epistemologies is required to render visible knowledge-generating practices that have been overlooked or ignored by mainstream social sciences. In this context, approaches to scientific knowledge generation, such as 'complex science' or a more popular one called 'citizen science', allow for the involvement of bottom-up dynamics and the acknowledgement and activation of citizens as creators of knowledge (Sousa Santos (de), 2007; Jiménez-Bueno and Ramos, 2009).

In this context, I prioritised a sociological approach to the study of scaling-up strategies of CASE with a twofold objective. On the one hand, it allowed to expand the interest of sociology of culture in the area of how innovations get diffused, a topic of interest for sociologists for various decades now (Wejner, 2004). On the other hand, I aim to 'de-managerialise' some mainstream approaches to the interplay between 'innovation' and 'culture' by incorporating the role of actors and collective dynamics.

2.2.1 Conceptualising Social Enterprise

Social enterprises, beyond their recent growing recognition as a useful and innovative tool for employment creation and social cohesion, have a long-standing tradition in Europe (Light, 2005; Nicholls, 2006; Green, 2020).[1] However, they are far from being acknowledged by the general public: 'social enterprise' remains a polysemic and contested concept (Huybretchs and Nicholls, 2012), much as social innovation represents a quasi-concept (Jenson and Harrisson, 2013). Indeed, research indicates that there have been up to 45 different definitions of social enterprise between 1994 and 2014 (Fisac-García, 2015), clearly indicating that no shared definition currently exists (Galera and Borzaga, 2009; Defourny and Nyssens, 2021). Moreover, the concept continues to evolve over time (Kerlin, 2010; Teasdale, 2012).

Nevertheless, there is an understanding of the core traits of social enterprises that is shared by researchers – and, to some extent, by practitioners and policymakers – including the existence of a social mission aimed towards society's general interest, a sustained economic activity and a participatory mode of governance (Borzaga and Defourny, 2001; Defourny and Nyssens, 2021; EC, 2020). Regarding the most characteristic mode of creation of social enterprises in Europe, the first mapping study of social enterprises conducted across the 27 EU member states (plus Switzerland) identified that they are 'citizen-led' – that is, created under the impulse of a group of citizens (EC, 2014). Social enterprises are also created out of a marketisation trend of non-profit organisations and of the restructuring of the public sector in the form of spin-out organisations (EC, 2014).

For scholars who have been studying this phenomenon since the 1990s, it is now clear that the notion of social enterprise refers both to a brand-new organisation and to a new, entrepreneurial dynamic reshaping of existing ones (Borzaga and Defourny, 2001). Social enterprises constitute a structural trend that expands throughout all member states, although they have developed very differently from one member state to another: in some countries they have a strong presence and are integrated into public policies, while in other countries they are both poorly developed and understood (Galera and Borzaga, 2009; EC, 2020).

Usually, three main schools of thought are identified around social enterprise depending on which organisational dimension is emphasised (Defourny and Nyssens, 2012, 2021). First is the 'social economy school of thought', which is grounded in the long-lasting European experience with socioeconomic initiatives led by a group of individuals to address immediate social needs (Defourny, 2014). Around the 1970–1980s, specific policies supporting civil society to provide responses to unemployment emerged across Europe, creating the first well-documented wave of social enterprises, namely 'work integration social enterprises' (also known by their English acronym WISE). The goal of these enterprises was to reintegrate vulnerable people into the labour market by involving them in a productive activity; they were initiated by civil society actors in the 1970s in a crisis context with high unemployment (Nyssens et al., 2012). The comparative research carried out at the time showed that this type of enterprise was multi-goal and multi-stakeholder, with personal services being the most active in the activity fields.[2] Later on, as social enterprises became more well known, many continued to improve the field of personal services, while others began to innovate in fields such as renewable energies, fair trade and culture.[3] Despite this expansion of field boundaries, some actors, including public administrations, continued to promote a restricted view on the area of activity of social enterprises, which severely hampered their development (Galera and Borzaga, 2009).

The research of the EMES International Research Network (EMES), created by European researchers in 1996, included perspectives from sociology, political sciences and economics, among others. The subsequent European projects led by EMES used a set of criteria consisting of three dimensions captured in Table 2.1: economic and entrepreneurial, social, and participatory governance (Borzaga and Defourny, 2001; Nyssens, 2006).

This initial work led by researchers paved the way for recognition in other sectors, including policy-making at all levels. Indeed, in 2011, the European Commission adopted a definition within the first European strategy aimed at supporting the development of social enterprises in Europe – the Social

Table 2.1 EMES criteria for an ideal type of social enterprise

Dimension 1. Economic and entrepreneurial
1. A continuous activity of producing goods and/or selling services
2. A significant level of economic risk
3. A minimum amount of paid work
Dimension 2. Social
1. An explicit aim to benefit the community
2. An initiative launched by a group of citizens or civil society organisations
3. A limited profit distribution
Dimension 3. Participatory governance
1. A high degree of autonomy
2. A decision-making power not based on capital ownership
3. A participatory nature which involves various parties affected by the activity

Business Initiative (EC, 2011), which falls within this first 'social economy school':

> A social enterprise is an operator in the social economy whose main objective is to have a social impact rather than make a profit for their owners or shareholders. It operates by providing goods and services for the market in an entrepreneurial and innovative fashion and uses its profits primarily to achieve social objectives. It is managed in an open and responsible manner and, in particular, involves employees, consumers and stakeholders affected by its commercial activities.

Secondly, the 'earned-income school of thought' is based on market-based approaches to income generation and social change. For this approach, social enterprises are to become full market actors as a way to address social problems and find solutions for them (Defourny and Nyssens, 2010). To fully grasp this approach, the idea of a continuum of social entrepreneurial activity is useful (Dees, 1998; Nicholls, 2006), although it results in a too large number of operational social enterprise models.[4]

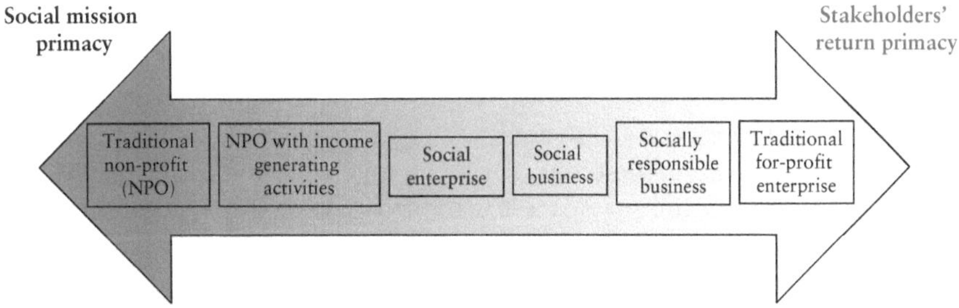

Figure 2.1 Social entrepreneurial activity spectrum.
Source: Adapted from Nicholls (2008) and Alter (2004).

Within this approach, any earned-income business or strategy undertaken by a non-profit to generate revenue in support of its social mission can be considered a social enterprise, including the 'social business' which is 'a non-loss, non-dividend company designed to address a social objective' (Yunus, 2010).

The third approach to social enterprise is the 'social innovation school of thought' which focuses on the innovations brought about by entrepreneurs who find 'new combinations' following Schumpeter's theory of innovation as a process of creative destruction (Defourny and Nyssens, 2013). Organisations like Ashoka have used this approach and considered entrepreneurs as 'change makers', although it is still to be confirmed whether the results of their action really have had an impact in the space occupied by social enterprises, since the opportunities for innovating in this type of social entrepreneurship appear to be found more and more often in the traditional private sector (Defourny and Nyssens, 2012).

Despite the focus of the current volume on social innovation and the apparently logical connection to this last school of thought, for the current research, I will consider mainly the EMES approach, which also inspired the European Commission to create a definition. By doing so, I am sure to deploy elements that are relevant to research and policy-making. Therefore, I consider social enterprises as

> organisations with an explicit aim to benefit the community, initiated by a group of citizens and in which the material interest of capital investors is subject to limits. Social enterprises also place a high value on their autonomy and on economic risk-taking related to ongoing economic activity.
>
> (Nyssens, 2006)

Before moving on to clarify conceptually similar concepts, I will provide a definition of social entrepreneurship. This is a challenge given the contextual and contingent set of activities it encompasses that are all subject to interpretive analysis and measurement (Bacq and Janssen, 2011; Huybrechts and Nicholls, 2012). Social entrepreneurship covers a broad range of socially innovative initiatives in a spectrum from for-profit to voluntary organisations. Ultimately, it is the agents' perspective that determines the various meanings or scopes of social entrepreneurship. If we consider the perspective of civil society actors, social entrepreneurship may be a driver of systemic social change (Nicholls, 2006), but it may also constitute a unique space for hybrid partnerships (Austin et al., 2006; Battilana and Lee, 2014), or a political transformation and citizens empowerment strategy (Alvord et al., 2004). From the point of view of public administrations, social entrepreneurship may represent a possible solution to state failures in welfare provision (Nyssens, 2006; Borzaga and Tortia, 2019). With regard to the traditional business sector, social entrepreneurship can offer a new market opportunity (Huybrechts and Nicholls, 2012).

2.2.1.1 Social Enterprise, the Social Economy, the Solidarity Economy and the Third Sector

There are three important notions that need to be clarified when talking about social enterprises: the 'social economy', the 'solidarity economy' and the 'third sector'. They are the wider economic areas from where social enterprises have traditionally emerged and thus provide the explanation to understanding their evolution and relevance in present-day Europe.

The 'social economy' appeared in France at the end of the nineteenth century and carries an enormous historical relevance for social enterprises. Indeed, arguably, most European social enterprises are rooted in the social economy, which gathers all those organisations whose major goal is to serve their members (or a larger community) rather than to seek profit for their investors. The social economy relies on democratic decision-making processes, which function as a structural procedure to control the actual pursuit of the goals of the organisation. The types of organisations gathered under the social economy term are associations, cooperatives and mutual organisations, including, more recently, foundations and social enterprises. The Charter of Principles of the Social Economy promoted by the EU-level representative institution for these four forms of social economy organisations emphasises the following core traits of social economy organisations:[5]

- The primacy of the individual and the social objective over capital.
- Voluntary and open membership.
- Democratic control by membership (which does not concern foundations, as they have no members).
- The combination of the interests of members/users and/or the general interest.
- The defence and application of the principle of solidarity and responsibility.
- Autonomous management and independence from public authorities.
- Most of the surpluses are used in pursuit of sustainable development objectives, services of interest to members or the general interest.

Not all social economy organisations can be considered social enterprises, as a part of them carry out economic activities without a general-interest objective and therefore do not meet the primary social objective requirement. Social enterprises seek, above all, to maximise the general-interest or collective benefit dimension through the pursuit of an entrepreneurial or economic activity.

A second concept that is extremely relevant to understanding different developmental paths of social enterprise is the 'solidarity economy', which can be defined as 'all economic activities subject to a determination to act democratically, in which social relations of solidarity have priority over individual interest or material profit' (Cattani and Laville, 2005: 253–259). The two main elements of the definition are the democracy and solidarity dimensions, which come before any economic mission of the organisation. Such a counter-mainstream approach is sustained by the recognition of a variety of economic resources and principles, going beyond the sophistry that 'economy equals the market' (Laville and Amaro, 2016). Indeed, it relies on the work of critical political sociologists and unorthodox economists such as Karl Polanyi who advanced several allocation mechanisms such as redistribution, reciprocity and exchange.

Vital factors in the solidarity economy are the plurality of economic principles and hybridisation of resources, in the context of a plural economy and plural democracy (Laville, 2010), as well as a co-construction logic in the definition of the supply and demand of services and products implemented by both professionals and users (Brandsen and Pestoff, 2007). Proximity services are very often used in the context of solidarity economy as they combine all these dimensions (Gardin, 2006). Figure 2.2 illustrates the main elements that explain a plural economy, which were captured in a different way by Figure 2.1.

Among the many elements the solidarity economy aims to reinvigorate are 'public spaces' where stakeholders can debate the social needs

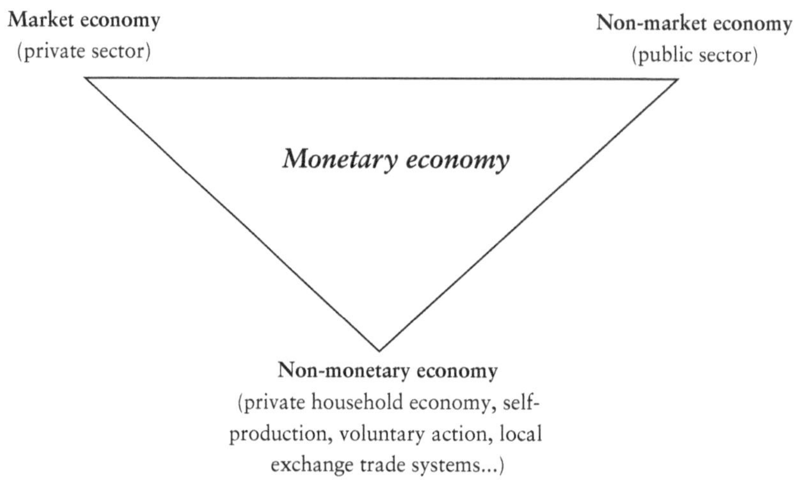

Figure 2.2 The structure of the plural economy.
Source: Adapted from Roustang et al. 1997.

to be addressed and the means to do it. Ultimately, solidarity economy organisations seek to achieve an economic democracy for all citizens as the necessary step required to achieve a full political democracy (Coraggio, 2011). Increasingly, the word 'social' is being added resulting in the broader encompassing term 'social and solidarity economy'.

A third macro-economic concept often brought into the discussion when talking about social enterprises is the 'third sector'. Traditionally a much-contested notion across countries, efforts to articulate a consensus definition of the 'third sector' have been carried out (Salamon and Sokolowski, 2014). This term was originally used in scientific literature to overcome the differences between the many national models referring to organisations that are not owned by the public sector and not active in the market. When using 'third sector organisations', authors emphasise the intermediary nature of these organisations, and as we have seen, in most countries they include non-profit organisations, but exclude cooperatives and other trading-intensive social enterprises. Beyond the institutional way of approaching the third sector (through the legal form of the organisation), an important number of individual and informal activities are included, including volunteering, pro-bono work or participation in social movements or advocacy activities (Salamon and Sokolowski, 2014). Figure 2.3 below illustrates the combination of various actors, logics of action and resources that social enterprise represents.

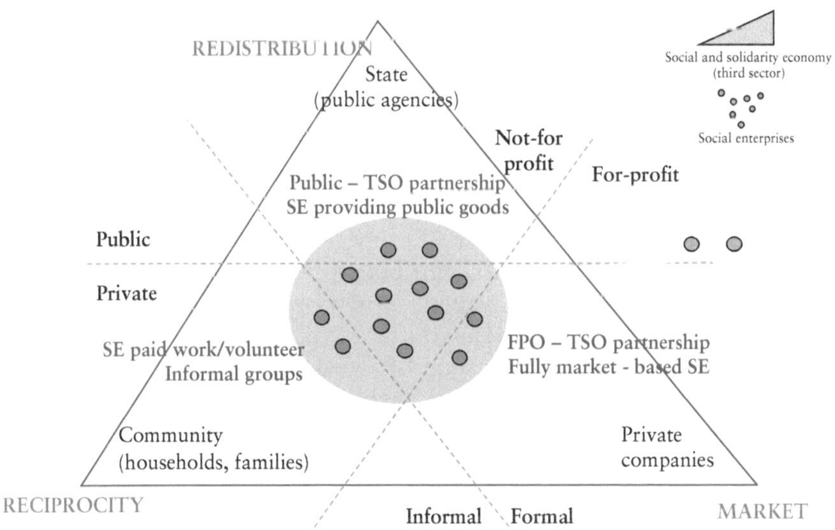

Figure 2.3 Social enterprise as a combination of various actors, logics of action and resources.

Source: Adapted from Pestoff (2008 and 2005) Defourny and Nyssens (2021).

2.2.1.2 Recent Developments in Social Enterprise Research, Policy and Practice

The study of social enterprise in Europe was initiated by economists, political scientists and sociologists with a focus on WISEs (Nyssens, 2006). Since then, other disciplines have joined the effort, especially management sciences, psychology, anthropology and even design. Sociologists have devoted most of their attention to the crossing of governance and participation (Spear and Hulgård, 2006) within social enterprises as well as their 'schools of democracy' dimension, where citizen learn the ins and outs of functioning democratically (Eschweiler and Hulgård, 2012). Such wide disciplinary interest stems in part from the abovementioned emergence of new fields of practice, from renewable energies to finance and culture (Galera and Nogales Muriel, 2021). In parallel, or probably at the root of this field expansion, we have witnessed an upsurge in social movements not only seeking a change in political rule but also aiming at the economic emancipation of citizens as a prior step to full political democracy (Laville, 2010; Laville and Eynaud, 2019).

Those social enterprises which are constructed from the bottom up by collective citizen movements represent one of the ways to achieve economic emancipation, and as such, they continue to be created to tackle recent challenges such as urban regeneration and citizen participation and larger-scale ones such as the refugee crisis or the climate crisis. In this sense, a shift in focus can be seen in the study of social enterprise: while a decade ago the focus was on proving the entrepreneurial potential of these organisations and learning how to manage them in a more efficient manner, it seems to be now on how they can effectively articulate aspirations of citizens to transform a society led by collective interest and the common good.

Policymakers are increasingly formulating legal frameworks, policy initiatives and support mechanisms for social enterprises in response to recognition of their contributions to tackling societal and environmental challenges and fostering inclusiveness. The Social Business Initiative (SBI), launched in November 2011 by the European Commission, was the first transversal strategy that aimed to contribute to developing socially innovative enterprise projects through introducing new investment models for social entrepreneurs and enterprises to support their typical hybrid funding model[6] and pushing for greater consideration of social aspects in public procurement practices (EC, 2011).[7] The latter goal builds on a directive that offers detailed suggestions to public authorities on how to design and introduce socially responsible public procurement of services, modelled on European social policy[8] in an attempt to harmonise policy objectives in different member states.[9] A consultative multi-stakeholder group on social entrepreneurship (*Group d'experts de la Commission en entrepreneuriat social* – GECES), including representatives from all member states and European civil society, examines the progress of the measures envisaged in the SBI and the European Social Economy Action Plan.[10] The European Commission presented its second transversal policy strategy on social economy in December 2021. The European Social Economy Action Plan gathers 10 concrete actions to further support the development of social economy in collaboration with member states and stakeholders. The Action Plan builds on the results of the 2011 SBI and the 2016 Start-Up and Scale-Up Initiative and will be assessed in 2025 to monitor its successful implementation.[11]

Looking at how social enterprises have developed in Europe, we can conclude that the relevance of this new institutional arrangement could be considered the result of four trends (the first two being converging transformational trends within the traditional social economy/solidarity economy/third sector):

1. The turn towards more market-based strategies on the part of third sector organisations (e.g. associations) that did not carry out any trading activity.
2. The opening of the social mission of social economy organisations (e.g. cooperatives, mutual societies) to the wider community or society at large (general interest), going beyond their members' interests.
3. The creation of organisations not emerging from the traditional social economy/third sector but that adopt a newly created social enterprise form.
4. The existence of de facto social enterprises, which are driven by the mobilisation of a group of citizens, regardless of the legal form they adopt (this will be determined by the specific legal system). These are locally rooted and enjoy a wide participation, making them more strategic in how to access varied resource mixes. They often remain invisible.

This European-based understanding has developed, however, against a myriad of international definitions and approaches. Indeed, the global relevance of the social enterprise concept and the connectedness among actors have facilitated the exchange of experiences worldwide, but Europe and the EEUU remain the main sources of reference. However, alternative dynamics appearing in 'peripheral' countries (e.g. Colombia, Brazil and India) are questioning this hegemony (Hulgård and Shajahan, 2013; Laville and Amaro, 2016). Parallel to the ongoing efforts to delimit the boundaries of a definition for social enterprise, a categorisation of social enterprises and social enterprise models was conducted in the framework of some ambitious international comparative research projects (e.g. International Comparative Social Enterprise Models).[12]

Such projects take into account one of the key elements introduced by the literature on social enterprise, which relates to the extreme importance of the macro-institutional framework in the conditions of emergence and development of social enterprises (Kerlin, 2009). Indeed, social enterprises are embedded in their sociopolitical contexts, and the tensions between the various actors of the economic and political systems increase as their position in these systems consolidates (Nyssens, 2006). The sociological neo-institutionalist approach developed by DiMaggio and Powell (1983) has inspired many studies in the field of social enterprises. For instance, there is a tradition of research in this area that has looked at how existing institutions influence the development of the non-profit sector in various countries (Salamon et al., 2000; Salamon, 2010), as well as addressed path dependency and isomorphism issues in the interaction of social enterprises with the public and traditional private sectors (Nyssens, 2006). Moreover, most EU-funded comparative research on social enterprises begins with a description of the institutional context and its evolution, so as to provide the necessary framework for understanding their development. Drawing on sociological and political science historical institutionalism, Kerlin gathers macro-level information on institutions to see how they appear to shape social enterprise models in five countries. I follow Kerlin's conception of 'institution' after Rueschemeyer's definition (2010: 210): 'Institutions are clusters of norms with strong but variable mechanisms of support and enforcement that regulate and sustain an important area of social life.'

In her model, Kerlin proposes that these macro-institutional processes act as causal paths for the emergence of social enterprise models. Usually five factors are identified as the main components of such models: recent culture and history, type of government, stage of economic development, model of civil society and international influences (Kerlin, 2010). This model will be applied in the present research in the three-country case studies selected to analyse more in-depth national adaptations of a social enterprise model.

2.2.2 *Social Enterprise and Social Transformation*

As suggested above, the issue of social transformation is a complex one and far from being solved. Indeed, it entails many actors and disciplines such as sociology, political science, social work, developmental studies and psychology. Recently, interest in capturing and measuring social transformation (and social innovation) has been increasing. The way to approach this has been through the measurement of social value created by the social initiative, particularly social enterprises. Despite the problem of defining value across cultures (González et al., 2010; Mulgan, 2010) and its intangible nature (Nicholls and Cho, 2006), several ways to capture it have been developed, most of them stemming from the management sciences and focused on the concept of 'social impact'. The term 'social impact' is usually accompanied by the word 'positive' so as to indicate that the term 'impact' can be ambivalent and the result ultimately depending on the goals sought (Evers et al., 2014; Nicholls et al., 2015). There exist a number of ways to capture the notion of social impact, which is often used to refer to the contribution made by social actors to social change. These methods are based on the quantification of results (outputs), the most common standardised methodologies for measuring social value (including social return on investment – SROI) and cost–benefit analysis. However, the main challenge for social enterprises remains the intangible part of this value or impact creation process, which remains elusive to all measurement attempts (e.g. 'Social Added Value Evaluation' by A. Bassi and 'Social Value Measurement' by R. Contreras).

When it comes to social enterprises, their aim is clearly to address a social need or tackle societal and environmental challenges. Indeed, they can enhance physical, mental and social well-being and thus daily living conditions.[13] The range of these daunting challenges in the last decades includes climate change and pollution, ageing populations, structural unemployment, health, migration and global conflict (Borzaga and Galera, 2016).

Therefore, social enterprises are increasingly being recognised as important actors in the fight against some of society's structural problems, such as unemployment, social exclusion and racism (Borzaga and Becchetti, 2011). In addition to the economic relevance of the third sector, Laville and Lallement (2000) and Pestoff (2009) emphasise the unmatchable capacity of the third sector to generate innovative organisational practices; it offers novel ways to tackle urgent social needs, covers a wide spectrum of services, contributes to reducing the bureaucracy involved in the provision of services by public administrations and mobilises untackled resources that exist in civil society. A central question, however, remains as to why these resources have remained untapped: according to some scholars, many of these citizen-based resources have been made invisible in the name of progress and rationalisation, thus impoverishing the process and the result (Sousa Santos (de), 2007; Calle et al., 2017). In any case, some social enterprises tend to create other positive externalities such as the promotion of bond capital and responsible behaviour among employees, volunteers, customers and beneficiaries; mobilising social and civic capital; and fostering citizens' democratic behaviour (Godbout, 1992; Pestoff, 2009).

Rooted in the longer tradition of the social and solidarity economy, social enterprises are also contributing to emerging areas of activity with innovative services and products (from recycling in the 1990s to renewable energy in the 2000s), but also with a participatory and collective way of delivering and producing them (Nyssens, 2006). Since social enterprises are often launched by a collective group of citizens who share a sense of urgency and together design a way to address it, they enjoy a social legitimacy that enables them to attain the social mission they sought to achieve. Although not central yet, we will see later how the field of culture is emerging as one of these new areas of activity where the social economy (and particularly social enterprises) is becoming more present.

Transformation is very often thought of as the result of a process of innovation. As such, literature on change theory and related topics has observed several possible results of social transformation, at the level of institutional transformation, transformation of social relations and political transformation (Wright, 2010). Regardless of the results of transformation, they usually include processes of empowerment for the participating actors as they become actors of change (Wright, 2010; Moulaert et al., 2010). The upsurge in concepts like the *new commons* or *buen vivir* can be located in this process by conceiving social transformation as a prioritisation of the general interest of societies, future generations and the planet over the private interest of a few with crucial consequences for the rest of society (Ostrom, 1990; Hess, 2008; Haberl et al., 2011; Fernández Casadevante et al., 2018). The present research locates social enterprises and their contribution to social innovation precisely in that space for social transformation, more particularly in the field of culture.

The next section covers social innovation in detail and links it to social enterprises and social transformation. As part of this connection, social enterprises are recognised as a useful actor to achieve such transformation, especially by policymakers:

> At all levels of the political arena, strategies are being drawn up to encourage social entrepreneurs to contribute to the work of solving problems by delivering and developing social services in a period marked by cross-pressures arising from demographic changes, higher expectations and ever greater global competition.
>
> (BEPA, 2010)

However, this connection has not been scientifically proven (Evers et al., 2014). Moreover, I problematise the often-recommended scaling-up and replication strategies of social innovation and social enterprises by exploring the factors that affect such replication and the adaptation required for it to be successful.

Lastly, I would like to advance four dimensions of social enterprises (as understood in this book) that may contribute to social transformation processes in the long term and that will be tested in the framework of the fieldwork to be completed:

1. *Rootedness in the social and solidarity economy:* As already mentioned, European social enterprises enjoy a unique framework of reference in the social and solidarity economy/third sector. They are 'knowledgeable about the best way to preserve an identity while interacting with the market, the public authorities and civil society', particularly when social enterprises are to find a way forward 'under all these isomorphic pressures' (Defourny and Nyssens, 2011: 27). At the same time, there is still a lot of room for innovation at the more sectoral level, particularly when it comes to finding ways to articulate the tensions emerging from some of the developmental trends pointed out above.
2. *Interaction with public authorities:* While the risk social enterprises are taking in the market (including financial markets) seems to be increasing, the sustained interaction with public authorities at all levels constitutes a unique and relevant trait of European social enterprises (EC, 2020).

Indeed, a possible increasing marketisation should not neglect the development of public contracts and co-construction logics (whereby public authorities act as commissioning parties), other types of private contributions (e.g. membership) or volunteering.

3. *Collective dimension:* There exists within the social economy and the third sector across Europe a tradition of collective entrepreneurship – either joint (leader and supporters) or team-based entrepreneurship – driving the setup of entrepreneurial initiatives (Borzaga and Defourny, 2001), which in turn results in higher levels of social capital (Nyssens 2006). In some cases, this collective dimension may even facilitate the organisation of social action around an economic activity (Laville et al., 2005).
4. *Participatory governance:* The governance structure of social enterprises has been identified as one of the most innovative dimensions of this institutional arrangement (Defourny et al., 2014; Borzaga and Depedri, 2015). Indeed, European social enterprises are embedded in the third sector or social economy tradition, which frames them in 'a long-lasting quest for more democracy in the economy' (Defourny and Nyssens, 2012).

2.3 Approaching Social Transformation through Social Innovation

2.3.1 Social Innovation as a Novel Institutional Space

Despite its popularity among policymakers and social scientists, social innovation remains a contested concept through which different worldviews, epistemologies and socioeconomic and political contexts meet. As a matter of fact, depending on not only the discipline but also the epistemological tradition, social innovation can be conceptualised differently. Ultimately, as explained by Nicholls et al. (2015), 'each case of social innovation … will need its own epistemology and set of boundaries and logics if it is to be understood clearly. This is, of course, a methodological, as well as theoretical, challenge for researchers'. Moreover, some authors think that when it comes to social science itself, there is not even a 'consensus regarding its [social innovation's] relevance or specific meaning in the social science or humanities' (Pol and Ville, 2009: 878).

Such lack of a unified definition stems both from the complexity of the concept and also from the fragmented community of practitioners and researchers in the social sciences and humanities. Many approaches to, and definitions of, social innovation coexist across different disciplines (sociology, business administration, economics, political science, communication studies, etc.), which is positive for advancing science but, at the same time, results in repetition and overlap while recurring gaps remain unaddressed (Brandsen et al., 2016).

Many elements have been identified that make it particularly difficult to define social innovation. Whether because of the different scales at play and actors involved (Moulaert et al, 2005), or the various disciplines from which it is approached (van der Have and Rubalcaba, 2016) or the large array of institutional settings and geographic areas in which it can take place (van Wijk et al., 2019), the truth is that social innovation remains an elusive concept. And still, despite weak theoretical foundations, social innovation has quickly expanded across the world (Borzaga and Bodini, 2014). This is especially true in Europe, where the concept was embraced by the 2010–2014 European Commission and maintained by the 2014–2019 one.[14] The dramatic increase in political attention to social innovation in Europe can be explained inter alia by its alleged capacity to leverage initiatives that address inequality and to increase social cohesion in specific settings by adapting social innovation initiatives to other contexts. Such development adds to the urgency to understand at least a group of core traits that can help us understand the phenomenon.

In terms of the nature of the concept itself, social innovation has been defined as a 'quasi-concept' (Jenson and Harrisson, 2013; EC, 2014) in the sense that it is a non-stabilised concept working across academic and policy communities precisely because of its hybridity, ambiguity and polysemy. This view joins Gallie's idea of 'contested concepts' which are 'conceptually imprecise and used in ways which we may see as disagreeable' (Ayob et al. 2016). In this context, a kaleidoscopic view needs to be developed by researchers working with social innovation, given the multiple sets of theories, traditions and experiences gathered under such an umbrella, which also includes positivist and critical perspectives.

Having said this, each research endeavour on social innovation needs to contextualise and provide its own definition of social innovation. This section sets out not only to provide such a contextual definition but also to go a step beyond by identifying a set of common traits that seem to be widely accepted by the scientific community, with a view to delimiting a 'definitional core' of social innovation. Before doing so, I will summarise the main schools of thoughts and traditions within social innovation with a critical eye. Lastly, I will select the elements from the various schools and approaches that allow us to build a working definition with the support of the article by Ayob et al. (2015) that traces the evolution of the concept.[15]

2.3.1.1 Main Approaches to Social Innovation: Technological versus Emancipatory

Although the exact origin of the term 'social innovation' is unclear, its sociological origin is currently accepted among social scientists. There were some predecessors in the social sciences who named it 'social invention', while others studied the dimensions of social innovation without naming it as such. However, the work of Gabriel Tarde (1899) is often cited as one of the first to study the increasingly networked dimension of the economy, which resulted in a proliferation of innovations or new 'production techniques' within society (Ayob et al., 2016; Nicholls et al., 2015). A few years later (and in parallel to a subsequent work by Tarde focusing on the diffusion of these innovations in society), the first journal paper to include the term 'social innovation' was Hoggan's 'The American negro and race blending' in the *Sociological Review* (Ayob et al., 2016).

Fast-forwarding a few decades, I focus for the present research on the issues social innovation referred to when it began to be widely used in the 1960s in relation to collective action and social transformation (Jessop et al., 2013). Schumpeter's theory of innovation is very often cited as one of the crucial theoretical references to social innovation, as it aimed to develop a 'comprehensive social theory' that exceeded the boundaries of economic logic and mobilised other sociologies that are able to provide a worldview from where one could analyse development and innovation (MacCallum et al., 2009). This ambitious endeavour is sometimes mistakenly reduced to his theory of innovation and entrepreneurship, which has been often used to explain the development of social enterprise and social entrepreneurship. Moving beyond a restrictive outcome- and management-based view of social innovation, literature in recent years has shown how disciplines such as sociology and political science have reapproached social innovation, opening the door to more dynamic and relational conceptions.

The first systemic study of the evolution of the term 'social innovation' by Ayob et al. (2016) covers a 25-year period (from 1989–2013) and distinguishes five phases: (1) the accidental emergence of a concept (1989–1993); (2) social relations vs. technological innovation (1994–1998); (3) early signs of contestation (in the sense of conflict about meaning) (1999–2003); (4) progressive competition – challenging extant power relations or creating utilitarian societal value (2004–2008); and (5) the apparent decontestation of social innovation (2009–2013).

Their study confirms that most publications reviewed do not define social innovation explicitly, but rather describe only the main dimensions of a particular innovation. Based on these characterising dimensions, three broad themes were found: *societal impact* (focused on the output created to address a given problem or need), *social relations* (emphasising new social processes or forms of social relations created) and *technological innovation* (when innovation is driven by technology or is technology-based). Since all social innovations do take society into account (even when they highlight the technological contribution of the innovation), the authors further refined the last category into 'technological innovation and societal impact' and 'technological innovation and social relations'. Although these categories gradually converged over time, they were useful to make distinctions based on whether the authors focused on (1) the social or technological component of the innovation or (2) the social relations or societal impact.

Although most research funding has been channelled towards technological innovation, it is becoming widely accepted that social innovation is a complement to technology-driven solutions. Indeed, in technology-intensive areas such as energy, health care and transport, the social dimension of innovation is seen as crucial (WILCO, 2014).

The boundaries between technological and social innovation are also bridged by increasing awareness of the limits of technocratic innovation (Moulaert et al., 2005) along with the belief that the future of innovation lies in social and service innovation (Mulgan, 2006). Additionally, there is a notion that economic development relies increasingly on social innovation (Vienna Declaration) and the new models of systemic innovation under the concept of the quadruple helix of university–industry–government–civil society (Carayannis and Campbell, 2009).

The conditions of the emergence for social innovation relate to a number of growing social problems caused by societal changes. These deeply rooted problems include issues related to material deprivation (growing inequalities, economic exclusion, deprivation, long-term unemployment, etc.) as well as to human subjectivities that hinder citizen participation in society, including social and cultural exclusion, ageing, political and civic alienation or even climate change (Chambon et al., 1982; Moulaert et al., 2013; Nicholls et al., 2014). Frank Moulaert and colleagues see the empowerment of citizens who participate in social innovations as a central aspect and refer to it as 'socio-political mobilisation' (Moulaert et al., 2013: 19).

In this context, a critical reading of the technological approach to social innovation is crucial for revealing the possibility of 'emancipatory' readings. In this sense, Laville and Amaro (2016) criticise the limited view of the historical lineage of the social innovation concept and the need to connect it to the idea of solidarity for it to be truthful to the European tradition. Indeed, the appearance of the concept of social innovation at the end of the twentieth century is linked to the crisis of the historically short-lived synergy between the market and the state. But it would be fairer to speak of 'crises' in plural, as we can distinguish two crises that occurred and became established.

The first one is a somewhat forgotten crisis of a cultural nature. As the 'ideology of progress' was being eroded, new social movements, such as the feminist and the ecological movement, emerged to question forms of domination in the formerly paternalistic welfare state which treated citizens as customers. Laville and Amaro (2016) identify many of these social innovation initiatives as grounded in the social and solidarity economy: they could be considered to some extent as a repoliticisation of the social economy and as a reaction against its earlier trivialisation, which focused on the economic and social dimensions while leaving out the political one.

However, over time, these dynamics became linked to changes in the forms of public engagement, characterised by an emphasis on pragmatism, local action and concrete experiences, which in turn led to a change of terminology. This was a critical moment when a shift from the 'new social movements' to 'social innovations in civil society' occurred, and many of these initiatives for social innovation were grounded in the idea of solidarity and implemented through forms of social and solidarity economy.

All the issues that have been raised in the course of this cultural crisis remain timely, since none of them has been truly resolved. However, the urgency of dealing with the subsequent economic crises took over after 2008: indeed, social innovation ceased to be perceived in relation to citizen initiatives and began to be taken in relation to economic performance. This process of rendering invisible the political search for transformation by citizen-led initiatives explains, according to Laville, the more utilitarian, technology-driven approaches to social innovation.

This focus on performance corresponds to the second major conception of social innovation described above. With the slowdown in economic growth in the 1980s, the idea that technological innovation contributed to economic recovery began to spread and became a major issue for political scientists. Furthermore, broadening the understanding of technological innovation led to the idea that a condition for success was the transition to organisational innovation as a way to ensure that technological 'insertion' was not rejected by workers.

The main differences between the two main approaches to social innovation (technological vs. emancipatory) explain the difficulty in understanding what is happening in terms of social innovation. Furthermore, over time, there has been a certain crossover between these two distinct ways of looking at social innovation, and new promising combinations are being developed. Thus, we currently see citizens' initiatives as a result of democratic and emancipatory demands to follow an entrepreneurial dynamic, and the questions raised about economic performance have led to the identification of new problems and ways to tackle them.

Indeed, within this emancipatory approach to social innovation, Subirats and García Bernardos (2015) propose a 're-constitutive' social innovation that acknowledges the need to enlarge the notion of innovations to include new decision-making and democratic participation formats that reflect the non-passive acceptance of the established order. Both of these approaches avoid the conception of social innovation processes as individual, heroic ones and frame it within a social ecology logic (Subirats and García Bernardos, 2015).

The abovementioned approaches to emancipatory social innovation constitute the most critical views which have been able to integrate issues such as real transformation and participation into the debate, beyond the utilitarian (innovations planned in detail and used at scale) or technologist (innovations in society driven by technology) approaches.

Since the issue of barriers that prevent the emergence, development, scaling and/or replication of social innovations is key to this research, I will now dwell a bit longer on them. Specific research on social innovation barriers shows that not only are they very context-specific, but they are found on different levels (individual and society) and have different formalisation degrees (some are formal and other informal). Indeed, Hougaard and Lauritzen (2014), building on the work of Danish colleagues, attempts to put forward a framework visually summarised in a matrix with two axes covering the individual–society continuum and the formal–informal continuum.[16] Based on this matrix, four categories of barriers can be described:

Formal barriers related to society such as regulation and legal frameworks. They can be tackled by decisive action and it is the type of barrier usually addressed by policy-making.

Informal barriers related to society that are connected to culture, both societal and organisational culture. They are pervasive and take a long time to alter.

Informal barriers related to the individual innovator, which are connected to the lack of trust driven by the existence of hidden motives.

Formal barriers related to the individual that are associated with the lack of competences of the social innovator who needs to actively seek to overcome this lack by (for instance) training. However, it is not fully dependent on the individual since the possibility of accessing these competences needs to be available (such as relevant education).

An interesting intermediate level between the individual and the social is the organisation-level barrier identified by Fonović et al. (2016) when describing the barriers to third sector development: they range from environment-level barriers (regulations and resistance within local communities) to organisation-level barriers (organisational rigidities and scarce resources, prevailing discourses and practices). Learning about these barriers could allow us to define organisational and environmental arrangements to overcome them. Another set of barriers can be more specifically defined for the scaling-up and replication of social innovation.

2.3.1.2 Types of Social Innovation

In addition to definitions, the *types* of social innovation are important in determining the ambition, effect and duration of social innovations over time. The most commonly accepted types of social innovation are *incremental* (an effective, concrete solution in the form of goods or services usually focused on a disadvantaged group), *organisational* (when existing institutional arrangements are reshaped or new ones are created to reconfigure market structures and patterns and increase the social value created) and *disruptive* (aiming to change cognitive frames of references, alter power relations and social systems and reframe social issues) (Nicholls et al., 2015).

These three types are associated with three complementary perspectives to the social dimension of social innovation, namely the *social demand perspective* (the narrowest approach which focuses on solving urgent problems for given society groups with a logic of complementing a market or state provision failure), the *societal challenge perspective* (which balances the economic and social creation of value with a logic of making societal problem-solving a crucial part of economic development) and the *systemic changes perspective* (the hardest approach which focuses on sustainable systemic transformation to be reached through processes of institutional development and changes in relations between institutions and stakeholders) (BEPA, 2010). Table 2.2 provides examples of social innovations according to their perspective and type. Although a common perspective type pairing is suggested, there may be occasions in which they combine differently (e.g. an incremental type of social innovation can lead to addressing a societal challenge). In any case, it is important to note that the widest type of social innovation usually includes the previous levels; thus, systemic (disruptive) social innovation includes meso (organisational) and micro (incremental) and that organisational social innovation usually includes a concrete incremental type of social innovation.

The importance of the systemic transformation dimension of social innovation is covered in the literature. Geels' contribution focuses on how social innovation moves from a local to systemic level, while others offer 'recipes for social innovation' (Boyer et al., 2011). The aim of creating sustainable systemic transformation involves the idea of reshaping society with the solutions created and the processes implemented to find those solutions. The idea of the systemic level of social innovation has also driven the growing recognition that innovation is not just technological or organisational but also inter-institutional in a given territory and thus is a deeply social process that necessitates the crystallisation of a number of actors, dynamics and processes into a conducive ecosystem (Geels, 2005, 2006). A potential negative effect of this local-to-global evolution, identified by researchers, could

Table 2.2 Social innovation examples per perspective and type

Perspective	*Type*	*Example*
Social demand (micro)	Incremental	• Health and care services for the elderly • Educational services and care of children • Urban regeneration
Societal challenge (meso)	Organisational	• Fair trade • Migrants' and asylum-seekers' dispersed accommodation
Systemic change (macro)	Disruptive	• Gender mainstreaming public policy reforms • Collaborative economy • Social movements and self-conscious political actors

be the intensive push for scaling-up and replication (without the adaptation required by the specific context) that has driven policy-making in the last decade.

Given the ambiguity of the term, social innovation has even been limited to a technological trend, a specific policy area, a corporate social responsibility strategy or even a form of organising. As for the various research approaches, they represent different perspectives on how social innovation can be studied: as a concrete output (new service or product), a process (whereby new groups of citizens are activated and empowered to carry out the transformation) or a combination of both. Beyond the initial objectives, context is of utmost importance: the wider political system in which social innovations are embedded as well as the reaction of the socioeconomic actors are crucial for determining its success or failure (Osborne and Brown, 2011; Montagut, 2014).

2.3.1.3 A Working Definition of Social Innovation for the Current Research

After some initial attempts at setting the boundaries of social innovation with a view to finding a definite shared definition, there seems to be an emerging feeling among the loose community of social innovation researchers that such a task may be not only unrealistic but also futile. This debate mirrors the development of social enterprise with some actors defending the need for an agreed-upon concept and others rejecting such possibility and still others offering some tools for locating ideal types of institutional arrangements that reflect what happens in the field (Defourny and Nyssens, 2010, 2021).

Based on the above, I distinguish two main conceptions of social innovation. The first one is concerned with the role of citizens in the construction of a society where processes leading to new forms of social relations matter as much as those aimed at solving societal problems. These new processes can be mediated by technology, but in no case does technology become the centre of social innovation. In this approach, the added value brought about by a given social innovation can be evaluated, but the emphasis is not on quantifiable economic indicators. The second conception is concerned with the utilitarian performance (in many cases economic) of a given initiative and its social impact, thus focusing on the outputs produced, its measurable impact and its scaling-up and replication.

Needless to say, the 'new ways of doing things' in relation to the Social Polis project emerged through 'acts of citizenship' from collective actors capable of creating new spaces for public debate and for claiming new rights. Such a research line joins other views about associationism and its role in the construction and shaping of the public sphere (Laville and Sainsaulieu, 1997) as well as about the need to integrate the political discussion about what kind of improvements and transformations are sought and brought about by social innovations and interventions, well beyond functionalist approaches (Montagut, 2014).

An interesting dialectic seems to emerge from the analysis of all these definitions and approaches to social innovation: the tension between competition and solidarity. Indeed, one crucial distinction that can be made between the two main approaches to social innovation is the value they assign to competitiveness and solidarity. Economic and managerial approaches to social innovation put forward the value of competitiveness and technology, while perspectives including social movements and empowerment (change in social relations and political change) emphasise the need to cooperate and create spaces for solidarity-based exchanges (as opposed to monetary ones). Such a dialectic, together with the systemic transformation angle, represents an interesting analytical framework for the current research. Therefore, the main elements of the working definition within the framework of this research stem from all the above elements as well as from Nicholls et al. (2015). I summarise the definition below.

Table 2.3 Dimensions included in the working definition of social innovation

Dimensions	*Explanation*
Needs satisfaction	Social innovation is about addressing problems via specific outputs and outcomes. The value created goes beyond financial profit and is distributed beyond the originators of the social innovation.
Process	New forms of interaction are established in the dynamics and processes at play within social innovation; it is considered as important as the outputs/outcomes.
Change in social relations	Rebalancing power disparities of economic inequalities in society.
Improvement	Social innovation results in increased 'social value' or 'social impact', therefore improving existing conditions and solutions understood as a process where all concerned actors participate.
Empowerment	It translates into the sociopolitical mobilisation of citizens involved in social innovations.
Specific form	It may have multiple forms (covering formal to informal): ideas, actions, frames, models, systems, processes, services, rules and regulations as well as new organisational forms.
Originators and leaders	It may have multiple originators: the public and private sectors or the social economy/third sector as well as users and communities.
Unforeseeable nature	Social innovation cannot be controlled, and expected or intended results are affected by a variety of factors.

With the dimension-based working definition, I avoid the unnecessary challenge of adopting a simplistic definition to carry on with this research. In order to reach a systemic level, social innovation needs to be truly transformative, which implies a change in attitudes, values and practices. When planning an initiative or intervention, the aim should be on reaching a shared well-being and governance patterns and shared social justice criteria (Montagut, 2014). Indeed, social innovation means 'fostering inclusion to and wellbeing through improving micro and macro social relations and empowerment processes' (Moulaert et al., 2013: 16). In the next section I will focus on framing social enterprise within the larger context of transformative social innovation.

2.3.2 *Framing Social Enterprise within Social Innovation*

Insofar as social innovation actors commit to addressing societal challenges at a level that is broader than the immediate one, they are de facto engaged in institutional work (Lawrence et al., 2009). It has been observed that such work usually takes the form of either groups or individuals creating institutional arrangements leading to new organisational forms (Rao et al., 2000; Tracey et al., 2011). This approach links with the societal challenge perspective of social innovation aiming at the meso level of social transformation illustrated by Table 2.3. According to Nicholls (2010), the resulting institutional arrangements can be 'radical' (aiming to overthrow some of the existing institutions), 'incremental' or 'institutional' (with a focused scope and challenging only institutions that challenge their development).

Some authors consider social entrepreneurship as 'a subset of social innovation – the organisational enactment of social innovation ideas and models' (Nicholls et al., 2015: 5), and social enterprise would be the most concrete institutional example of this subset (Alter, 2006; Nyssens, 2006). This approach links with the societal challenge perspective of social innovation aiming at the meso level of social transformation explained above.

The timeliness of the contribution of social enterprises to solving some societal challenges is being brought to light now in parallel with a broader context of policies aimed at boosting social innovation in Europe. As we have seen, social innovation is widely understood as new solutions to existing social problems, usually in the form of services, products or new institutional arrangements (BEPA, 2010; Evers et al., 2014; Moulaert et al., 2014). Indeed, Moulaert and Nussbaumer (2005: 2071) point out that social innovation rests on two pillars: 'institutional innovation (innovation in social relations, innovations in governance including empowerment dynamics) and innovation in the sense of the social economy – i.e. satisfaction of various needs in various communities'.

A nascent body of literature on social innovation tends to confirm this connection, although not to the extent suggested in the grand political discourse (Evers et al., 2014). While the exact relationship between social innovation and social enterprises requires further research (Borzaga and Bodini, 2014), social enterprises are widely recognised as key actors for social innovation (Hulgård, 2014) and are capable of being vehicles of social innovation insofar as they provide institutional innovation and are embedded in the social and solidarity economy (Gardin, 2006; Brandsen and Pestoff, 2007). For instance, according to the abovementioned 'social demand approach' to social innovation, the social entrepreneur is often seen as a main agent of social innovation. The key players of social innovation have been described as being pioneers in their fields, accepting high levels of risk arising from the unknown and agreeing to interact with attitudes that are risk-averse (BEPA, 2010). The ability of social enterprise initiators to forge partnerships, cooperate and create networks is also compared to that of social innovation initiators (BEPA, 2010). Moreover, social enterprises engage in sustainable economic activities aiming to increase the well-being of society at large or ample groups of society seeking financial relief, with profits only reinvested back into the organisation so that it can continue to fulfil its social mission.

Departing from the elements included in the Schumpeterian definition of innovation, Defourny and Nyssens (2013) explain how social enterprises have driven social innovation in the form of:

- New products/services or improved quality of products/services (work integration, personal banking, recycling and reusing, ethical banking, etc., which social enterprises provide in response to the severe social problems that Europe faces);
- New methods of organisation and/or production (which define the management, organisation, financing structure and sources, ownership structure and control mechanisms, or the idea of social integration via labour and work training); and
- New production factors (the authors mention volunteering or atypical forms of employment, among many others).

The link between social innovation and social enterprise also remains underresearched with regard to the transformation of social relations. Defined as one of the core aspects of social innovation, and one of the added values of social enterprises, the empowerment of social actors involved in the activity of social enterprise deserves further study. A way to address this gap would be to consider what mostly francophone authors have said about the relationship between social innovation and social and solidarity economy, in which social enterprises are embedded. Indeed, the social and solidarity economy has been considered as 'a laboratory for social innovation' (Lévesque, 2007; Bouchard, 2013) due to its contribution to the creation of non-capitalist legal forms (co-ops, mutual societies, not-for-profit organisations, etc.) seeking societal goals through economic action and the promotion of self-management practices and multi-stakeholder governance. Crucially, the social and solidarity economy also unveils traditionally hidden, non-capitalist economic practices and economies (economy of care, informal and non-monetary economy, ecological economy, alternative currencies, etc.) and promotes them as instrumental for achieving social well-being and environmental regeneration (Riutort, 2016); the area has the potential to produce new representations of the economy based on solidarity, cooperation and democracy (Fraisse, 2013). However, not all social and solidarity organisations are innovative, and they are at constant risk of institutional isomorphisms through the pressures of market or government instrumentalisation (DiMaggio and Powell, 1983; Fraisse, 2013). Therefore, although social innovation cannot be reduced to the social and solidarity economy, the latter plays a crucial role in channelling the former within society in collaboration with public administrations and other economic and non-economic players (Montagut, 2014).

Lastly, a growing number of multidisciplinary studies exist around the relationship between social enterprises and social innovation and the processes whereby they can be scaled up and replicated (Weber et al., 2012). Indeed, social enterprises have progressively been perceived as a policy-friendly way to support social innovation, which could explain the focus on the start-up phase of social enterprise development (e.g. incubators, social finance, scaling-up strategies) when talking about social innovation. Precisely because the connection between the two has been presented as a policy construct that is still to be confirmed by evidence, examples of social enterprises operating in the field of culture that do produce socially innovative solutions offer unique insights into this relationship. In this sense, this volume is very timely as it questions some of the assumptions that exist about the diffusion of social innovation via the replication of social enterprises.

The current research supports the claim that social enterprises active in the field of culture are vehicles of social innovation at three levels: first, the transformational potential embedded in their institutional form; second, their activity area, namely, culture and the arts; and third, their embeddedness in the wider social and solidarity economy. In this section we are concerned with the first level – how the institutional characteristics of social enterprises relate to social innovation not only at the outcome level but also mostly at the process level, particularly related to the social relations among groups (Defourny and Nyssens, 2013). I would emphasise the following four characteristics of social enterprise that are particularly relevant to social innovation:

1. The involvement of wide categories of stakeholders in the activity of the social enterprise.
2. The governance mechanisms that ensure their participation.
3. The identification of new fields of activity, such as culture, for social enterprises driven by citizens themselves.

4. An organisational form that contributes to the scaling-up and replication of socially innovative solutions, even while their conditions and contexts are of utmost importance.

Specifically, three major features linking the connection between social enterprise and social innovation have been analysed, namely the satisfaction of human needs, the relation among human beings and social groups and the empowerment of people trying to fulfil their needs (the latter acts as a bridge between the former two) (Defourny and Nyssens, 2013).

However, there is a body of literature that questions the relationship discussed above, mostly on the grounds of the weakness of social innovation as a lasting concept. For instance, some say that justifying the activity of social enterprises by the creation of social impact does little service to the real contribution of social enterprises, insofar as the measurement of social impact is far from being a solid or agreed-upon methodology. The transformative dimension of social enterprises would be neglected if all the emphasis is put on its productive capacity. Indeed, that would be limiting it to the narrowest level of transformation, whereas transformative dimensions such as the participatory governance directly affecting the processes of empowerment and coordinated lobbying via networks may result in effective systemic effects, whether at the level of political reforms (e.g. incipient reforms on the energy market to allow for citizen-led initiatives), modification of the attitude of vast groups of citizens (e.g. responsible or ethical consumption) or the creation of specific markets (e.g. social finance). This book aims to contribute to that under-researched area by exploring the conception of culture and the arts as a transmitter of social innovation where social enterprises can thrive.

Notes

1 A relevant illustration in the field of health is the argument built by the World Health Organisation for social enterprises as public health intervention agents to reduce persisting and widening inequalities.

2 WISE were the leading innovators in areas such as recycling and reutilising, well before these areas constituted a market worth entering by traditional businesses.

3 Culture is meant in the widest sense – from sustainable tourism and heritage conservation to artist cooperatives and citizens revitalisation initiatives through the arts.

4 According to some authors, this continuum does not contribute to the categorisation effort of social enterprise insofar as all of them could be considered as 'intermediate organisations' and labelled 'hybrids' (Doherty et al., 2014; Defourny and Nyssens, 2016).

5 Social Economy Europe, formerly known as the European Standing Conference on Co-operatives, Mutual Societies, Associations and Foundations (CEP-CMAF). See www.socialeconomy.eu.org.

6 Many social enterprises derive their income from a mix of resources, like the sale of goods and services to the public or private sector, government subsidies and grants, private donations and voluntary work (EC, 2014).

7 Follow-up actions include the European Commission's mapping study to identify social enterprise ecosystems and good practice (EC, 2014, 2020) and the draft of a European Foundation Statute. Detailed documentation of follow-up actions, related programmes, initiatives and updates on implementation is available here: https://ec.europa.eu/growth/sectors/proximity-and-social-economy/social-economy-eu/social-enterprises_en [accessed 25 January 2022].

8 Actions range from introducing ethically traded coffee in cafeterias of public institutions to purchasing service delivery for vulnerable groups by social enterprises or other service providers who demonstrate social considerations. This can be in the form of offering equal employment opportunities for people who are hard to integrate in the regular labour market, offering decent pay and working conditions or displaying an exceptional sustainability portfolio.

9 Including social clauses in procurement procedures can be a complex task, especially for larger contracts. Legal advisors and tutors can help authorities who wish to 'buy social', with the European Commission providing financial support via the EU structural funds.

10 See https://ec.europa.eu/growth/sectors/proximity-and-social-economy/social-economy-eu/social-enterprises/expert-groups_en [accessed 8 March 2022].

11 The Action Plan is available here: https://ec.europa.eu/social/BlobServlet?docId=24986&langId=en [accessed 8 March 2022].

12 The ICSEM project began in 2011 and ended in 2017, although it merged into the Empower-SE COST Action, which lasted until 2021. A webpage with the project results is available here: https://emes.net/research-projects/social-enterprise/icsem-project.

13 Understanding health inequalities on the line of income inequities, social enterprises can tackle the inequitable distribution of power, money and resources through their participatory governance 'that can be significantly empowering' (Roy et al., 2013: 62–63).

14 See 'Social innovation as part of the Europe 2020 strategy', available on a devoted webpage of the European Commission: ec.europa.eu/growth/industry/innovation/policy/social/index_en.htm.

15 In the original PhD thesis, a review of the seven most relevant EU-funded research projects on social innovation was included, but removed from this volume.

16 A blog dedicated to social innovation research no longer active (http://siresearch.eu) included contributions on the various topics related to social innovation, such as barriers and drivers.

References

Alter, S. K. (2006) Social Enterprise Models and Their Mission and Money Relationships. In A. Nicholls (ed.), *Social Entrepreneurship: New Models of Sustainable Social Change*, 205–232, New York: Oxford University Press.

Alvord, S. H., Brown, L. D. and Letts, C. W. (2004) Social Entrepreneurship and Societal Transformation: An Exploratory Study, *Journal of Applied Behavioral Science*, Vol. 40 (3), pp. 260–282.

Austin, J., Stevenson, H. and Wei-Skillern, J. (2006) Social and Commercial Entrepreneurship: Same, Different, or Both? Entrepreneurship: Theory & Practice, Vol. 30 (1), pp. 1–22.

Ayob, N., Teasdale, S. and Fagan, K. (2016) How Social Innovation 'Came To Be': Tracing the Evolution of a Contested Concept, *Journal of Social Policy*, Vol. 1, pp. 1–19.

Bacq, S. and Janssen, F. (2011) The Multiple Faces of Social Entrepreneurship: A Review of Definitional Issues Based on Geographical and Thematic Criteria, *Entrepreneurship & Regional Development*, Vol. 23 (5&6), pp. 373–403.

Bassi, A. (2012) How to Measure the Intangibles: Towards a System of Indicators (S.A.V.E.) for the Measurement of the Performance of Social Enterprises. In H.-W. Franz, J. Howaldt and J. Hochgerner (eds), *Challenge Social Innovation*, 325–350, Berlin: Springer.

Battilana, J. and Lee, M. (2014) Advancing Research on Hybrid Organizing: Insights from the Study of Social Enterprises, *Academy of Management Annals*, Vol. 8 (1), pp. 397–441.

Borzaga, C. and Becchetti, L. (2011) *The Economics of Social Responsibility: The World of Social Responsibility*, London: Routledge.

Borzaga, C. and Bodini, R. (2014) What to Make of Social Innovation? Towards a Framework for Policy Development, *Social Policy and Society*, Vol. 13 (3), pp. 411–421.

Borzaga, C. and Defourny, J. (eds) (2001) *The Emergence of Social Enterprise*, London: Routledge.

Borzaga, C. and Depedri, S. (2015) Multi-Stakeholder Governance in Civil Society Organizations. In J. L. Laville, D. R. Young and P. Eynaud (eds), *Civil Society, the Third Sector and Social Enterprise: Models and Outcomes*, 109–122, London: Routledge.

Borzaga, C. and Galera, G. (2016) Innovating the provision of welfare services through collective action: the case of Italian social cooperatives, International Review of Sociology, 26(1): 31–47.

Bouchard, M. J. (ed.) (2013) *Innovation and the Social Economy: The Quebec Experience*, Toronto: University of Toronto Press.

Boyer, B., Cook, J. W. and Steinberg, M. (2011) *In Studio: Recipes for Systemic Change*, Helsinki: Helsinki Design Lab. Available at http://helsinkidesignlab.org/instudio/ [accessed 12 August 2016].

Brandsen, T., Cattacin, S., Evers, A. and Zimmer, A. (eds) (2016) *Social Innovations in the Urban Context*, New York, Springer International. Available at www.springer.com/gp/book/9783319215501 [accessed 15 November 2016].

Brandsen, T. and Pestoff, V. (2007) *Co-production: The Third Sector and the Delivery of Public Services*, London: Routledge.

Bureau of European Policy Advisers (BEPA) (2010) *Empowering People, Driving Change. Social Innovation in the European Union*, Brussels: Bureau of European Policy Advisors and European Commission.

Calle, A., Suriñach, R. and Piñeiro, C. (2017) Comunes y economías para la sostenibilidad de la vida. In A. Calle (ed.), *La Rebeldía en Común*, 15–46, Madrid: Editorial Libros en Acción.

Carayannis, E. G. and Campbell, D. F. J. (2009) 'Mode 3' and 'Quadruple Helix': Toward a 21st Century Fractal Innovation Ecosystem, *International Journal of Technology Management*, Vol. 46 (3), pp. 201–234.

Cattani, A. D. and Laville, J. L. (2005) *Dictionnaire de l'autre économie*, Paris: Editions Desclée de Brouwer.

Chambon, J.-L., David, A. and Devevey, J.-M. (1982) *Les Innovations sociales*, Paris: Presses Universitaires de France.

Coraggio, J. L. (2011) *Economía social y solidaria. El trabajo antes que el capital*, Quito: Abya Yala.

Dees, J. G. (1998) *The Meaning of Social Entrepreneurship*, Kansas City, MO: The Kauffman Center for Entrepreneurial Leadership.

Defourny, J. (2014) From Third Sector to Social Enterprise: A European Research Trajectory. In J. Defourny, L. Hulgård and V. Pestoff (eds), *Social Enterprise and the Third Sector. Changing European Landscapes in a Comparative Perspective*, 17–41, London: Routledge.

Defourny, J. and Nyssens, M. (2010) Conceptions of Social Enterprise and Social Entrepreneurship in Europe and the United States: Convergences and Divergences, *Journal of Social Entrepreneurship*, Vol. 1 (1), pp. 32–53.

Defourny, J. and Nyssens, M. (2012) The EMES Approach of Social Enterprise in a Comparative Perspective, EMES Working Paper No. 12/03, Liege: EMES European Research Network. Available at www.emes.net/site/wp-content/uploads/EMES-WP-12-03_Defourny-Nyssens.pdf [accessed 11 October 2016].

Defourny, J. and Nyssens, M. (2013) Social Innovation, Social Economy and Social Enterprise: What Can the European Debate Tell Us? In F. Moulaert, D. MacCallum and A. Mehmood (eds), *The International Handbook on Social Innovation: Collective Action, Social Learning and Transdisciplinary Research*, 40–52, Cheltenham: Edward Elgar.

Defourny, J. and Nyssens, M. (2021) *Social Enterprise in Western Europe: Theory, Models and Practice*, London: Routledge.

DiMaggio, P. J. and Powell, W. (1983) The Iron Cage Revisited: Institutional Isomorphism and Collective Rationality in Organizational Fields, *American Sociological Review*, Vol. 48, pp. 147–160.

Doherty, B., Haugh, H. and Lyon, F. (2014) Social Enterprises as Hybrid Organizations: A Review and Research Agenda, *International Journal of Management Reviews*, Vol. 16, pp. 417–436.

Eschweiler, J. and Hulgård, L. (2012) Social Innovation and Deliberative Democracy, EMES Working Paper No. 12/04, Liege: EMES International Research Network. Available at www.emes.net/site/wp-content/uploads/EMES-WP-12-04_Eschweiler-Hulgard_Final.pdf [accessed 2 September 2015].

European Commission (EC) (2011) *Social Business Initiative: Creating a Favourable Climate for Social Enterprises, Key Stakeholders in the Social Economy and Innovation*, Brussels: European Commission.

European Commission (EC) (2014) *Mapping Study of Social Enterprises and Their Ecosystem in Europe*, Brussels: European Commission.

European Commission (EC) (2020) *Social Enterprises and Their Ecosystems in Europe. Comparative Synthesis Report*. Luxembourg: Publications Office of the European Union. Available at https://europa.eu/!Qq64ny [accessed 23 March 2021].

Evers, A., Ewert, B. and Brandsen, T. (eds) (2014) *Social Innovations for Social Cohesion. Transnational Patterns and Approaches from 20 European Cities*, Brussels: WILCO Project. Available at www.wilcoproject.eu/ereader [accessed 15 November 2016].

Fernández Casadevante Kois, J. L., Morán Alonso, N., Calle Collado, A. and del Viso, N. (2018) *Cultivating Commons in the Heart of the City. Madrid Community Gardens against Austerity Urbanism*, ECSP-3EMESPolanyi-04, Liege: EMES International Research Network. Available at https://emes.net/publications/conference-papers/3rd-emes-polanyi-international-seminar/cultivating-commons-in-the-heart-of-the-city-madrid-community-gardens-against-austerity-urbanism/ [accessed 11 December 2019].

Fisac-García, R. (2015) *Modelo de análisis organizativo para la mejora del desempeño de empresas sociales*, doctoral thesis, Polytechnic University of Madrid. Available at http://oa.upm.es/33676 [accessed 15 November 2016].

Fonović, K., Zimmer, A. and Benedikt Pahl, J. (2016) Growing Risks in a Demanding Environment: Policy Recommendations for a Sustainable Development of the Third Sector, Working Paper No. 12. Available at http://thirdsectorimpact.eu/site/assets/uploads/documentations/tsi-policy-brief-no-12-growing-risks-in-a-demanding-environment/TSI-Policy-Brief-12-Comparative_FromBarriersToRecommendations.pdf [accessed 11 May 2017].

Fraisse L. (2013) The Social and Solidarity-Based Economy as a New Field of Public Action: A Policy and Method for Promoting Social Innovation. In F. Moulaert, D. MacCallum, A. Mehmood and A. Hamdouch (eds), *The International Handbook of Social Innovation*, 361–371, Cheltenham: Edward Elgar.

Fraisse, L. and Gardin L. (2010) L'action politique des organisations de l'économie sociale et solidaire: entre banalisation et contestation. In É. Dacheux and D. Goujon (eds), *Réconcilier démocratie et économie: la dimension politique de l'entrepreneuriat en économie sociale et solidaire*, 17–20, Paris: M. Houdiard Éditeur.

Galera, G. and Borzaga, C. (2009) Social Enterprise: An International Overview of Its Conceptual Evolution and Legal Implementation, *Social Enterprise Journal*, Vol. 5 (3), pp. 210–228.

Galera, G. and Nogales Muriel, R. (2021) Sustaining and Growing One of the Largest International Communities of Social Enterprise Scholars: The Empower-SE COST Action, Empower-SE Stakeholder Brief No. 11, Liege: EMES/COST. Available at www.empowerse.eu/wp-content/uploads/2021/12/EURICSE_Brief11-1.pdf [accessed 11 December 2021].

Gardin, L. (2006) *Les initiatives solidaires. La reciprocité face au marché*, Toulouse: Ed. Erès.

Geels, F. W. (2005) Processes and Patterns in Transitions and System Innovations: Refining the Co-evolutionary Multi-Level Perspective. *Technological Forecasting and Social Change*, Vol. 72 (6), pp. 681–696.

Geels, F. W. (2006) Analysing the Breakthrough of Rock 'n' Roll (1930–1970): Multi-Regime Interaction and Reconfiguration in the Multi-Level Perspective, *Technological Forecasting and Social Change*, Vol. 74 (2007), pp. 1411–1431.

Godbout, J. T. (with the collaboration of A. Caillé) (1992) *L'esprit du don*, Paris: La Découverte.

González, S., Moulaert, F. and Martinelli, F. (2010) 'How to analyse social innovation at the local level', in Moulaert, F., Martinelli, F., Swyngedouw, E. & Gonzalez, S. (eds) Can Neighbourhoods Save the City? Community Development and Social Innovation, Oxford and New York: Routledge, pp. 49–67.

Green, K. R. (2020) Dis/ability Arts and Systemic Innovation in the UK and Sweden, *Journal of Social Entrepreneurship*, Vol. 13 (3), pp. 366–389.

Haberl, H., Fischer-Kowalski, M., Krausmann, F., Martinez-Alier, J. and Winiwarter, V. (2011) A Socio-Metabolic Transition towards Sustainability? Challenges for Another Great Transformation, *Sustainable Development*, Vol. 19 (1), pp. 1–14.

Hess, C. (2008) *Mapping the New Commons*. Available at https://ssrn.com/abstract=1356835 [accessed 19 March 2022].

Hougaard, K.F. and Lauritzen, J.R.K. (2014) Sammen om velfærd: bedre løsninger med social innovation. [Together for Welfare: Better Solutions with Social Innovation], Copenhagen: Gyldendal A/S.

Hulgård, L. (2014) Social Enterprise and the Third Sector: Innovative Service Delivery or a Non-Capitalist Economy? In J. Defourny, L. Hulgård and V. Pestoff (eds), *Social Enterprise and the Third Sector: Changing European Landscapes in a Comparative Perspective*, 66–84, London: Routledge.

Hulgård, L. and Shajahan, P. K. (2013) Social Innovation for People-Centred Development. In F. Moulaert, D. MacCallum and A. Mehmood (eds), *The International Handbook on Social Innovation*, 93–104, Cheltenham: Edward Elgar.

Huybretchs, B. and Nicholls, A. (2012) Social Entrepreneurship: Definitions, Drivers and Challenges. In C. K. Volkmann, K. O. Tokarski and K. Ernst (eds), *Social Entrepreneurship and Social Business: An Introduction and Discussion with Case Studies*, 31–48, Wiesbaden: Springer-Gabler.

Jenson, J. and Harrison, D. (2013) *Social Innovation Research in the European Union. Approaches, Findings and Future Directions*, Luxembourg: European Union.

Jessop, B., Moulaert, F., Hulgård, L. and Hamdouch, A. (2013) Social Innovation Research: A New Stage in Innovation Analysis? In F. Moulaert, D. MacCallum and A. Mehmood (eds), *The International Handbook on Social Innovation*, 110–130, Cheltenham: Edward Elgar.

Jiménez-Bueno, M. and Ramos, I. (2009) *¿Más allá de la ciencia académica?* Arbor: Ciencia, pensamiento y cultura.

Kerlin, J. (2010) A Comparative Analysis of the Global Emergence of Social Enterprise, *Voluntas: International Journal of Voluntary and Nonprofit Organizations*, Vol. 21 (2), pp. 162–179.

Lautermann, C. (2013) The Ambiguities of (Social) Value Creation: Towards an Extended Understanding of Entrepreneurial Value Creation for Society, *Social Enterprise Journal*, Vol. 9 (2), pp. 184–202.

Laville, J.-L. (2010) Solidarity Economy/Plural Economy. In K. Hart, J.-L. Laville and A. D. Cattani (eds), *The Human Economy*, 225–235, Cambridge, MA: Polity Press.

Laville, J. L. and Amaro, R. (2016) *Social Innovation in Europe: What Relation with Solidarity Economy? Towards a Plural European Vision of Social Innovation*. Available at www.socioeco.org/bdf_fiche-document-4518_en.html [accessed 6 December 2016].

Laville, J. L. and Eynaud, P. (2019) A Cross-Disciplinary and International Perspective about Social Enterprise. In P. Eynaud, J. L. Laville, L. L. Dos Santos, S. Banerjee, H. Hulgard and F. Avelino (eds), *Theory of Social Enterprise and Pluralism: Social Movements, Solidarity Economy, and Global South*, 44–66, London: Routledge.

Laville, J. L. and Lallement, M. (2000) Qu'est-ce que le tiers secteur? Associations, économie solidaire, économie sociale (What Is the Third Sector? Associations, Solidarity Economy, Social Economy), *Sociologie du Travail*, Vol. 42 (4), pp. 523–529.

Laville, J.L. and Sainsaulieu, R. (1997) *L'association. Sociologie et économie*. Paris: Desclée de Brouwer.

Lawrence, T. B., Suddaby, R. and Leca, B. (2009) *Institutional Work: Actors and Agency in Institutional Studies of Organizations*, Cambridge: Cambridge University Press.

Lévesque, B. (2007) L'innovation dans le développement économique et sociale. In J. L. Klein and D. Harrisson (eds), *L'innovation sociale*, 43–68, Québec: Presses de l'Université du Québec.

Light, P. C. (2005) *The Search for Social Entrepreneurship*, Washington, DC: Brookings Institution Press.

MacCallum, D., Moulaert, F., Hillier, J. and Vicari-Haddock, S. (eds) (2009) *Social Innovation and Territorial Development*, Aldershot: Ashgate.

Mendell, M. and Alain, B. (2015) Enabling the Social and Solidarity Economy through the Co-Construction of Public Policy. In P. Ütting (ed), *Social and solidarity economy: Beyond the fringe*, 166–184, London: Zed Books.

Montagut, T. (2014) De la innovación a la Innovacion Social, *Documentación Social*, Vol. 176, 15–30.

Moulaert, F., MacCallum, D., Mehmood, A. and Hamdouch, A. (eds) (2010) *The International Handbook on Social Innovation: Collective Action, Social Learning and Transdisciplinary Research*, 528, Cheltenham: Edward Elgar.

Moulaert, F., MacCallum, D., Mehmood, A. and Hamdouch, A. (eds) (2013) *The International Handbook on Social Innovation: Collective Action, Social Learning and Transdisciplinary Research*, Cheltenham: Edward Elgar.

Moulaert, F., Martinelli, F., Swyngedouw, E. and Gonzalez, S. (2005) Towards Alternative Model(s) of Local Innovation, *Urban Studies*, Vol. 42 (11), pp. 1969–1990.

Moulaert, F. and Nussbaumer, J. (2005) Defining the Social Economy and Its Governance at the Neighbourhood Level: A Methodological Reflection, *Urban Studies*, Vol. 42 (11), pp. 2071–2088.

Mulgan, G. (2006) The Process of Social Innovation, *Innovations: Technology, Governance, Globalization*, Vol. 1 (2), pp. 145–162.

Mulgan, G. (2010) *Measuring Social Value: Stanford Social Innovation Review*, Stanford, CA: Stanford Center on Philanthropy and Civil Society.

Nicholls, A. (ed.) (2006) *Social Entrepreneurship: New Models of Sustainable Social Change*, Oxford: Oxford University Press.

Nicholls, A. (2010) The Legitimacy of Social Entrepreneurship Reflexive Isomorphism in a Pre-Paradigmatic Field, *Entrepreneurship Theory and Practice*, Vol. 34, pp. 611–633.

Nicholls, A. and Cho, A. (2006) Social Entrepreneurship: The Structuration of a Field. In A. Nicholls (ed.), *Social Entrepreneurship: New Models of Sustainable Social Change*, 99–118, Oxford: Oxford University Press.

Nicholls, A., Simon, J. and Gabriel, M. (2015) *New Frontiers in Social Innovation Research*, Hampshire: Palgrave Macmillan.

Novkovic, S. (2020) Multi-Stakeholder Cooperatives as a Means for Jobs Creation and Social Transformation In B. Roelants, H. Eum, S. Eşim, S. Novkovic and W. Katajamäki (eds), *Cooperatives and the World of Work* 220–233, London: Routledge.

Nyssens, M. (ed.) (2006) *Social Enterprise. At the Crossroads of Market, Public Policies and Civil Society*, London: Routledge.

Osborne, S. and Brown, L. (2011) Innovation, Public Policy and Public Services Delivery in the UK. The Word That Would Be King? *Public Administration*, Vol. 89 (4), pp. 1335–1350.

Osburg, T. (2013) Social Innovation to Drive Corporate Sustainability. In T. Osburg and R. Schmidpeter (eds), *CSR, Sustainability, Ethics & Governance*, 13–22, New York: Springer.

Ostrom, E. (1990) *Governing the Commons: The Evolution of Institutions for Collective Action*, Cambridge: Cambridge University Press.

Parsons, T. (1951) *The Social System*, New York: Free Press.

Pestoff, V. A. (1991) *Between Markets and Politics: Co-operatives in Sweden*, Frankfurt am Main: Campus-Verlag.

Pestoff, V. A. (2009) *A Democratic Architecture for the Welfare State*, London: Routledge.

Pol, E. and Ville, S. (2009) Social Innovation: Buzz Word or Enduring Term? *Journal of Socio-Economics*, Vol. 38 (6), pp. 878–885.

Rao, H., Morrill, C. and Zald, M. N. (2000) Power Plays: How Social Movements and Collective Action Create New Organizational Forms, *Research in Organizational Behavior*, Vol. 22, pp. 239–282.

Riutort, S. (2016) *Energía para la democracia*, Madrid: FUHEM Ecosocial, Catarata.

Roy, M. J., Donaldson, C., Baker, R. and Kay, A. (2013) Social Enterprise: New Pathways to Health and Well-being? *Journal of Public Health Policy*, Vol. 34 (1), pp. 55–68.

Rueschemeyer, D. (2009) *Usable Theory: Analytic Tools for Social and Political Research*, Princeton, NJ: Princeton University Press.

Salamon, L., Sokolowski, S. W. and Anheier, H. K. (2000). Social origins of civil society: Anoverview (Working Paper of the Johns Hopkins Comparative Nonprofit Sector Project, No.38.). Baltimore, MD: The Johns Hopkins Center for Civil Society Studies.

Salamon, L. (2010) 'Putting the Civil Society Sector on the Economic Map of the World', *Annals of Public and Cooperative Economics*, Vol. 81 (2), pp. 167–210.

Salamon, L. M. and Sokolowski, S. W. (2014) The Third Sector in Europe: Towards a Consensus Conceptualization, Working Paper No. 02/2014. Available at: http://thirdsectorimpact.eu/site/assets/uploads/documentations/tsi-working-paper-no-2-third-sector-europe-towards-consensus-conceptualization/TSI-Wrkg-Ppr-2-Conceptualiza-fnl-2-17-15-.pdf [accessed 9 September 2016].

Sousa Santos (de), B. (2007) *Beyond Abyssal Thinking: From Global Lines to Ecologies of Knowledges*. Available at www.boaventuradesousasantos.pt/media/pdfs/Beyond_Abyssal_Thinking_Review_2007.PDF [accessed 3 November 2016].

Spear, R. and Hulgård, L. (2006) Social Entrepreneurship and the Mobilisation of Social Capital in European Social Enterprises. In M. Nyssens (ed.), *Social Enterprise: At the Crossroads of Market, Public Policies and Civil Society*, 85–108, London: Routledge.

Subirats, J. (ed.) (2005) Democracia, participación y transformación social, *Polis. Revista Latinoamericana*. Available at http://polis.revues.org/5599 [accessed 3 October 2016].

Subirats, J. and García Bernardos, A. (eds) (2015) *Innovación social y políticas urbanas en España. Experiencias significativas en las grandes ciudades*, Barcelona: Icaria editorial.

Tarde, G. (1899) *Social laws: An outline of sociology*, New York: Macmillan.

Teasdale, S. (2012) What's in a Name? Making Sense of Social Enterprise Discourses, *Public Policy and Administration*, Vol. 27 (2), pp. 99–119.

Tracey, P., Phillips, N. W. and Jarvis, O. (2011) Bridging Institutional Entrepreneurship and the Creation of New Organizational Forms: A Multilevel Model, *Organization Science*, Vol. 22 (1), pp. 60–80.

van der Have, R. P. and Rubalcaba, L. (2016) Social Innovation Research: An Emerging Area of Innovation Studies? *Research Policy*, Vol. 45 (9), pp. 1923–1935.

van Wijk, J. C., Zietsma, C., Dorado, S., de Bakker, F. G. A. and Martí, I. (2019) Social Innovation: Integrating Micro, Meso, and Macro Level Insights from Institutional Theory, *Business and Society*, Vol. 58 (5), pp. 887–918.

Weber, C., Kröger, A., and Lambrich, K. 2012. Scaling social enterprises – A theoretically grounded framework, Frontiers of Entrepreneurship Research, 32 (19), Article 3. Available at: http://digitalknowledge.babson.edu/fer/vol32/iss19/3

Wejnert, B. (2014) *Diffusion of Democracy: The Past and Future of Global Democracy*, New York: Cambridge University Press.

WILCO (2014) *Policy Brief: Lessons Learnt about the Sustainability and Diffusion of Social Innovation, Based on the Evidence of the WILCO Project*. Available at https://ec.europa.eu/research/social-sciences/pdf/policy_briefs/wilco_eu_policy_brief_032014.pdf [accessed 22 March 2016].

Wright, E. O. (2010) *Envisioning Real Utopias*, London: Verso.

Yunus, M. (2010) Social Business: A Step toward Creating a New Economic and Social Order, Working Papers No. 2383, eSocialSciences.

Zamagni, V. N. (2012) Interpreting the Roles and Economic Importance of Cooperative Enterprises in a Historical Perspective, *Journal of Entrepreneurial and Organizational Diversity*, Vol. 1 (1), pp. 21–36.

3 Culture as a Field for Social Innovation and Social Enterprise

3.1 The Complex Relationship between Culture and Social Transformation

There is no agreed-upon definition of culture, and therefore, despite the ubiquity of the term, it should be clarified every time it is discussed. The term 'culture' became a key scientific concept as mainly sociologists (but also anthropologists and economists) in the US began to reinterpret and use the contributions of Tylor, Boas, Durkheim and Lévy-Bruhl (Cuche, 2010). Culture has been conceptualised in a universal-versus-individualistic sense as well as in general-versus-specific views, depending on the theories, approaches and logics being used. The advent of 'the cultural turn' in the 1970s contributed to bridging academic disciplines and creating symbiotic expressions such as Bourdieu's 'cultural capital' (Jameson, 1998).

Since then, 'cultural' has been used either in a restricted sense in reference to 'the symbolic creations socially endorsed stemming from the field of the arts at large' (Cuche, 2010: 80) or in a larger ethnological sense of a set of 'attitudes, beliefs, customs, values and practices which are commonly shared by a group' (Throsby, 2001: 4), which also includes artistic production. More recently, two additional developments took place within the continuum space between these two definitions of 'culture': on the one hand, the explosion of activity areas using the label 'culture' (such as 'work culture' or 'enterprise culture') and, on the other hand, the diversification of mechanisms and tools involved in the production, mediation and consumption of cultural goods and services (e.g. self-production of culture, technology-supported home consumption, etc.).

Throsby (2001) complemented the definition of culture in his influential work *Economics and Culture*. For Throsby, culture encompasses the activities undertaken by a group of people and the product of these activities, drawing upon enlightenment and education of the mind. The author characterises particular expressions of culture as incorporating some degree of creativity, generating and communicating symbolic meanings and including, to some extent, intellectual property. One of the virtues of this definition is that it bypasses the trap of selecting a specific sector of activity to label something

DOI: 10.4324/9781003342144-4

as 'cultural', thus allowing the inclusion of other emerging cultural practices, the creative and cultural industries and other traditional/artisanal practices.

In the past, culture as a human and economic activity field was usually conceptualised around poles that included production, mediation and consumption. Indeed, Becker (1982) and Moulin (1997) offer well-known descriptions of the complex system of artistic production and how these three main cultural functions (production, mediation and consumption) are fulfilled by different socioeconomic agents. Even though these three elements can still be found in numerous examples in the cultural field, they have undergone profound mutations (Rodríguez Morató, 2012; Muñoz López, 2007).

Some elements of this transformation, such as changes in working arrangements, have had a direct impact on the objective and subjective conditions of artists and creators. For the present research, I will focus on three aspects of this ongoing transformation, with the aim to set the ground for understanding the emergence of attempts to counteract some of these negative effects for cultural workers: the progressive blurring of the producer–consumer boundary in the field of culture and the arts, the increased social and political commitment of artists and other cultural workers and the real social transformation that is being brought about by culture and the arts.

Firstly, regarding the production function of culture, the dichotomy between producer or creator and receiver or consumer has tended to blur. Compared to only a few decades ago, today, such blurring has been accelerated by technology: production tools have become more accessible to the public, and the production process has become simplified. Coupled with the increased leisure time at the disposal of potential artists and creators, a 'creativity explosion' has taken place. In this context, public administrations have tackled culture (and particularly the creative industries) as a promising professional development pathway, in many cases ending in self-employment and/or a freelance relationship with intermittent employers (Menger, 2005). Research on this 'flexibility' suggests that flexible work arrangements do not follow rational calculations on the part of workers, but are the result of a predominantly individualistic culture composed of autonomy and short-term vision, producing social insecurity and new work–life (im)balances (Nanteuil (de) and El Akremi, 2005). Making ends meet in this uncertain and unstable environment directly impacts the economic autonomy of artists and culture professionals.

Secondly, as the above-described conditions come about, professionals in the arts and culture sector have become increasingly active, forming from scratch and/or joining what are known as 'new social movements' and political activism in general. In short, in the last two decades, there has been a revival of socially and politically committed artists and cultural workers (BAVO, 2011; Hope, 2017; Byrne et al., 2018). What seems clear is that, for a growing number of artists, 'art has long ceased to be about what it says, represents or reflects, but about what the work "does", effects or generates in the social context in which it operates' (BAVO, 2011: 289), although there is no agreement on how to strengthen the potential of arts and culture as a main vehicle for protest, social demand and contestation in the public space (Bishop, 2012; Jackson, 2011; Harvie, 2013). These 'pragmatic art' practices try to counteract the negative effects of neoliberal policies, but since they often fail to engage in reflection about transforming the underlying structures through sustained political action, they remain restricted to a humanitarian type of action (the authors refer to them as 'NGO artists').[1] Terry Eagleton (2000) explained how the relationship between the arts and politics is historically determined and that it is useful to remember that specific periods in history have required explicit political activism as a precondition for the production of meaningful art (BAVO, 2011; Hope, 2017; Sanz and Rodríguez-Labajos, 2021). One of the underlying assumptions of this book is that by forming active, committed and connected communities, cultural workers and artists might have a better chance to articulate a shared political project within their own artistic discipline and beyond. The initial basis of such transformation could possibly be the values put forward by the social and solidarity economy, as already embraced by many cultural organisations adhering to them.

Lastly, new emerging practices (as well older ones that had remained in the fringes) are bringing together the notion of culture and social innovation. Some case studies have illustrated how culture and the arts achieve real social transformation in given contexts.[2] Although most of the research has been done in urban settings, some highly innovative experiences of rural-based networks are also emerging (Nogales Muriel, 2023). It is crucial for a study like the present one to keep in mind those countermovements that have emerged in reaction to, or on the margins of, this mainstream evolutionary track just described. Two trends worth following are the development of social creativity in rural areas (and the emergence of rural-based networks of culture around them) and the reappropriation and rehumanisation of urban spaces via culture and the arts. Related to the former, good examples of social innovation in rural and sparsely populated areas driven by culture and the arts are found in the experience of Montemor-o-Novo, in the deprived Alentejo region of Portugal and in the Ecopoetry Festival of the Jerte Valley in Spain. As for the latter, initiatives like Olinda in Milan, Italy, and the Bookstore project in the Netherlands constitute paradigmatic examples of all that has been said above.[3]

3.1.1 The Invisibilisation of the Social Value of Culture and Its Progressive Return

My main assumption on the relationship between culture and social innovation is that the disjunction between 'social value' (in the sense of social transformation as seen above) and 'artistic or cultural quality' when referring to the contribution of artists has been artificially constructed. A historic look at the evolution of these two notions can offer support for this assumption. Indeed, at one point in modern history, the connection between art and society was engineered to be interrupted, the most notable example being Greenberg's 'art for art's sake' in the post–World War II period (Greenberg, 1979). Such interruption consisted of at least two logics that were rapidly accepted and normalised: the increase in canonisation processes (whereby artists were allowed to access 'Mount Olympus' that was formerly reserved for only a few), and the growing complexity of the aesthetic languages that were officially considered as 'contemporary art' (including the traditional visual arts, performing arts and the more radical ones like performance art, video art and graffiti). Both logics rendered contemporary arts accessible to only a reduced group of citizens, which in turn caused the relationship between the artist (production) and the public (consumption) to either disappear or suffer a high degree of mediatisation (shown by the boom in arts managers and cultural agents). Such constatation made cultural agents to realise that culture without wider audiences would not last long and would have a limited impact. This was the beginning of the next turning point: slowly, around the 1990s, there was an interest in the engagement of audiences on the part of cultural agents specialised in mediating and presenting culture (especially museums of all types, symphonies, operas, etc.). The separation between social value and cultural value would not last long because, among other reasons, culture continued to be created outside these institutionalised circles within communities and as part of the independent cultural scene, although these alternative 'agencies of action' were invisibilised.

A decade later, economists and 'marketers' around the world appropriated the values and practices of culture and the arts in order to promote their value as tools for economic and social development. These processes of intensive economisation also took place in spheres such as politics (Laville and Salmon, 2015) and healthcare (Roy et al., 2013). This turn made some scholars to appeal to 'put the arts back into arts policy making' (Caust, 2003), but unfortunately, policy-making did not escape the rationalisation of what some called 'instrumental cultural policy' (Belfiore, 2002). Several authors have insisted on the danger of putting the emphasis on the 'economic justifiers' for public arts and culture in general, and especially for artists and artistic organisations, 'since serving the state as an economic generator is very different from taking risks artistically, or being innovative and creative generally' (Caust, 2003: 54).

The notion of 'creative industries' appeared around this time and represented the epitome of this process of instrumentalisation. In a context of high unemployment and initial budget cuts in publicly funded culture, the cultural industries generated a large quantitative basis for its legitimation, which resulted in their adoption and promotion across Europe. Arguably, two positive consequences of this instrumentalisation of culture and the arts as an economic tool by local, national and European public bodies have been, first, the benefit for a few cultural organisations and, second, the bridging of culture to other policy areas such as social and labour policies (Pascual i Ruiz, 1998).

The trend towards the rationalisation of culture and the arts culminated in the implementation of the 'creative class' idea proposed by Florida (2002), which rapidly turned into an ambiguous and contested notion. The creative city narrative aimed to create liveliness in urban centres through the creativity of its inhabitants resulting in wealth and inner satisfaction, as exemplified by numerous examples. The 'spectacle' and 'Cultural Temples' have become part of the daily life of citizens, particularly in urban centres and cities that seem to have begun a never-ending competition for spectacularity through architecture, large-sized festivals, blockbuster exhibits and other events (Moulaert et al. 2005; OECD, 2005). However, the dark side of the notion was savage processes of gentrification, banalisation of cultural and creative proposals and the pressures of financial speculation on urban contexts (Harvey, 2012). In other words, social cohesion, equality and real participation for all citizens remained an unmet goal of the 'creative city'. For instance, the private sector was often the first to exploit some of the positive externalities produced by regeneration processes using strategies such as real estate speculation, which was a major factor in the failure of the 'creative city' approach that targeted citizens without financial power.

3.1.2 Culture and Creativity as Drivers for Social Innovation

The relationship between creativity and culture, and innovation is a complex one. Firstly, as we have seen in the case with culture, there is not just one definition of innovation that can be applied to culture as there are many heterogeneous cultural fields and actions as well as different economic logics at play in each of them. Moreover, different ideological and political – and thus economic – interpretations emanate according to which notion of culture is used (Eagleton, 2000). Music, literature, performing arts and visual arts constitute unique systems of production, mediation and consumption – each with different industries and value scales behind them (YProductions, 2009).

Some think that it is tautological to speak of innovation in culture and the arts, as they are seen to be always 'pushing the boundaries'. However, the dominant discourse around innovation in Europe in the last ten years, characterised by an economic and managerial nature, has also percolated to culture and the arts. Adorno and Horkheimer's classical criticism of the influence of mass production and commodification on culture has been strengthened by critical voices that justify culture as a means for something else, such as developmental, social or economic goals benefitting large groups of citizens or the general interest (Yúdice, 2002; Moulaert et al., 2005; Sanz and Rodríguez-Labajos, 2021).

At this point, the issue of the autonomy of the arts within society rises. Some deem it crucial for maintaining their independence from elements that aim to instrumentalise the arts, but to talk about such autonomy in the current capitalist economy can be considered a utopian exercise (YProductions, 2009). Therefore, considering the difficulty of securing total autonomy for the arts, as well as the fact that some cultural actors do not subscribe to the quest of such autonomy, what seems clear is that for a cultural and artistic artefact or expression to be considered innovative, it must contribute to legitimating the very artistic category to which it belongs (YProductions, 2009). Therefore, identifying the category of a given cultural or artistic production, as well as its goals and contexts, is crucial for determining its innovation potential.

Returning to the social innovation literature, creativity has been identified as a driver of social innovation (BEPA, 2010; Tremblay and Pilati, 2013). The assumption that the field of culture is a locus of creativity has led to the deduction that it has a high potential for social innovation. Although initial studies and an explosion of initiatives may suggest so, their sustainability and real transformational power are yet to be confirmed by social science research. Some cultural initiatives are delivering social innovation for local communities, but experience tells us that most of them remain local and reduced in scale, so replication is certainly not the average.

A possible key to the link between social innovation and culture is offered by André and Abreu (2010) – turning creativity into 'social creativity'. Creativity is usually recognised as a human ability related to cognitive abilities to produce novel thoughts, ideas and images (Sternberg, 1999). When applied to a group of individuals, we can speak of *social* creativity and the preconditions it requires to emerge: diversity, tolerance and open-mindedness, as well as learning and critical thinking (André and Abreu, 2010). These authors also identify a set of preconditions for social innovation to flourish: participation, collective references and memories, leadership and adequate geographical scales. Table 3.1 briefly defines and compares these preconditions.

A second related but distinct concept for understanding how social innovation comes about in the field of culture is 'collective intelligence'. A term borrowed from studies of the animal world, collective intelligence is different from the sum of its parts (the intelligence of individuals) and depends on properties that are only found in the whole: in this sense, it is an 'emergent' property that, when the right level of integration is in place, can produce outputs similar to those associated with rational agency (Landemore, 2013).[4] Collective intelligence is distributed, that is, not concentrated in one place or unit of a system, be that an organisation or country. Needless to say, people included in the group or collective unit continue to have their own individual intelligence which, in the field of culture, is of paramount importance for creative processes.

Table 3.1 Preconditions for social creativity and social innovation

Social creativity	*Social innovation*
Diversity: understood as a variety of experiences, ideas and perspectives brought together **Tolerance and open-mindedness:** understood as the general acceptance of failure, risk-taking is encouraged **Learning and critical thinking:** understood as the capacity to appropriate, deconstruct and reconstruct new information so as to imbue old institutions and structures with new meanings	**Participation:** understood as collective cooperation, dialogue and, whenever necessary, conflict (in a critical and positive understanding of the latter) **Collective references and memories:** understood as necessary anchors that ensure the resilience of places and their ability to embrace what is new without degenerating into fragmentation **Leadership:** understood as the initial vision and impulse for consequent collective action **Adequate geographical scales:** understood as the lack of destructive tensions from the places involved. This results in 'plastic' places that modify their shape without sacrificing the internal structure and coherence (Lambert, 2004).

Source: Adapted from André and Abreu (2010).

In the current knowledge economy driven by neoliberal policies, it has been the trend to appreciate more the prospects and initiatives stemming from social groups whose relevance as an economic resource is increasing (YProductions, 2009). Therefore, to be considered an innovation in culture, any breakthrough in social creativity needs to reach a market, thus leading to the necessary economisation of cultural practices (YProduction, 2009). Then, regarding social innovation, André and Abreu point out that it 'takes social creativity a step forward, in the sense that it puts greater emphasis on the social appropriation and dissemination of socially creative "novelties"' (2010: 63).

From this standpoint, social innovation in culture faces the challenging task of distributing and capitalising on collective intelligence so as to contribute to the general interest and not to private interests. Plus, it supposedly should do so in a way that protects the creative autonomy of artists and cultural workers (Dubetz et al., 2015). This translates, in practice, into the capacity for combining the *potential* for conceiving of human, viable and sustainable alternatives (a de facto creative social laboratory) with the *concreteness* of interventions in society via human, viable and sustainable initiatives that are effective and efficient vis-à-vis the *territory* and the *human community* they target (Dubetz et al., 2014). Saying so does not imply that the supra-local level should be ignored; on the contrary, supra-local instances that work for the recognition of 'culture as the fourth pillar' of sustainable development (together with the economic, social and environmental dimensions) should be promoted (Stone, 2004; Hawkes, 2006). However, such promotion should be bottom-up, as a top-down approach to the creation of representative bodies usually results in a low level of representation; plus, such bodies should be governed in the same democratic and equalitarian manner that they defend.

Regarding civil society initiatives, international umbrella organisations such as Culture Action Europe (CAE) and the European Network of Cultural Centres (ENCC) are crucial for exchanging best practices and conducting a lobbying action vis-à-vis public authorities and the market. In so doing, a sense of community is created which reinforces the willingness to contribute to the building of such community with participation and commitment. For instance, CAE focuses on the collectively identified needs and challenges facing the sector and works from within the field to create ties with other activity fields and actors. A member-based organisation – CAE – organises annual events and ad hoc campaigns and has become a crucial interlocutor with European organisations such as the European Commission (EC), the European Economic and Social Committee and the European Parliament. At the national level, the experience of the network of entities and agents of community culture in Spain (*Red de Espacios y Agentes de Cultura Comunitaria* – REACC) has provided a unique environment in which to articulate over 300 initiatives, collectives and agents who are a self-described part of community culture.[5]

3.1.3 Social Innovation and Culture: Revealing the Implicit Connection

The relationship between culture and innovation remains a conflicting one, inter alia, due to the mainstream economics approach to innovation. As we have seen, innovation has become a necessary element to every aspect related to the public and private financing of culture. However, in order to understand the implications of innovation in culture, we need to grasp the ideological underpinnings that explain the production systems – including actors and goals – mobilised within 'innovation' and 'culture'.

For the present research, I have adopted the approach to innovation in culture proposed by YProductions and used the notion of 'social creativity' and its connection to social innovation developed by two researchers who participated in the Katarsis European project.[6] Before doing so, though, a word of caution must be put forward, seconding the warning of these authors. These distinctions and categorisations should be taken for what they are: an analytical aid to help us navigate the unknown and heterogeneous field of innovation and culture. All categories mentioned below are tightly interwoven, are not mutually exclusive and cannot be conceived on their own because they influence each other.

According to YProductions, innovation in culture can be considered analytically as moving around three dimensions: *auto-generative innovation* (the cultural field itself advances in the sense of emerging culture or new cultural categories/practices/styles), *instrumentalising innovation* (a modification in processes, practices and/or behaviours is sought by actors outside of the cultural field to advance political, economic and ideological goals) and *traditional market-driven innovation* (innovation happens in the cycle of demands based on needs via traditional cultural markets). Together, they form the space for innovation in the cultural sphere.

Connected to these dimensions are three dominant strategies for 'economising' cultural practices, so as to meet the request of 'reaching a market' needed to speak about innovation in culture. These categories of innovation are a *culture of innovation* through the creation of an environment that supports creative thinking and shapes a cultural framework to drive innovations (Karnaukhova, 2015); *innovating culture* through the simulation of demand of cultural products; and *emergent culture* through the endogenous development of the cultural sphere. Each of these aims at different objectives and has different promoters or actors. Table 3.2 summarises all three dimensions and categories of innovation in culture.

The way in which the cultural sphere interacts with social creativity and vice versa is important to analyse. This two-way relationship between culture and social creativity results in the embeddedness of culture in social creativity, to which it contributes in new and innovative ways. However, this embeddedness could be achieved in a socially innovative way – or

Table 3.2 Possible types of innovation in culture

	Innovation category	*Goals*	*Promoters/main actors*	*Examples*
Instrumentalising innovation	Culture of innovation	Planned economic and territorial development	Policymakers and public administrations	Urban regeneration, cultural tourism
Traditional market-driven innovation	Innovating culture	Stimulation of the demand of cultural products	Public administrations and for-profit actors operating in the field of culture	Blockbuster exhibitions, series of cities of culture
Auto-generative innovation	Emergent culture	Endogenous development of the cultural sphere	Cultural actors and related institutions	Reflective cultural praxis, co-created cultural processes and events

Source: Adapted from YProductions (2009).

not.[7] Figure 3.1 visually captures the complexity of the spaces and forms of innovation in culture and the notions of 'social creativity' and 'collective intelligence'.

I have intended to enrich the original model by including collective intelligence in the area of social creativity. Furthermore, I suggest that a specific type of social creativity originates in the specialised cultural sphere. While the cultural sphere obviously feeds from society's wider social creativity and contributes to it in a mutually enriching loop (designated by the arrows in Figure 3.1), I claim that a collective intelligence can be put into motion when the social creativity of individuals in the cultural sphere is activated. We refer to this type of ability as *specialised cultural creativity* to distinguish it from cultural intelligence (Ang et al., 2015), culture-based creativity (Karnaukhova, 2015) and creative intelligence (Nussbaum, 2013). It is surprising to see how these terms have been combined in all possible forms by experts and academics to create novel concepts that, in themselves, combine innovation, creativity, a social /collective dimension and intelligence. Very briefly, we would like to illustrate that 'cultural intelligence' – coined by Early and Ang in 2003 – is the capability to relate and work effectively in culturally diverse situations. The term 'cultural creatives' was first coined by Ray and Anderson (2000) to refer to citizens with specific values which combine a focus on their spirituality with a strong passion for social activism. A third term is 'culture-based creativity', which emanates from the fact that

> culture feeds creativity to the extent of conventions under which community exists and influence sociality through cultural environment (including education and training), cultural capital, and specific skills.

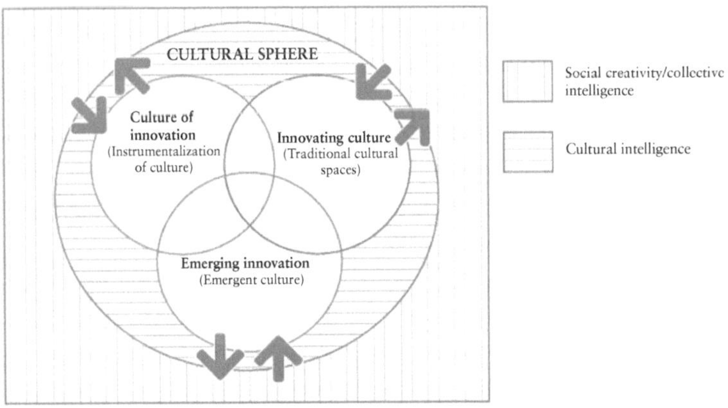

Figure 3.1 Possible spaces and categories of innovation in culture.
Source: Adapted from YProductions (2009).

> It is when creativity is the expression of human sensibility (such as imagination, intuition, memories, affects) that it becomes culture-based creativity.
>
> (Karnaukhova, 2015: 204)

As we can see, these three definitions approach culture in the wide and large sense, and therefore are relevant only tangentially to our discussion. 'Creative intelligence' (Nussbaum, 2013) is the ability to go beyond the existing to create novel and interesting ideas and so is too vague and large to fit our purposes.

Far from contributing to the terminological confusion, it is my aim to emphasise the specific ability to produce novel solutions – ideas that people involved in (or are in touch with) the cultural sphere share can take the form of any of the three types of innovation (culture of innovation, innovating culture and auto-generative innovation).

These three strategies for economising culture and making innovation apparent are not the only ones possible. Indeed, this economisation does not necessarily imply a market-based economy and can function within different models of economy such as the 'substantive' economy (Laville, 2010). The substantive economy (or 'plural economy' as it has been called since recently) proposes that a plurality of economic principles exists beyond the rational market-based and scarcity approaches to include a more substantive relationship among humans and between humans and nature. The work of Karl Polanyi, and his notion of substantive or plural economy, draws on history and anthropology to help us understand the different possible logics at play in the economic realm. Literature on the plural economy (Roustang et al. 1996), including the work of Polanyi ([1944] 1975), shows that the dominance of the market is relatively recent. Such dominant positions should be relativised with the inclusion of the mechanisms of redistribution and reciprocity. As explained in Chapter 2, reciprocity constitutes the integrating principle within the solidarity economy and takes the form of voluntary work, solidarity networks, donations and so on (Gardin, 2005).

The reciprocity aspect and plural economy approach have received little attention in the field of culture, except in France where the works of sociologist Jean-Louis Laville and other scholars, the Opale association and the manifesto published in 2007 by the *Union fédérale d'intervention des structures culturelles* (UFISC – Federal Union of Intervention of Cultural Structures) have paved the way for a line of work daring to combine innovation and solidarity in the field of culture through a formal allegiance to the principles of solidarity economy. As we saw above, the core value of the social and solidarity economy is to place human beings at the heart of the functioning of each activity area (including culture) which is conducted in a sustainable way. Such value translates into concrete organisational principles that can be summarised as: primacy of the general interest over private interest, democratic or participatory decision-making, equality of rights and reinvestment of profits generated by the organisation. These cultural structures in France have the following characteristics (Colin and Gauthier, 2010):

- They are multi-goal, multi-activity and multi-stakeholder organisations;
- They give priority to the articulation of different and plural voices in the public space;
- They are embedded in their territories and activate local actors and institutions;
- They follow logics of collaboration and cooperation and, when they reach a significant size, tend to invest in the emergence of other organisations, rather than securing a hegemonic position;
- They implement participatory or democratic governance, thereby assuring the commitment of key stakeholders and the relevance of actions and mission;
- They tend to be small to middle-sized organisations, mostly of an associative form, which allows them to enjoy some flexibility in terms of financing and also workers with a poly-competency in various areas;
- They mobilise the three types of resources already mentioned (market, redistribution and reciprocity);
- Their (auto-generative) innovation is related to experimentation and it is welcomed insofar as it respects the values described.

In the last decade, cultural actors, mainly from civil society but in partnership with public administrations and private firms, have gradually begun to recognise the values in common with this way of conceiving and practising the economy. Indeed, external factors mentioned in this text (globalisation, shrinking public budgets, social conflicts emanating from large-scale immigration, etc.) are forcing cultural actors to revise the way in which they conceive, finance, produce and disseminate their product in order to survive and be sustainable (Dubetz et al., 2015). Although the most obvious way to identify the cultural initiatives that adhere to such principles could seem to be through the type of legal form chosen (associations, social cooperatives, etc.) or the public they target (e.g. disadvantaged audiences), these are too limited to provide an accurate enough picture of the field (Colin and Gauthier, 2010). Some of the challenges facing such recognition are (1) the sectoral nature of culture and the arts, which tends to prevent identification with larger values and goals; (2) the lack of awareness of the nature of the social and solidarity economy on the part of cultural actors; and (3) the limited resources available to organisations for developing partnerships beyond their day-to-day operations and for participating in debates and discussion.

Despite these challenges, the number of organisations and actors that informally adhere to the social and solidarity economy values (economic autonomy, participation, collaboration, empowerment, etc.) is growing; they are also beginning to constitute a political and economic force with relevant transformational potential, mostly at the local level, but also at the national and international levels. The transformation I am referring to has little to do with the vision of unlimited growth based on the exploitation of natural and human resources around the globe that drove the industrial and technological transformations of the nineteenth and twentieth centuries: it is human- and environment-centred.

Polanyi was one of the precursors of such an approach, saying:

> The substantive meaning of economic derives from man's dependence for his living upon nature and his fellows. It refers to the interchange with his natural and social environment, in so far as these result in supplying him with the means of material want satisfaction.
>
> (Polanyi et al., 1957: 243)

Indeed, the substantive (or plural) approach to the economy puts to the test the statement that 'the promotion of culture and the arts within the context of local development strategies may provide a crucial contribution to harmonising the goals of economic competitiveness and social cohesion (as well as those of economic innovation and social innovation)', but 'will not be a broad-based, participatory approach to culture and the arts that is able to (re)combine collective memory and collective creation' (André and Abreu, 2010: 60).

When it comes to policy-making, the goal is to create 'virtuous synergies' between several development axes related to culture (e.g. historical and natural heritage, artistic creation, etc.) and social inclusion (e.g. participation, cohesion, emancipation, etc.) (André and Abreu, 2010).

The emphasis social innovation puts on social transformation is acknowledged to be a '*relative* detriment of the creative act *per se*', but this should not mean an inherent loss of creativity (André and Abreu, 2010: 63, original emphasis). On the contrary, finding the right context where collaborations and institutional arrangements can combine all three dimensions (the social, the artistic/cultural and the economic) becomes urgent both for culture (conceived as embedded in society) and for social innovation (incorporating the cultural dimension as a crucial element in any process of transformation). I suggest that social enterprises constitute one of these choices through which we can hope for the development of a cultural field that not only is aware of and promotes social justice but also makes it a central element of its raison d'être.

An interesting case at hand is that of 'community culture' which is gaining momentum in countries like Spain after decades of being invisibilised. The formal entities active in this area are increasingly being recognised for adhering to the principles and values of the social and solidarity economy and adopting its legal forms (REACC, 2022). Despite the well-being, involvement and sustainability this proximity-based culture generates, many of these initiatives work with reduced resources and support from public administrations. These limitations, together with the proximity and trust required to make community culture thrive, result in a difficulty to adapt well to the messages, codes and channels characteristic of mainstream media and traditional cultural institutions (Rowan, 2016; REACC, 2021).

3.2 Social Enterprises and the Field of Culture

3.2.1 An Emerging Type of Organisation: Cultural and Artistic Social Enterprise

The study of social enterprises has focused on their contribution to the social, economic and environmental aspects of sustainable development. Indeed, they have played a crucial role in the provision of services for disadvantaged groups as well as in the creation of new products and services via innovative processes. Unfortunately, so far, the potential of culture for social enterprise development has received very limited attention (Caruana and Nogales Muriel, 2020). Culture has been considered a mere activity field for social enterprises, which has hampered the recognition of the true meaning of (social) creativity and innovative processes in cultural and artistic initiatives in the field of social and solidarity economy. So far, culture has been studied in relation to the well-being of individuals and groups (Guetzkow, 2002; Keaney, 2006), social cohesion of various groups (Bisballe, 2006), the integration of people with disabilities and groups at risk of social exclusion (Jermyn, 2004) and the competitiveness and liveliness of cities (Florida, 2002; Arts Victoria, 2008).

Only recently has culture began to be approached from the social innovation perspective, which has unveiled the complex locus of culture in the transition process and the transformation of societies (Moulaert et al., 2014; ENCC, 2021). Through their promotion of a new model of sustainable development, based on the creation of social, economic, environmental and (more recently) cultural value, social enterprises rooted in the social and solidarity economy have the potential to bring about *true* social innovation through *real* social transformation. Therefore, the potential of culture within an integrated framework of solidarity and sustainability has been overlooked in part by ignoring social enterprises active in the field of culture.

The emergence of 'Cultural and Artistic Social Enterprise' (CASE) consolidates culture as a promising field of activity for the larger social and solidarity economy. The main activity areas where CASE is active include: the arts, especially visual and performing arts, via associations and cooperatives of dancers, musicians and actors; handcrafts and artisanry (jewellery, ceramics, sewing, etc.); publishing and illustration by independent publishing houses supported by IT solutions (print-on-demand, self-publishing, etc.); artistic and cultural education, using the associative form as the basis for creating schools; and innovative disciplines at the crossroads of other traditional disciplines such as multicultural products (fashion, cooking, festivals, etc.), multicultural tourism, heritage and conservation and urban planning. From a political perspective, social enterprises involved in culture tend to defend culture as a basic social need and treat it as a public good, regardless of whether they are active in the field of production, mediation or consumption. Moreover, by being financially independent from external bodies, they claim to be 'schools of democracy', empowerment and emancipation (Spear and Hulgård, 2006; Eschweiler and Hulgård, 2012).

The enlargement of the field of social and solidarity economy to include culture can be considered the result of at least three phenomena: firstly, the economic crisis after the stock market crash in 2007–2008, which resulted in a profound reformulation of welfare traditions and a sense of urgency to find alternative recipes for employment and solidarity; secondly, the advent of the 'culture society', which has erased borders typically separating culture from other spheres of society and brought in the creative industries as a leading productive sector of society; and thirdly, the reactivation of the field of culture and the arts as a test-bed for imagining alternative political, economic and environmental arrangements.

Culture and the social and solidarity economy share unique, essential values insofar as they put people and their capabilities at its centre: people as the core of cultural and/or social transformation for sustainable development. Based on praxis, CASE offers a rare example of organisational settings embracing all four dimensions of sustainable development (social cohesion, economic growth, environmental balance and culture). As shown in Figure 3.2, CASE shows organisational traits of both social enterprises and cultural organisations, which adds to the already complex 'multi-goal nature' and hybridity of this institutional arrangement (Battilana and Lee, 2014 Nyssens, 2006). However, it must be said that most CASEs show a typical characteristic of the cultural sector – the artistic vision taking precedence over market considerations (Colbert, 2011).

The trust social enterprises are able to mobilise among workers/members, and between them and customers or beneficiaries, originates in the multi-goal nature of an organisation that accepts 'a satisfactory rather than a maximal return on their capital' (Pestoff, 2009: 101) in exchange for meeting other non-financial goals. Such lack of primacy for profit-maximising, market-based transactions might reduce one traditional conflict at play in the cultural field: the ambivalence of the artist in the face of money and her related plea for autonomy. The core of this conflict has been located in the market-based exchange of a cultural or artistic artefact (be it the commissioning or the salary-based relationship) (Chiapello, 1998).

The few CASE initiatives that are well known are locally focused and develop activities for close audiences. Moreover, only some of them

Figure 3.2 Multi-goal nature of CASE.

have been integrated into second-level representative or transversal sectoral organisations, which hinders the possibility of their needs being addressed. In this context, there are only a few examples of CASEs that have expanded geographically. SMart is the most well-known case of a social innovation in culture in the form of a social enterprise. It reinvented collaboration in the field of culture by putting in place a mutualistic perspective: the sharing of gains and losses of cultural actors as the only way to grow in a sustainable way and to 'exist' as a sector. Mutualisation means that both risks and benefits are shared by all members, something that has not traditionally characterised artistic and cultural creation, except in the case of some sectors such as actors' or painters' cooperatives. Although a detailed history of the coming together of culture and social enterprises is still to be made, this book attempts to make a contribution in that direction.

3.2.2 Current Context for Working in the Field of Culture in Europe

The current way in which the field of culture functions is having a direct effect on the traditional spheres of cultural production, mediation and consumption. This section summarises some of the factors mentioned above, but also introduces the missing elements that conform to the context for cultural creation nowadays and frames the creation of responses from the field itself, as has been found in the SMart case.

The dismantling of the public culture system as a result of neoliberal public policies and the 2007–2008 crisis has resulted in massive layoffs of culture agents, the closing down of venues and activities and the drastic reduction of financing available for cultural initiatives (Belfiore, 2022).

Moreover, in the case of Spain, the exorbitant tax raise implemented in 2013 (21% TVA) equated culture to luxury activities and products. Overall, the public support model for culture is disappearing, despite the fact that the European Parliament recognised already in 1999 that 'artists, whether creators or performers, are essential to ensuring that our society is both self-renewing and properly balanced' and so their 'role takes on a new significance as the voice which asks questions about the future and argues about the present, goes against the tide, helps society to develop a critical faculty and in general invigorates the entire social fabric'.

However, back then, the EC reported that in the European Union (EU) only 20% of artists had an 'adequate' income, meaning they make a living out of their work.[8] The situation has increasingly worsened in the last few decades for both large-scale public institutions and citizen-driven initiatives. For instance, the Reina Sofia Museum in Spain saw its budget decrease by 45% in 2008, although it was able to double its attendance figures in eight years. As stated by its director, it did so, despite the 'ecological destruction' caused by neoliberal policies, by mobilising resources other than direct public funding (income-generating activities, artwork loans, private and corporate donations and exhibit co-production) and by making a conscious effort to connect the museum to the world and place it within society in a meaningful way (Mora and Pastor, 2016). This combination of new resource mobilisation with a quest for meaning and relevance in society is shared by a neighbouring initiative, the 'Lavapiés Barrio de Teatros', which is radically different insofar as it stems from organised civil society in the form of social and solidarity economy entities (mostly associations but also cooperatives and foundations). After an initial success around 2008, backed by a steadily growing audience support, the grassroots movement that originated in the performing arts sector, based on alternative theatre spaces in the Lavapies neighbourhood of Madrid, saw stagnation in attendance numbers. This phenomenon was explained to be as a result of a glass ceiling related to the limited space available, increasing precariousness of its workers and a damaging competition among the alternative theatre spaces (Serrano Vidal, 2012). These circumstances drove some emblematic representatives to close down (e.g. La Bagatela, home of the 'teatro despojado' that originated in Argentina), and so in February 2014, in response to the economic, social and cultural crises, a network of theatre spaces 'diverse in form, spirit and content was born … with a common ground: theatre and dignity in our job' (Lavapiés Barrio de Teatros, 2014). This search for dignity, the network's manifesto states, is aimed at the level of not only theatre production but also its diffusion. Since its launch, the network has heavily relied on technology via a simple but efficient online platform, social media and an app for mobile devices.

The crisis and the austerity measures undertaken by the European institutions raised the level of precariousness throughout the continent,

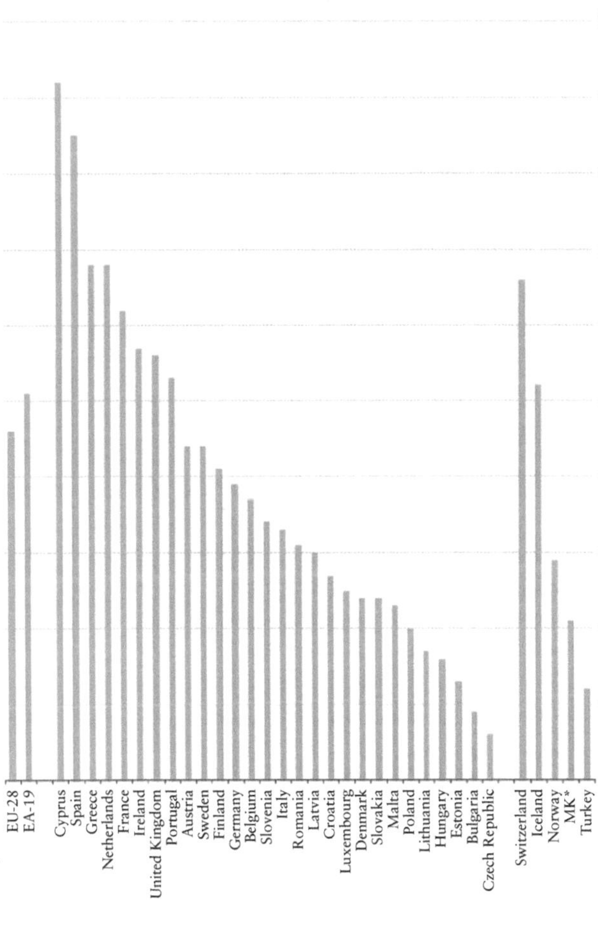

*The abbreviation MK used for the former Yugoslav Republic of Macedonia is a provisional code. The definitive nomenclature for this country will be agreed following current negotiations at UN level.

Graph 3.1 Underemployed part-time workers, persons aged 15–74, all countries, EA-19 and EU-28, annual average, 2015 (percentage of total employment).

thus adding a sense of urgency to the idea of exporting models like SMart to other contexts (see Graph 3.1). The ILO defines precarious employment as a 'work relation where employment security, which is considered one of the principal elements of the labour contract, is lacking. This term encompasses temporary and fixed term labour contracts, work at home, and sub-contracting' (ILO, 2011).

As for culture, according to Eurostat estimations, 6 million people were employed in the cultural field in the EU (about 3% of the total number of workers) in 2014.[9] Nearly half (49%) of the almost 2 million artists formally accounted for by Eurostat were self-employed, a much higher percentage compared with general workers who were self-employed (15%). Therefore, precariousness and work instability are higher in the cultural field than in other fields and are also characterised by high levels of temporality and short-term contracts. Other factors ultimately come into play, such as the size and structure of the market, the degree of competition and the luck factor as well as the stage the artist has reached in his or her career. In short, there are as many categories of entrepreneurs as there are practices in the creative professions.

In addition to the cuts in funding and the increased precariousness of culture professionals, creative production has also shrunk. In the specific case of creative industries, the 2010 UNCTAD (UN Conference on Trade and Development) report on creative economy said that, since the crisis started in 2008, international trade has shrunk by 12%. Unfortunately, this percentage has shrunk even further after the Covid-19 pandemic, with an average of 31% income loss and peaks of up to 90% in some sub-sectors (Goethe-Institut, 2021). For instance, in the case of community culture in Spain, only 5% of agents had earnings that enabled them to lead sustainable lives (REACC, 2022). The current, precarious and unstable context has added a sense of urgency to the plea launched in 1990 by the UNESCO to develop and implement a legal and institutional framework for creative workers and artists to have access to decent and stable jobs, social security and rights. The European Parliament continues to call upon policymakers 'to introduce a European Framework for Working Conditions in the cultural and creative sectors and industries (CCSI), which would provide guidelines and principles with a view to improving working conditions in the CCSIs'.[10] As a model stemming from the social and solidarity economy, this book illustrates how SMart provides one way of achieving this goal.

Notes

1 The discussion about boundaries and balance between culture (particularly the arts) and politics is an interesting one. Particularly, the notion of the tension between the search for 'autonomy' and a place of its own in society on the part of the arts and the struggle for 'heteronomy' so as to fuse with social reality and

use it as material that can be reconfigured according to artistic rules, put forward by Rancière (2006), are noteworthy. The grey zone where they meet is what the author refers to as 'the zone of indistinction of art and life'.

2 I cite three cases described in literature written in English. The first two are social enterprises: Olinda (Italy) by Thomas Emmenegger, which relates to the integration of patients of former psychological hospitals, and Kulturkælderen (Denmark) by Lise Bisballe, which relates to the integration of immigrants and asylum-seekers. The third case is a municipality-led development strategy that includes cultural activities: Montemor-o-Novo (Portugal) by Isabel André and Alexandre Abreu.

3 For more information on these initiatives, see the abovementioned case by Isabel André and Alexandre Abreu on Montemor-o-Novo (available at http://cordis.europa.eu/documents/documentlibrary/124376771EN6.pdf), the blog of the Ecopoetry Festival in the Jerte Valley (http://vocespoesiajerte.blogspot.com/), Olinda (www.olinda.org) and the Bookstore project websites.

4 This concept has been widely used with quite different meanings. For instance, in political theory it can refer to the 'democratic reason' of societies (Landemore, 2013), while in business and management studies, it is treated as 'empathy capital' to be exchanged in the era of 'invisible capitalism' (Tasaka, 2011).

5 See https://reacc.org.

6 The EU-funded Katarsis project (2006–2009) took the multidimensionality of social innovation into consideration and overcame fragmented analyses and strategies in the fight against social exclusion. See http://katarsis.ncl.ac.uk/index.html.

7 An example of this two-way dynamic used in a non-socially innovative manner is the way that commercial firms use culture and the arts to increase their sales. The issue of appropriation of culture by major corporations has often been in the media in Spain (see www.elconfidencial.com/cultura/2016-07-05/creatividad-desigualdad-paradojas-de-lo-cool_1226078/#lpu6AT6ErG36oDuw) in parallel to the publication of the book *Paradojas de lo cool. Arte, literatura, política* (*Paradoxes of the Cool. Art, Literature, Politics*) by Alberto Santamaría (Textos (in)surgentes, 2016).

8 See the two reports of the European Parliament: *Report on the Situation and Role of Artists in the European Union* (1999) (available at www.europarl.europa.eu/sides/getDoc.do?pubRef=-//EP//TEXT+REPORT+A4-1999-0103+0+DOC+XML+V0//EN) and the *Report on the Situation of Artists and the Cultural Recovery in the EU* (2021) (available at www.europarl.europa.eu/doceo/document/TA-9-2021-0430_EN.html).

9 This figure grew up to 7.4 million people in cultural employment across the EU (3.7% of total employment) even after the 10% drop that had occurred between 2019 and 2021 (Source: Eurostat).

10 *Report on the Situation of Artists and the Cultural recovery in the EU* (EU, 2021).

References

André, I. and Abreu, A. (2010) Understanding the Dynamics of Social Innovation through Arts: The Case of Montemor-o-Novo, Portugal. In F. Moulaert, D. MacCallum, A. Mehmood and A. Hamdouch (eds), *The International Handbook on Social Innovation: Collective Action, Social Learning and Transdisciplinary Research Project*, 60–66, Cheltenham: Edward Elgar. Available at http://cordis.europa.eu/documents/documentlibrary/124376771EN6.pdf [accessed 3 April 2015].

Arts Victoria (2008) The Role of Arts and Culture in Liveability and Competitiveness. Available at www.arts.vic.gov.au/files/89c10592-c289-453f-a7a0-9b6700df155d/Role_of_ArtsnCulture_in_Liveability-AV_submission_VCEC_liveability.pdf [accessed 20 April 2015].

Battilana, J. and Lee, M. (2014) Advancing research on hybrid organizing: Insights from the study of social enterprises. *Academy of Management Annals*, Vol (8), pp. 397–441.

BAVO (Gideon Boie and Matthias Pauwels) (2011) Artists, One More Effort To Be Really Political. In L. Carter (De), R. Roo and K. Vanhaesebrouck (eds), *Art and Activism in the Age of Globalization*, 288–297, Reflect #8, Rotterdam: NAi Publishers.

Becker, H. S. (1982) *Art Worlds*, Oakland, CA: University of California Press.

Belfiore, E. (2002) Art as a Means of Alleviating Social Exclusion: Does It Really Work? A Critique of Instrumental Cultural Policies and Social Impact Studies in the UK. *International Journal of Cultural Policy*, Vol. 8 (1), pp. 91–106.

Belfiore, E. (2022) Who cares? At what price? The hidden costs of socially engaged arts labour and the moral failure of cultural policy, *European Journal of Cultural Studies*, Vol. 25(1), pp. 61–78.

Bisballe, L. (2006) *Intercultural Social Entrepreneurship*, Copenhagen: COMEDIA.

Bishop, C. (2012) *Artificial Hells: Participatory Art and the Politics of Spectatorship*, New York: Verso Books.

Bureau of European Policy Advisers (BEPA) (2010) *Empowering People, Driving Change. Social Innovation in the European Union*, Brussels: Bureau of European Policy Advisors and European Commission.

Byrne, E., Elliott, E., Saltus, R. and Angharad, J. (2018) The Creative Turn in Evidence for Public Health: Community and Arts-Based Methodologies. *Journal of Public Health*, Vol. 40, pp. 24–30.

Caruana, V. and Nogales Muriel, R. (2020) Unlocking the Transformative Potential of Culture and the Arts through Social Enterprise, Empower-SE Stakeholder Brief No 5, Liege: EMES/COST. Available at https://bit.ly/2KR9n2S.

Caust, J. (2003) Putting the 'Art' Back into Arts Policy Making: How Arts Policy Has Been 'Captured' by the Economists and the Marketers. *International* Journal of Cultural Policy, Vol. 9 (1), pp. 51–63.

Chiapello, E. (1998) *Artistes versus Managers*, Paris: Métailié.

Colbert, F. (2011) Management of the Arts. In R. Towse (ed.), *A Handbook of Cultural Economics*, 266–272, Cheltenham: Edward Elgar.

Colin, B. and Gauthier, A. (2010) *Pour une autre économie de l'art et de la culture*, Paris: Editions érès.

Cuche, D. (2010) *La notion de culture dans les sciences sociales*, 4th ed., Paris: La Découverte.

Dubetz, E., Huchet, E., Cadic, P., Meresse, F., Burton, R. and de Mesmaeker, S. (2015) *Économie sociale, secteur culturel et creative. Vers une nouvelle forme d'entrepreneuriat social en France*, Cahiers #35, Brussels: Pour la Solidarité/SMart. Available at www.cresspaca.org/storage/files/actualites/economie-sociale-secteur-1074.pdf [accessed 11 March 2016].

Eagleton, T. (2000) *The Idea of Culture*. Oxford: Blackwell.

Eschweiler, J. and Hulgård, L. (2012) Social Innovation and Deliberative Democracy, EMES Working Paper No. 12/04, Liege: EMES International Research Network. Available at www.emes.net/site/wp-content/uploads/EMES-WP-12-04_Eschweiler-Hulgard_Final.pdf [accessed 2 September 2015].

European Network of Cultural Centres (ENCC) (2021) *Invisible Damage: Cultural Centres across Europe Warn against Severe Long-Term Effects on the Foundations of Socio-Cultural Work*, Brussels: ENCC. Available at https://encc.eu/sites/default/files/2021-09/encc_report_invisible_damage.pdf [accessed 15 December 2021].

Florida, R. (2002) *The Rise of the Creative Class*, New York: Basic Books.

Galera, G. and Nogales Muriel, R. (2021) Sustaining and Growing One of the Largest International Communities of Social Enterprise Scholars: The Empower-SE COST Action, Empower-SE Stakeholder Brief No. 11, Liege: EMES/COST. Available at www.empowerse.eu/wp-content/uploads/2021/12/EURICSE_Brief11-1.pdf [accessed 11 December 2021].

Gardin, L. (2005) La reciprocité. In J.-L. Laville and A. D. Cattani (eds), *Dictionnaire de l'autre économie*, 520–525, Toulouse: Ed. Erès.

Goethe Institute (2021) *Status and Working Conditions of Artists and Cultural and Creative Professionals*. Available at https://voicesofculture.eu/wp-content/uploads/2021/07/VoC-Brainstorming-Report-Working-Conditions-2.pdf [accessed 11 December 2021].

Greenberg, C. (1979) Modern and Postmodern, *Arts*, Vol. 54 (6).

Guetzkow, J. (2002) How the Arts Impact Communities: An Introduction to the Literature on Arts Impact Studies, Working Paper No. 20, Princeton, NJ: Princeton University.

Harvey, D. (2012) *Rebel Cities: From the Right to the City to the Urban Revolution*, London: Verso.

Harvie, J. (2013) *Fair Play: Art, Performance and Neoliberalism*, London: Palgrave Macmillan.

Hawkes, J. (2006) *The Fourth Pillar of Sustainability: Culture's Essential Role in Public Planning: A Summary*. Available at http://culturaldevelopment.net/downloads/FourthPillarSummary.pdf [accessed 27 June 2015].

Hope, S. (2017) From Community Arts to the Socially Engaged Art Commission. In A. Jeffers and G. Moriarty (eds), *Culture, Democracy and the Right to Make Art*, 203–222, London: Bloomsbury.

International Labour Organisation (ILO) (2011) *Policies and Regulations to Combat Precarious Employment*. Available at www.ilo.org/wcmsp5/groups/public/---ed_dialogue/---actrav/documents/meetingdocument/wcms_164286.pdf [accessed 22 October 2016].

Jackson, S. (2011) *Social Works: Performing Art, Supporting Publics*, London: Routledge.

Jameson, F. (1998) *The Cultural Turn. Selected Writings on the Postmodern, 1983–1998*, London: Verso.

Jermyn, H. (2004) The Art of Inclusion. Available at www.artscouncil.org.uk [accessed 3 April 2015].

Karnaukhova, O. (2015) Culture-Based Creativity in the Regional Strategy of Development: Is Russia in Game? In B. Christiansen and J. Koeman (eds),

Nationalism, Cultural Indoctrination, and Economic Prosperity in the Digital Age, 203–221, Hershey: IGI Global.

Keaney, E. (2006) *From Access to Participation: Cultural Policy and Civil Renewal*, London: Institute for Public Policy Research.

Landemore, H. (2013) *Democratic Reason: Politics, Collective Intelligence, and the Rule of the Many*, Princeton, NJ: Princeton University Press.

Lavapiés Barrio de Teatros (2014) *Manifiesto (Manifest)*, Madrid: Lavapiés Barrio de Teatros. Available at www.lavapiesbarriodeteatros.es/wp-content/themes/JointsWP-master/library/pdf/LavapiesBarriodeTeatros-Manifiesto.pdf [accessed 15 October 2016].

Laville, J.-L. (2010) Solidarity Economy | Plural Economy. In K. Hart, J.-L. Laville and A. D. Cattani (eds), *The Human Economy*, 77–83; 225–235, Cambridge, MA: Polity Press.

Laville, J.-L. and Salmon, A. (2015) *Associations et action publique*, Paris: Desclée de Brouwer.

Menger, P.-M. (2005) *Les intermittents du spectacle. Sociologie du travail flexible*, Paris: EHESS.

Mora, M. and Pastor, F. (2016) Queremos demostrar que otra economía del arte es posible, *Contexto y Acción*. Available at http://ctxt.es/es/20161019/Culturas/9004/entrevista-Manuel-Borja-Villel-director-Museo-Reina-Sofia-coleccion-permanenente-exposiciones.htm [accessed 23 October 2016].

Moulaert, F., MacCallum, D., Mehmood, A. and Hamdouch, A. (eds) (2014) *The International Handbook on Social Innovation: Collective Action, Social Learning and Transdisciplinary Research*, Cheltenham: Edward Elgar.

Moulaert, F., Martinelli, F., Swyngedouw, E. and Gonzalez, S. (2005) Towards Alternative Model(s) of Local Innovation, *Urban Studies*, Vol. 42 (11), pp. 1969–1990.

Moulin, R. (1997) *L'artiste, l'institution et le marché*, Paris: Flammarion.

Muñoz López, B. (2007) De las industrias culturales a los circuitos culturales la metamorfosis de un proceso ideológico [From cultural industries to cultural circuits: the metamorphosis of an ideological process], *Sociedad y utopía: Revista de ciencias sociales*, No 29, 19–36.

Nanteuil (de), M. and El Akremi, A. (eds) (2005) La société flexible. Travail, emploi, organisation en débat, Ramonville Saint-Agne: Editions Eres.

Nogales Muriel, R. (2023) Sembrando para quienes nos sucederán: Resignificación de 'lo rural' a través del arte y la cultura en un contexto de crisis ecosocial (R-Rural) [Sowing for those who will succeed us: Resignification of 'the rural' through art and culture in a context of eco-social crisis (R-Rural)], *Periférica Internacional. Revista para el análisis de la cultura y el territorio*, vol. 23, 164–180, Cadiz: Editorial UCA.

Nussbaum, M. C. (2003) Capabilities as Fundamental Entitlements: Sen and Social Justice. *Feminist Economics*, Vol. 9 (2&3), pp. 33–59.

Nyssens, M. (ed.) (2006) *Social Enterprise: At the Crossroads of Market, Public Policies and Civil Society*, London: Routledge.

Organisation for Economic Co-operation and Development (OECD) (2005) *Culture and Local Development*, Paris: OECD.

Pascual i Ruiz, J. (1998) *EMPIRIC: Third System, Culture, Employment*, Brussels: European Commission/Interarts.

Pestoff, V. A. (2009) *A Democratic Architecture for the Welfare State*, London: Routledge.

Polanyi, A., Polanyi, K., Arensberg, C. M. and Pearson, H. W. (1957) *Trade and Market in the Early Empires: Economies in History and Theory*, New York: Free Press.

Polanyi, K. (1944) *The Great Transformation*, Boston, MA: Beacon Press.

Rancière, J. (2006) Democracy, Republic, Representation, *Constellations*, Vol. 13 (3), pp. 297–307

Ray, H. P. and Anderson, S. R. (2000) *The Cultural Creatives: How 50 Million People Are Changing the World?* New York: Harmony Books.

Red de Espacios y Agentes de Cultura Comunitaria (REACC) (2021) *Articular las artes y la cultura transformadoras desde la participación ciudadana y la justicia social: La germinación y proceso de consolidación de la Red de Entidades y Agentes de Cultura Comunitaria, REACC*, Madrid: Ministry of Culture and Sports. Available at https://culturayciudadania.culturaydeporte.gob.es/dam/jcr:46253c44-1832-4476-9ddf-5fa6b7f21188/reacc.pdf [accessed 13 December 2021].

Red de Espacios y Agentes de Cultura Comunitaria (REACC) (2022) *Delineando horizontes comunes para el arte y la vida en España: Resultados del primer estudio de la Red de Espacios y Agentes de la Cultura Comunitaria*. Available at https://reacc.org/primerinformediagnostico [accessed 3 March 2022].

Rodríguez Morató, A. (2012) The Culture Society: A Heuristic for Analyzing Cultural Change in the Global Age. In A. Sales (ed.), *Sociology Today: Social Transformations in a Globalizing World*, 316–336, London: Sage.

Roustang, G., Laville, J.-L., Eme, B., Mothé, D. and Perret, B. (1996) *Vers un nouveau contrat social*, Paris: Desclée de Brouwer.

Rowan, J. (2016) *Cultura libre de Estado*, Madrid: Traficantes de Sueños.

Roy, M. J., Donaldson, C., Baker, R. and Kay, A. (2013) Social Enterprise: New Pathways to Health and Well-Being? *Journal of Public Health Policy*, Vol. 34 (1), pp. 55–68.

Sanz, T. and Rodríguez-Labajos, B. (2021) Does Artistic Activism Change Anything? Strategic and Transformative Effects of Arts in Anti-Coal Struggles in Oakland, CA, *Geoforum*, Vol. 122, pp. 41–54.

Serrano Vidal, A. (2012) Nuevos proyectos culturales en el entorno madrileño: una alternativa a la crisis actual (New Cultural Projects in Madrid: An Alternative to the Current Crisis), *Heritage & Museography*, Vol. 4 (3). Available at www.raco.cat/index.php/Hermus/article/view/313475/403594 [accessed 3 May 2016].

Spear, R. and Hulgård, L. (2006) Social Entrepreneurship and the Mobilisation of Social Capital in European Social Enterprises. In M. Nyssens (ed.), *Social Enterprise: At the Crossroads of Market, Public Policies and Civil Society*, 85–108, London: Routledge.

Sternberg, R. J. (ed.) (1999) *Handbook of Creativity*, New York: Cambridge University Press.

Stone, J. H. (ed.) (2004) *Culture and Disability: Providing Culturally Competent Services*, Newbury Park, CA: Sage.

Throsby, C. D. (2001) *Economics and Culture*, Cambridge: Cambridge University Press.

Tremblay, D.-G. and Pilati, T. (2013) Social Innovation through Arts and Creativity. In F. Moulaert, D. MacCallum, A. Mehmood and A. Hamdouch (eds), *The*

International Handbook on Social Innovation: Collective Action, Social Learning and Transdisciplinary Research, 67–79, Cheltenham: Edward Elgar.

YProductions (2009) *Innovación en cultura. Una introducción crítica a la genealogía y usos del concepto*, Madrid: Traficantes de sueños. Available at www.traficantes.net/var/trafis/storage/original/application/84acd361547fa013662de900c47cc390.pdf [accessed 13 February 2016].

Yúdice, G. (2002) *Usos de la cultura en la era global*, Barcelona: Gedisa Editorial.

4 Diffusing Social Innovation

4.1 Diffusion of Innovation

Diffusion of social innovation has attracted considerable scholarly attention. Sociology has a longstanding interest in learning about the factors influencing the diffusion of innovation across groups, communities, societies and countries, and more recently the focus has been on modelling this process (Wejnert, 2002). Although most of the research has been conducted following analytical frameworks and theories developed for purely market-based firms, in a few years it has evolved from being solely an adaptation of traditional commercial strategies to developing unique approaches specific to the social field. The main challenge when conducting research on scaling-up and replication in the 'social' field is failing to recognise some of the essential factors at work in the social and solidarity economy and the third sector, such as the existence of different economic logics (i.e. redistribution and reciprocity) as opposed to market exchange (Gardin, 2005). Other factors to consider are the embeddedness of the social innovation in the local context (Nyssens et al., 2012) and the presence of participation mechanisms that allow internal and external stakeholders to play a central role (Defourny et al., 2014).

In this chapter I will focus on the factors that influence the spreading of a social innovation. Since social enterprise is considered a class of institutional arrangement that carries or enacts social innovation (Defourny and Nyssens, 2014; João-Roland and Granados, 2020), several institutionalist theories can be mobilised to understand the processes behind its diffusion, even though they were not originally conceived to explain 'social innovations' but only 'innovations'. Before moving on to the theoretical discussion, some terms need to be clarified given that diffusion, replication, adaptation and scaling can be used differently. Table 4.1 summarises these definitions.

4.1.1 Main Theoretical Frameworks Addressing Diffusion

The first study of diffusion was Gabriel Tarde's book *The Laws of Imitation* (1903), but it had to wait an additional 40 years to reach a high level of

DOI: 10.4324/9781003342144-5

Table 4.1 Various notions of diffusion in this research

Adaptation	The process of making the required adjustments to the operational model in order to ensure a successful transfer to a new context.
Diffusion	The process by which an innovation is communicated through certain channels over time among the members of a social system (Rogers, 1962: 5).
Replication	Implementing an operational model in a new geographic location without any adjustment, which constitutes an exception when it comes to social enterprises and social innovation (Weber et al., 2012).
Scaling out	Increasing the size and/or spread of the social innovation (by replicating it in new locations, increasing memberships, turnover, etc.) (Westley et al. 2014, cited in Haxeltine et al., 2015).
Scaling up	The interaction of the social innovation with the 'regime level', with institutional change, and/or with whatever is required to bring about systemic change (Westley et al. 2014, cited in Haxeltine et al. 2015).

interest from researchers in fields such as agriculture, technology and policy (Wejnert, 2002). The pioneering contribution was made by Everett M. Rogers with his *Diffusion of Innovations Theory* published in 1962. According to Rogers, diffusion is 'the process by which an innovation is communicated through certain channels over time among the members of a social system' (1962: 5). For him, diffusion is a type of communication related to a new idea, and this newness involves a degree of uncertainty.[1] He furthermore distinguishes between centralised and decentralised diffusion systems; in the former, decisions about how, when and what to diffuse are made by a small number of individuals in power or with technical expertise, whereas in the latter, decision-making processes are shared among various stakeholders, including potential adopters. Rogers also defines five phases in the diffusion process: knowledge, persuasion, decision, implementation and confirmation. According to him, there are four main elements that influence the spread of a new idea: the innovation itself, communication channels, time and a social system. Rogers also warned that not all innovations are 'necessarily desirable' (1962: 12), a warning that has been applied extensively to social innovation by more recent scholars (Evers et al., 2014; Nicholls et al., 2015).

Norbert Alter's sociological approach to the diffusion of innovation represents an interesting complement to the more individual-based innovation decision process of Rogers, in that he incorporates two important dimensions to the diffusion process: collective and systemic dimensions. Indeed, according to the author, since innovation depends on collective creativity, it cannot be perfectly planned (Alter, 2002). Alter's basic realisation relies on the fact that innovation accelerates social impact but also creates a number of conflicts, operating not only inside the innovating agent but also externally (Alter, 2013). His reading of the process of innovation diffusion is more critical to the extent that he incorporates notions of deviation, conflict, negotiation and rules transgression.

In Alter's approach, the collective ability to identify and integrate complex and random phenomena (such as social innovations) constitutes a double-edged sword for innovation: it represents the strongest limitation to innovation but also the most enabling resource for reaching its potential. Moreover, following Schumpeter's creative destruction approach, collective creativity aimed at innovation has the destructive effect of altering (and sometimes destroying) agreed-upon collective conventions and ways of living (Alter, 2002). Departing from the idea that 'innovation cannot be the end in itself' (Alter, 2002: 9), he warns of the evaluation mechanisms created to measure innovations which may be ill-suited to capturing intangible value.

In addition to Rogers' and Alter's approaches, three additional theoretical contributions help us understand how innovations spread. The first one is offered by David Strang and John W. Meyer's theory of diffusion of innovation (1993) in institutions based on elements of 'theorisation' and 'cultural linkages' to create ties among disconnected social entities (later developed by Strang). Theorisation is the process whereby the experience of previous actors during diffusion and subsequent adaptation, together with the shared values and personal interpretations of the world by social actors, progressively transforms into shared knowledge that speeds up the diffusion. The power of theorisation is that, if done within specific institutional contexts and shared by a specific category of social actors, diffusion will take place more rapidly (Strang and Meyer, 1993; Strang and Soule, 1998). Later, Nee and Ingram (1998) stated that paradigm changes in the institutional environment (led by the government in most cases) make new organisational forms possible. Cultural linkages are the ties that connect the social entities (people or organisations) belonging to a common social category. Strang and Meyer argued that diffusion should be rapid among actors falling into the same category.

The second helpful idea is the notion of 'coalitions', developed by DiMaggio and Powell, which originated from institutional change theory. In their 1983 paper, the authors argue that coercion and mimicry between institutions lead to isomorphism of their practices. Particularly, they can do that through the achievement of patterns of coalition and mutual recognition between organisations that pursue the same objective. DiMaggio and Powell (1983: 148) define the organisational field as 'those organisations which, in the aggregate, constitute a recognised area of institutional life: key suppliers, resources and product consumers, regulatory agencies, and other organisations that produce similar services or products'. DiMaggio further developed the notion of 'organisational field' by emphasising the non-aggregative nature of the construct and approaching it as having full of meaning for the actors involved (DiMaggio, 1991). DiMaggio (1991) also introduced the notion of 'boundaries' from the perspective of actors and how these boundaries are defined based on their perceptions. This way of perceiving affects both organisational practices but also the representation of the field itself.

A third set of notions relevant to the SMart case study constitutes 'categories', 'boundary objects' and 'field boundaries' (Xhauflair et al., 2015). *Categories* are used to simplify complex information by setting discriminating boundaries, and *boundary objects* are 'artefacts of practice that are agreed and shared by communities, yet satisfy the informational requirements of each of them' (Sapsed and Salter, 2004: 1518, cited in Xhauflair et al., 2015). The idea of *field boundaries* (which expands previous work by DiMaggio) illustrates how SMartbe began by expanding its categories and field boundaries (first at a national level) before beginning the process of geographic replication. This confirms research stating that achieving scale in other countries tends to be more difficult than in one's own country and therefore should always be the second step (Weber et al., 2016). In the context of my research, however, the field boundary idea has the shortcoming of a unique institutional focus, understood at a particular organisational level, which limits the impacts of social innovation to the micro or, at the most, the meso level of analysis.

4.1.2 A Holistic Framework for the Diffusion of Innovation

Numerous variables have been defined in diffusion research in order to clarify the influence of the factors at play in the innovation replication processes, specifically on actors' decisions to adopt an innovation (Wejnert, 2002; De Keersmaecker et al., 2014). With a view to offer a conceptual framework on the diffusion of innovation that integrates all previous contributions, Wejnert (2002) groups diffusion variables into three major components: characteristics of innovations, characteristics of innovators and environmental context. The author also points out the contribution of these discussions to change theory insofar as diffusing an innovation involves changes of varying degrees, both in the agent proposing the innovation and in the recipient of the diffusion process.

As Wejnert points out, there is limitation in considering innovations themselves as a driving factor for the diffusion and adoption processes. Therefore, the first component relates to two factors connected to innovation: public versus private consequences, and benefit versus costs involved. The *public versus private consequences* factor captures how adopting an innovation impacts entities other than the actor (public consequences) as opposed to purely the actor itself (private consequence), and it is directly related to the scale of the impact. Public consequences involve collective actors (mainly countries, organisations and social movements) who are concerned with issues of societal well-being. Given the macro goal of these innovations, the public consequences of adopting these innovations often bring about reforms that constitute historical breakthroughs, including international regulation protecting the natural environment. Private consequences are the result of micro goal innovations addressing the needs of individuals or a community.

Both types of consequences result in social change, but they determine the content and way of communicating about an innovation, which in turn results in diffusion processes of a different nature. Particularly, innovations with public consequences are better diffused when they become deeply ingrained in society – institutionalised. The media is a key element in this process, although usually only after the goals of innovation have been clearly established and publicly accepted (Weiman and Brosius, 1994; Wejnert, 2002). On the contrary, when it comes to private effects of adopting an innovation, the nature of the process is characterised by 'spatial and temporal contiguity between the source of a new practice and a potential adopter' (Wejnert, 2002: 4). Despite the conceptual clarification this dichotomy offers to the analysis of innovation diffusion, Wejnert notes that usually real-life innovations combine both public (indirect and latent) and private (direct and manifest) consequences.

The *benefit versus cost factor* refers to the fact that direct and indirect costs, and/or the financial, technical or social uncertainty associated with an innovation, can affect its adoption rate. This has been underlined in recent models (Weber et al., 2012) as one of the main factors that determine the success of scalability processes at a time of financial uncertainty and budgetary austerity in welfare states.

The second component of Wejnert's model relates to the *characteristics of the innovators*, which relate to and can affect the previous set of characteristics. It includes six factors:

1. The *societal entity of innovators* relates to the scale of social entity of the innovator, ranging from individuals to kinship and friendship groups to communities and social movements that conform to 'societal microstructures' (Wejnert, 2002: 306). Collective entities tend to be involved in large scale innovations of public consequence and relate to new adopters through non-relational means, including the media, while individual innovators rely on direct ties and face-to-face interactions.
2. *Familiarity with the innovation* has to do with its radicality: the higher the novelty level, the lower the adoption rate. Familiarity aiming to decrease the radicality of the innovation is usually achieved by increasing understanding about it and its consequences and by drawing on different types of information sources.
3. *Status characteristics of adopters* refer to the relative position of an actor within a population of actors – that is, her/his social position. The adoption rate of innovations is directly related to an actor's high social position, which then promotes adoption on lower-status actors using influence and coercion. Usually, these high-profile actors adopt

non-controversial innovations that respect established values and norms, whereas low-profile actors are less afraid to lose popularity as a result of promoting controversial innovations.

4. *Socioeconomic characteristics* of the actor itself determine adoption rates insofar as they create 'objective feasibilities' (Wejnert, 2002: 305) within a given country. These characteristics include those of individual actors (e.g. educational level) as well as of collective actors (e.g. country's socioeconomic development – GNP or GDP; labour market practices; and political system). They may have potentiating and inhibiting effects and determine issues such as accessibility to the innovation (cf. Wejner, 2014 on the diffusion of democracy).
5. *Position in social networks of the actor* operates in relation to four areas of interactions: interpersonal networks for individual actors, organisational networks for collective actors, 'structural equivalence' or members' perceptions in relation to other members, and social density in relation to the lesser perception of risk in highly dense networks. Adoption can be explained as a network-based decision with a cumulative effect on the adoption of others. Variables such as network connectedness, closeness and density are crucial to understanding how diffusion is hampered or potentiated. The similarity of members in collective networks also determines a higher adoption rate. The horizontality or verticality of channels, through which influence circulates within the networks in an informative, conducive, educational or coercive manner, also determines the level of innovation adoption. The perceived structural equivalence of organisations is also key, as it predicts the homogeneity of behaviours in the adoption of the innovation.
6. *Personal characteristics*, particularly psychological ones such as self-confidence and independence, determine the rates of adoption but are affected by environmental context (see below), including societal culture, especially at the level of large subgroups or nations.

Lastly, the third component refers to the *environmental context* and includes the following:

- *Geographical settings* include elements such as ecological factors (e.g. climate), although this element affects more clearly social innovations that include the environment within its transformational process (e.g. the bio-agriculture or citizen-led renewable energy sources). Torsten Hägerstrand's 1967 observation that there was a direct effect of distance on the adoption of innovations was also seen in social innovations. For instance, the impact of distance on the diffusion of social innovations, such as policy reforms or even democracy, continues to be the focus of research (Moulaert et al., 2014). The density of adopters is related to the spatial factor of proximity, as well as helps to explain both the adoption rate and adoption potential of a given innovation.

- *Societal culture* includes belief systems, cultural tradition, cultural homogeneity and socialisation of citizens (Wejnert, 2014). Studies documenting the influence of societal culture over the diffusion of social innovations were numerous even though they were not termed such at the time.[2]
- *Political conditions* include political systems (including regulations and norms) and their stability; such variables are important as they may determine actors' behaviours, particularly those of collective actors, when adopting new policies (Wejnert, 2002). It is likely that the relevance of these variables becomes even more important in the context of social innovation, in which empowerment and change of social relations are a crucial part of the innovation itself.
- *Global uniformity* includes three variables – institutionalisation, global technology and world connectedness – reflecting 'the view of the contemporary world as one cultural community, characterised by collective development grounded in a synchronised, cohesive process of evolution' (Wejnert, 2002: 315). These variables mainly affect collective actors through institutionalisation, which is enhanced by scientific knowledge, reduced risk and ignorance about an innovation and the normalisation of practices by interest group politics. An interesting point is raised by Wejnert (2002: 318) when she states that this global uniformity means a 'Westernisation of the world' and that 'Western practices often connote symbolic meanings of socioeconomic advancement and elevated status'. In other words, the desire among developing countries to achieve those levels has constituted one of the major stimuli for the adoption of innovations coming from the West. However, more recent developments of world events have shown that the Western origin of social innovations may constitute a barrier for their adoption in some world regions.

In addition to the theoretical contributions described above, there are some useful literature reviews on spreading social innovation (Davies and Simon, 2013), which illustrate the various approaches that exist. Incubation is considered one of the most successful approaches (Miller and Stacey, 2014), but there are also other approaches. Considering the working definition of social innovation used in this research, scaling-up and replication of a social innovation is seen as the best way (from an efficiency and efficacy standpoint) to maximise the contribution to society it set out to create (Weber, 2012).

Table 4.2 summarises the relevant approaches just reviewed and provides some of the key notions they propose.

In addition to providing a theoretical context for the present research, these theoretical frameworks can be harnessed to understand unsuccessful social innovations, or scaling-up attempts, as well as to anticipate the performance of future adaptation processes of social innovations.

Table 4.2 Theories and notions mobilised for understanding the scaling-up of social innovation

	About diffusion	*Original contribution/relevant notions*
Rogers (1962)	The process by which an innovation is communicated through certain channels over time among the members of a social system.	*Phases:* Knowledge, persuasion, decision, implementation (or reinvention) and confirmation. *Elements:* The innovation itself, communication channels, time and a social system.
DiMaggio and Powell (1983)	Diffusion of innovation is usually more rapid within organisation fields.	*Organisational field:* Those organisations which, in the aggregate, constitute a recognised area of institutional life: key suppliers, resources and product consumers, regulatory agencies and other organisations that produce similar services or products.
Strang and Meyer (1993)	If done within specific institutional contexts and shared by a specific category of social actors, diffusion will take place more rapidly.	*Theorisation:* The experience of previous actors during diffusion and subsequent adaptation, together with the shared values and personal interpretations of the world by social actors, progressively transforms into shared knowledge that speeds up the diffusion. *Cultural linkages:* The ties that connect the social entities (people or organisations) belonging to a common social category.
Wejner (2002)	'The spread of abstract ideas and concepts, technical information, and actual practices within a social system, where the spread denotes flow or movement from a source to an adopter, typically via communication and influence' (similar to Rogers' definition from 1995).	Diffusion variables include three components: • Characteristics of innovations (public vs. private consequences; benefit vs costs) • Characteristics of innovators (societal entity, familiarity with the innovation, status characteristics, socioeconomic characteristics, position in social networks, personal characteristics) • Environmental context (geographical settings, societal culture, political conditions, global uniformity)

4.1.3 EU-Funded Research on Scaling Up Social Innovation

Shedding light on the issue of scaling-up and adaptability, a set of EU research projects has focused on the scaling-up and replication of social innovation. A salient feature across these research projects is the relevance of contextual factors, particularly when it comes to transnational scaling-up (Kerlin, 2013; Weber et al., 2012). Therefore, the subjective and micro-level approaches that characterised diffusion for early theorists are being complemented by recent research with a more objective and macro-level approach.

Given the focus of the present research, four recent projects and their contributions to the issue of replication of social enterprises as vehicles of social innovation will be highlighted. First, a major finding in the EU-funded project WILCO (Welfare Innovations at the Local Level in Favour of Cohesion)[3] is that 'diffusing innovations is not essentially different from innovating' (Brandsen, 2014), which resonates with Rogers' interpretation of the notion of reinvention: 'The degree to which an innovation is changed or modified by a user in the process of its adoption and implementation' which was measured as 'the degree to which an individual's use of a new idea departed from the "mainline" version of the original innovation' (1983: 16–17).

When it comes to intentionality of replication, WILCO researchers point out that, since social innovations are usually initiated to solve a local problem, wider diffusion tends to be of secondary importance to the innovators, and some cases even irrelevant. In any case, for a social innovation to thrive, it is especially important to have intermediaries, who know the situation on the ground, to assess what innovations require to take root elsewhere and to have translators capable of adapting the social innovators to new contexts. Furthermore, 'encouraging social innovation is therefore best done by allocating resources, not only to spreading information and building networks, but also to boundary spanning and translation activities' (WILCO, 2014). As we can see, the conceptual relevance of the notion of boundaries was identified by WILCO researchers as well as others (Xhauflair et al., 2015).

The second EU-level project to be reviewed is TRANSITION (Transnational Network for Social Innovation Incubation, 2013–2016),[4] which was not purely a research project but rather an experimental initiative to test how incubation methods and tools can better support, empower and scale up social innovation in Europe. There are two findings that relate to the present research. Firstly, concerning the perception of risks associated with transnational scaling-up, in this context, finding the 'right' partner was considered a precondition to scaling up transnationally as risk-free as possible. A right partner was 'a local actor who not only shared the social innovator's "vision" but who possessed good contextual knowledge of key stakeholders or the country's tax and legal systems' (Transition, 2016).

Secondly, it was demonstrated that strong networks – with peers, funders, customers, partners, collaborators, advisers and others – are crucial for social innovations to thrive.

The third project reviewed – BENISI (Building a European Network of Incubators for Social Innovation, 2013–2016) – focuses on incubators as a key element in the successful scaling-up of social innovations.[5] Together, the TRANSITION and BENISI projects published a joint report highlighting the following common lessons learned: firstly, the need to involve strong, committed and skilled teams composed of full-time employees in addition to volunteers, and secondly, the fact that business maturity is a key enabler to adapting to new markets (Benisi and Transition, 2015: 25). Four strategies for scaling up were identified and ad hoc support was offered to social innovators identified by these projects (Benisi and Transition, 2015: 10):

> Strategy 1 – Diffusion of knowledge: Scaling up requires using the experiences, knowledge and know-how of a successful social innovation applied to a new context and team. This could include support to individuals and groups seeking to bring small-scale innovations to a new local context, or to possible public authorities and other bodies that have a defined operating area.
>
> Strategy 2 – Capacity building: This strategy is aimed at social innovators who need to develop a suitable business model or business plan, or to secure public funding. Social innovators are provided with legal and business counseling through one of the 'clusters' defined by the consortium. This type of support typically concerns social enterprises that want to grow bigger in the same country.
>
> Strategy 3 – Joint venturing and franchising: This strategy is suitable for social innovations for which ongoing local adaptation is necessary, but which could also benefit from ongoing close partnerships with existing successful implementations of the social innovation. This method allows social innovations to explore options to develop legal agreements that govern differing degrees of cooperation, and to explore applying methods for adapting franchise models found in the private sector to social mission-driven enterprises and organisations.
>
> Strategy 4 – Creation of new sites: This type of support is appropriate for social innovations that are operational and looking to scale up to other countries. Alternatively, it would be possible to develop similar initiatives in the other countries that will benefit from this fourth path – based on the network created with this project and the transfer of information between a variety of clusters. With this path an organisation or an individual established in one country will be able to receive qualified support through one of their centres established elsewhere in the EU, as well as being able to explore opportunities to tap into local financing schemes and public contacts.

It is important to mention the people leading the replication processes, who are called 'scalers'. They are characterised as being entrepreneurial and exhibiting strong political skills (Benisi and Transition, 2015); they are socially astute, with the ability to influence others and develop or use existing networks, as well as being perceived by others as 'possessing high levels of integrity, authenticity, sincerity and genuineness'. Paradoxically, there was one counterintuitive finding: 'Most "scalers" (and virtually all those with a revenue-generating model) stated that they wished to scale alone, most commonly through building up their own capacity or branching' (Benisi and Transition, 2015: 22).

The fourth project reviewed is TRANSIT (TRANsformative Social Innovation Theory, 2014–2017), which developed a theory of social innovation that focuses on transformation in terms of empowerment and change in society, with an emphasis on the transnational scaling of social innovations.[6] Indeed, Haxeltine et al. (2015: 74) argue that 'for changes to be considered transformative they must in some way have sufficient scale'. One of the main findings of this project was that transnational social innovation networks applied different strategies for engaging with the transformative process of replicating social innovation. By 'transformative social innovation', TRANSITION researchers understood 'change in social relations, involving new ways of doing, organising, framing and/or knowing, which challenges, alters and/or replaces dominant institutions/structures in a specific social context' (Avelino et al., 2019). The five strategies described and covered by their dataset included different degrees of formalisation, institutionalisation, controversy, visibility and mainstreaming.

In connection with Alter's warning about the conflicting aspects of innovation diffusion, scale relationships are considered the result of contested and political negotiations and interactions; in other words, as transformative change is under way via specific social innovations, scale relationships can also be altered incrementally or fundamentally.

4.2 Spreading Social Innovation by Replicating Social Enterprises

There is vast literature on scaling-up and replication of social enterprises that, in only a few years, has evolved from being solely an adaptation of traditional commercial strategies to developing unique approaches specific to the social field (Lyon and Fernandez, 2012; Blundel and Lyon, 2015). Before going into more details of the model selected for the current research, it is useful to remember the stage theory initiated by Lewins (1951), which helps to recognise the four stages of changes in organisations, including social enterprises (Kaluzny and Hernandez, 1988):

1. Awareness: recognition of a problem and consideration of possible solutions.
2. Adoption: decision to adopt the innovation.

3. Implementation: redefinition of the innovation and modification of the organisational structures to accommodate it.
4. Institutionalisation: making the innovation part of the organisation's ongoing activities.

4.2.1 The Core Element of Replication: Operational Models of Social Enterprises

There is confusion caused by the interchangeable use of the terms 'business model' and 'operating model'. According to Campbell (2014), the former constitutes a larger notion that encompasses the second. Specifically, a business model defines the stakeholders of the organisation, the offer made to each stakeholder group (customers, employees, investors, internal and external suppliers, etc.), the resources available from each stakeholder (work from employees, money from customers), the financial models (income statement and balance sheet), and size and growth ambitions. The operating model is the 'nuts and bolts' that make it possible for the organisation to interact effectively with its stakeholders in order to achieve its goals.

Beyond this differentiation, there are plenty of volumes on strategic management and business architecture devoted to business models. Weill et al. (2005) created the MIT Business Model Archetypes (BMAs) based on a typology of 16 business models with a strong for-profit focus. Depending on whether the emphasis is put on one element or the other, there are different ways of conceptualising business models. According to Zott and Amit (2015), a business model captures the way in which a firm can configure its organisational structure and its interactions with external stakeholders, all of which is impacted by the technology used to facilitate processes.

However useful these perspectives can be for a first approach to business models, the bottom line in a discussion on business models for social enterprises is not only the components of the model but also the degree to which each of them matters regarding the goals of the organisation. In the case of social enterprises, the business model is the way in which inputs are transformed into outcomes, considering both values generated at the same time – social (measurable impact) and economic (revenue).[7] The fact that outputs are often intangible, and that social impact continues to be difficult to measure, has to be factored in when discussing the SMart business and operational models.

Indeed, the approach is often contingency-based and mechanistic, thus ill-suited for a knowledge economy where sharing and reciprocity are becoming more present and where issues of emancipation and democracy intertwine. As Perkmann and Spicer (2010) explain, academic literature treats 'business models' in three ways: as transactional structures, value-extracting devices and mechanisms for structuring the organisation. Adopting a more organisational sociology approach that activates performativity and cognition, they propose three alternative ways of looking at them: as narratives that convince, typifications that legitimate and recipes that guide social action. Although their study focuses on technology, it is relevant to this case study ultimately for seeking the political articulation and empowerment of a full segment of artists and creative workers.

There is far less literature describing the business and operating models of social enterprises. Those who do describe them usually approach social enterprises as hybrid models that combine several business models (Doherty et al., 2014; Grassl, 2012), which confirms the view that business models are not recipes to achieve a specific outcome (Perkmann and Spicer, 2010). Many types of social enterprises depend on the mobilisation of different business models (Dees, 1998; Emerson and Bonini, 2003; Alter, 2006; Nyssens, 2006; Ridley-Duff, 2008; Westall, 2009; Ridley-Duff and Bull, 2011). In general, the relevance of this discussion on business and operating models stems from the crucial questions of *what* is replicated in other countries, *how* it is done and *what is needed* for it to be done effectively and efficiently.

In this current research, 'the operational model corresponds to what in a commercial enterprise would be the business model' (Weber, 2016: 15). Considering that the social and financial dimensions are equally important for social enterprises, their operational model includes the combination needed to make it sustainable. Concretely, this refers to the actual actions or programmes developed to serve its social aim as well as the financial model that sustains it in the long term. However, for the sake of clarity, the operating model of SMart is reduced to the services offered (divided into core and accessory, as explained below) and the technology that makes them more efficient and accessible to a larger number of members.

4.2.2 A Model for Scaling Up Social Enterprises

The model mobilised for the present analysis departs from the contribution of Weber et al. (2012), developed specifically to analyse the scaling-up of social enterprises. The model was further tested in a study conducted on 358 social enterprises that scaled up their model. It includes two prerequisites and six success factors that play a role in the replication process. The two prerequisites are:

1. Viability of the operational model. As explained above, the centrality of the operational model in any process of replication is of paramount importance. Not only does the model need to be perceived as attractive and effective enough by possible initiators in their own countries, but it also needs to include a certain degree of flexibility over a given timespan before it can be implemented.
2. Commitment and readiness. Indeed, as noted by Rogers (1995), the timing of adoption depends on the interactions of social units.

As for the factors affecting the replicability of a viable operational model, provided there is commitment and readiness, Weber et al. (2016) distinguish six, which are briefly described below:

1. Management competences: Understood as the ability to apply business-oriented processes and structures in the social enterprise's daily operations.
2. Replicability: Understood as an organisation's ability to reproduce not only its products and services, but also, where appropriate, its structures and processes – nationally and internationally.
3. Mobilising the necessary resources: Ability to generate the diverse resources that the social enterprise will require in the various phases of the scaling process or, alternately, to mobilise those resources through third parties. To achieve this, its own social network has to be mobilised by deploying its social capital.
4. Control and dependency: Degree to which the social enterprise will want to work – or should work – with its partners.
5. Adaptation/Transfer costs: The concept of transfer costs derives from transaction cost theory and can be divided into two main types: internal transfer costs, resulting from adapting the operational model, and external transfer costs, resulting from the adaptation required for the different contexts in which the social enterprise is supposed to be scaled.
6. Legitimacy and reputation: These notions refer to the general perception or the understanding of third parties that an organisation's actions within a social system of standards and values are both desirable and appropriate.

The empirical research conducted in the framework of this volume relies on the model the authors developed and refined (Weber et al., 2012, 2016) with a view to assess the factors influencing the adaptation and replication of SMart in different European countries. The revision of the model entailed the inclusion of two prerequisites and the reduction of success factors from the original seven to six (Weber et al., 2016).

Notes

1 Rogers goes on to define uncertainty as the degree to which several alternatives are perceived with respect to the occurrence of an event and the relative probability of these alternatives.

2 These include reproductive patterns (Tolnay, 1995), welfare policy reforms (Abbott and DeViney, 1992) and sustainable agricultural practices (Sommers and Napiers, 1993).

3 WILCO, 2011–2014, http://wilcoproject.eu.

4 Outputs from TRANSITION can be found at https://cordis.europa.eu/project/id/604849.

5 Within BENISI, a total of 300 social innovations across Europe were selected based on their high potential for scaling, and the project provided the necessary support services for them to replicate. All intermediate and final project outputs can be found at www.benisi.eu.
6 All intermediate and final outputs from TRANSIT can be found at www.transitsocialinnovation.eu.
7 The typical legal form that social enterprises adopt is useful when looking at their business model, as in many cases it determines the kind of resources it is able to mobilise – or not.

References

Abbott, A. and DeViney, S. (1992) The Welfare State as Transnational Event: Evidence from Sequences of Policy Adoption, *Social Science History*, Vol. 16 (2), pp. 245–274.

Alter, N. (ed.) (2002) *Les logiques de l'innovation: Approche pluridisciplinaire*, Paris: La Découverte.

Alter, N. (2013) *L'innovation ordinaire*, 4th ed., Paris: Presses Universitaires de France.

Alter, S. K. (2006) Social Enterprise Models and Their Mission and Money Relationships. In A. Nicholls (ed.), *Social Entrepreneurship: New Models of Sustainable Social Change*, 205–232, New York: Oxford University Press.

Avelino, F., Wittmayer, J. M., Pel, B., Weaver, P., Dumitru, A., Haxeltine, A., Kemp, R., Jørgensen, M. S., Bauler, T., Ruijsink, S. and O'Riordan, T. (2019) Transformative Social Innovation and (Dis)empowerment, *Technological Forecasting and Social Change*, Vol. 145, pp. 195–206.

Benisi and Transition (2015) *Scaling Social Innovation: Experiences and First Success Stories of the Two European Networks of Incubators for Social Innovation.* Available at http://transitionproject.eu/scaling-social-innovation-experiences-and-first-success-stories-of-the-two-european-networks-of-incubators-for-social-innovation [accessed 20 March 2016].

Bishop, C. (2012) *Artificial Hells: Participatory Art and the Politics of Spectatorship*, New York: Verso Books.

Blundel, R.K. and Lyon, F. (2015) Towards a 'Long View': Historical Perspectives on the Scaling and Replication of Social Ventures, *Journal of Social Entrepreneurship*, Vol. 6 (1), pp. 80–102.

Brandsen, T. (2014) *The WILCO Project: A Summary of Findings*, Brussels: European Commission/EMES International Research Network. Available at www.wilcoproject.eu/wordpress/wp-content/uploads/WILCO-final-report_final.pdf [accessed 22 March 2016].

Byrne, E., Elliott, E., Saltus, R. and Angharad, J. (2018) The Creative Turn in Evidence for Public Health: Community and Arts-Based Methodologies. *Journal of Public Health*, Vol. 40, pp. i24–i30.

Campbell, A. (2014) Business Models and Operating Models. Andrew Ashridge Strategic Management Centre, 24 February. Available at http://ashridgeonoperatingmodels.com/2014/02/24/95/ [accessed 3 August 2015].

Davies, A. and Simon, J. (2013) Growing Social Innovation: A Literature Review. The Theoretical, Empirical and Policy Foundations for Building Social Innovation in Europe (TEPSIE), European Commission 7th Framework Programme, ID: 290771, Brussels: DG Research, European Commission.

Dees, J. G. (2001) *The Meaning of Social Entrepreneurship*, Durham, NC: Duke University Press.

Defourny, J., Hulgård, L. and Pestoff, V. (eds) (2014) *Social Enterprise and the Third Sector: Changing European Landscapes in a Comparative Perspective*, London: Routledge.

Defourny, J. and Nyssens, M. (2014) Social Innovation, Social Economy and Social Enterprise: What Can the European Debate Tell Us? In F. Moulaert, D. MacCallum and A. Mehmood (eds), *The International Handbook on Social Innovation: Collective Action, Social Learning and Transdisciplinary Research*, pp. 40–53, Cheltenham: Edward Elgar.

DiMaggio, P. J. (1991) Constructing an Organizational Field as a Professional Project: US Art Museums, 1920–1940. In W. W. Powell and P. J. DiMaggio (eds), *The New Institutionalism in Organizational Analysis*, 267–292, London: University of Chicago Press.

DiMaggio, P. J. and Powell, W. (1983) The Iron Cage Revisited: Institutional Isomorphism and Collective Rationality in Organizational Fields, *American Sociological Review*, Vol. 48, pp. 147–160.

Doherty, R., Haugh, H. and Lyon, F. (2014) Social Enterprises as Hybrid Organizations: A Review and Research Agenda, *Journal of Management Review*, Vol. 16, pp. 417–436.

Emerson, J. and Bonini, S. (2003) The Blended Value Map: Tracking the Intersects and Opportunities of Economic, Social and Environmental Value Creation, Working Paper. Available at https://community-wealth.org/content/blended-value-map-tracking-intersects-and-opportunities-economic-social-and-environmental [accessed 30 May 2016].

Evers, A., Ewert, B. and Brandsen, T. (eds) (2014) *Social Innovations for Social Cohesion: Transnational Patterns and Approaches from 20 European Cities*, Brussels: WILCO Project. Available at www.wilcoproject.eu/ereader [accessed 20 January 2015].

Gardin, L. (2005) La reciprocité. In J.-L. Laville and A. D. Cattani (eds), *Dictionnaire de l'autre économie*, 520–525, Toulouse: Ed. Erès.

Grassl, W. (2012) Business Models of Social Enterprise: A Design Approach to Hybridity, ACRN Journal of Entrepreneurship Perspectives, Vol. 1 (1), pp. 37–60. Available at www.acrn.eu/resources/Journals/JoE012012/Grassl_SE-Hybridity.pdf [accessed 27 June 2015].

Harvie, J. (2013) *Fair Play: Art, Performance and Neoliberalism*, London: Palgrave Macmillan.

Haxeltine, A., Kemp, R., Dumitru, A., Avelino, F., Pel, B. and Wittmayer, J. (2015) TRANSIT WP3 Deliverable D3.2: A First Prototype of TSI Theory. Available at http://bit.ly/2haqmxa [accessed 3 February 2016].

Hope, S. (2017) From Community Arts to the Socially Engaged Art. In A. Jeffers and G. Moriarty (eds), *Culture, Democracy and the Right to Make Art*, 203–221, London: Bloomsbury.

Jackson, S. (2011) *Social Works: Performing Art, Supporting Publics*, New York: Routledge.

João-Roland, I. d. S. and Granados, M. L. (2020) Social Innovation Drivers in Social Enterprises: Systematic Review, *Journal of Small Business and Enterprise Development*, Vol. 27 (5), pp. 775–795.

Kaluzny, A. P. and Hernandez, S. R. (1988) Organizational Change and Innovation. In S. M. Shortell and A. D. Kaluszny (eds), *Health Care Management: A Text in Organization Theory and Behavior*, 378–417, New York: Wiley.

Keersmaecker (De), A., Kandachar, P., Parmar, V., Vandenbempt, K. and Baelus, C. (2014) Factors Influencing an Upscaling Process of Grassroots Innovations: Preliminary Evidence from India. In B. Galbraith and F. Molinari (eds), *Social Innovation and Entrepreneurship: Case Studies, Practices and Perspectives*, 49–67, Reading, MA: Academic Publishing.

Kerlin, J. A. (2013) Defining Social Enterprise across Different Contexts: A Conceptual Framework Based on Institutional Factors, *Nonprofit and Voluntary Sector Quarterly*, Vol. 42 (1), pp. 84–108.

Lewin, K. (1951) *Field Theory in Social Science*, New York: Harper and Row.

Lyon, F. and Fernandez, H. (2012), Strategies for scaling up social enterprise: lessons from early years providers, *Social Enterprise Journal*, Vol. 8 No. 1, pp. 63–77.

Maeckelbergh, M. (2011) Doing Is Believing: Prefiguration as Strategic Practice in the Alterglobalization Movement, *Social Movements Studies*, Vol. 10, pp. 1–20.

Menger, P.-M. (2005) *Les intermittents du spectacle. Sociologie du travail flexible*, Paris: EHESS.

Miller, P. and Stacey, J. (2014) *Good Incubation: The Craft of Supporting Early-Stage Social Ventures*, London: Nesta. Available at www.nesta.org.uk/sites/default/files/whats_the_diff_wv.pdf [accessed 11 December 2016].

Moulaert, F., MacCallum, D., Mehmood, A. and Hamdouch, A. (eds.) (2014) *The International Handbook on Social Innovation: Collective Action, Social Learning and Transdisciplinary Research*, Cheltenham: Edward Elgar.

Nee, V. and Ingram, P. (1998) Embeddedness and Beyond: Institutions, Exchange, and Social Structure. In M. C Brinton, and V. Nee (eds), *The New Institutionalism in Sociology*, pp. 19–45, New York: Russell Sage Foundation.

Nicholls, A., Simon, J. and Gabriel, M. (2015) *New Frontiers in Social Innovation Research*, Hampshire: Palgrave Macmillan.

Nyssens, M. (ed.) (2006) *Social Enterprise. At the Crossroads of Market, Public Policies and Civil Society*, London: Routledge.

Nyssens, M., Defourny, J., Gardin, L. and Laville, J.-L. (2012) Work Integration Social Enterprises and Public Policy: An Analysis of the European Situation, Working Paper, Liege: EMES International Research Network.

Perkmann, M. and Spicer, A. (2010) What Are Business Models? Developing a Theory of Performative Representations. In N. Phillips, G. Sewell and D. Griffiths (eds), *Technology and Organization: Essays in Honour of Joan Woodward, Research in the Sociology of Organizations, Vol. 29*, 265–275, Bingley: Emerald Group.

Ridley-Duff, R. (2008) Social Enterprise as a Socially Rational Business, *International Journal of Entrepreneurial Behavior & Research*, Vol. 14 (5), pp. 291–312.

Ridley-Duff, R. and Bull, M. (2011) *Understanding Social Enterprise: Theory and Practice*, London: Sage.

Rodríguez Morató, A. (2012) The Culture Society: A Heuristic for Analyzing Cultural Change in the Global Age. In A. Sales (ed.), *Sociology Today: Social Transformations in a Globalizing World*, 316–336, London: Sage.

Rogers, E. M. (1995) *Diffusion of Innovations*, 4th ed., New York: Free Press.

Sanz, T. and Rodriguez-Labajos, B. (2021) Does Artistic Activism Change Anything? Strategic and Transformative Effects of Arts in Anti-Coal Struggles in Oakland, CA. *Geoforum*, Vol. 122, pp. 41–54.

Sapsed, J. and Salter, A. (2004) Postcards from the Edge: Local Communities, Global Programs and Boundary Objects. *Organization Studies*, Vol. 25 (9), pp. 1515–1534.

Sommers, D. G. and Napier, T. L. (1993) Comparison of Amish and Non-Amish Farmers: A Diffusion/Farm-Structure Perspective. *Rural Sociology*, Vol. 58 (1), pp. 130–145.

Stewart, E. and Tolnay, S. E. (1995) The Spatial Diffusion of Fertility: A Cross-Sectional Analysis of Counties in the American South, *American Sociological Review*, Vol. 60 (2), pp. 299–308.

Strang, D. and Meyer, J. W. (1993) Institutional Conditions for Diffusion. *Theory and Society*, Vol. 22 (4), pp. 487–511.

Throsby, D. (2001) *Economics and Culture*, London: Cambridge University Press.

Tolnay, S. E. (1995) The Spatial Diffusion of Fertility: A Cross-Sectional Analysis of Counties in the American South, 1940, *American Sociological Review*, Vol. 60 (2), pp. 299–308.

Transnational Network for Social Innovation Incubation (TRANSITION) (2016) Final Report Summary, European Commission 7th Framework Programme, ID: 604849, Brussels: DG Research, European Commission. Available at https://cordis.europa.eu/project/id/604849/reporting [accessed 15 March 2016].

Weber, C., Kröger, A. and Demirtas, C. (2016) *Scaling Social Impact in Europe: Quantitative Analysis of National and Transnational Scaling Strategies of 358 Social Enterprises*, Berlin: Bertelsmann Stiftung. Available at www.bertelsmann-stiftung.de/fileadmin/files/user_upload/BST_ScalingSocialImpactInEurope_final.pdf [accessed 12 December 2016].

Weber, C., Kröger, A. and Lambrich, K. (2012) Scaling Social Enterprises: A Theoretically Grounded Framework, *Frontiers of Entrepreneurship Research*, Vol. 32 (19), article 3. Available at http://digitalknowledge.babson.edu/fer/vol32/iss19/3 [accessed 12 December 2016].

Weill, P., Malone, T. W., D'Urso, V. T., Herman, G. and Woerner, S. (2005) Do Some Business Models Perform Better Than Others? A Study of the 1000 Largest US Firms, Working Paper No. 226, Cambridge, MA: MIT Center for Coordination Science.

Weimann, G. and Brosius, H.-B. (1994) Is There a Two-Step Flow of Agenda-Setting? *International Journal of Public Opinion Research*, Vol. 6 (4), pp. 323–341.

Wejnert, B. (2002) Integrating Models of Diffusion of Innovations: A Conceptual Framework. *Annual Review of Sociology*, Vol. 28, pp. 297–306.

Wejnert, B. (2014) *Diffusion of Democracy: The Past and Future of Global Democracy*, New York: Cambridge University Press.

Welfare Innovations at the Local Level in favour of Cohesion (WILCO) (2014) Policy Brief: Lessons Learnt about the Sustainability and Diffusion of Social Innovation, Based on the Evidence of the WILCO project. Available at https://ec.europa.eu/research/social-sciences/pdf/policy_briefs/wilco_eu_policy_brief_032014.pdf [accessed 22 March 2016].

Westall, A. (2009) Value and the Third Sector, Working Paper No. 25, Birmingham: Third Sector Research Centre.

Westley, F., Antadze, N., Riddell, D. J., Robinson, K. and Geobey, S. (2014) Five Configurations for Scaling Up Social Innovation: Case Examples of Nonprofit Organizations From Canada. *Journal of Applied Behavioral Science*, vol. 50 (3), pp. 234–260.

Xhauflair, V., Huybrechts, B. and Pichault, F. (2015) *From Art to Project: Cross-Border Diffusion of a Social Innovation on the Labor Market*, Liege: HEC Management School-ULg. Available at https://orbi.uliege.be/bitstream/2268/181172/1/XhauflairHuybrechtsPichault_FromArttoProject.pdf [accessed 15 February 2016].

Zott, C. and Amit, R. (2015) Business Model Innovation: Toward a Process Perspective. In C. E. Christina Ellen Shalley, M. A. Hitt and J. Zhou (eds), *The Oxford Handbook of Creativity, Innovation*, 395–406, Oxford: Oxford University Press.

5 The Case of SMart

A Unique European Social Enterprise in the Field of Culture

5.1 SMartbe and the SMart Model

The research setting selected is culture and, more specifically, cultural organisations in the field of social and solidarity economy. For this volume, I fuse the previously defined concept of social enterprise with the specialised cultural sphere defined by Sales (2012). The research is based on a revelatory case study focusing on 'understanding the dynamics present within single settings' (Eisenhardt, 1989: 534), with an eye on the depth and novelty of these dynamics. The selected organisation is SMartbe and its replication across seven European countries, with an emphasis on three of its national offsprings (Austria, Hungary and Spain). Even though SMart does not directly produce art as a main line of work, it illustrates a truly social and solidarity economy line of development, self-help and mutual support.

5.1.1 The Initiator: SMartbe

SMartbe was founded in 1998 as a small mutuality-based non-profit organisation in response to the growing demand of artists facing difficulties vis-à-vis the administrative aspects of their status and activities. SMartbe (acronym for 'Société Mutuelle pour artistes' or 'Mutual Society for artists') was created to act as an intermediary body to manage the contracts entered into between its members who engage in any kind of artistic performance and their customers. Therefore, the mission of SMartbe was not a priori directly aimed towards producing art, but supporting the creators.

This member-based association had several foci: first on the operational aspect of its services, then on developing more active member participation and more recently on expanding its presence in Europe. Its mission statement, as included in the original bylaws of the organisation, was

> to reinforce the autonomy of artists; to support the emergence of creative activities; to promote a legal framework for the artistic sector; to develop as a socio-professional association, the representativity of

DOI: 10.4324/9781003342144-6

their members; and to make available to its members administrative and financial tools for the exercise of their professional activities.[1]

In a nutshell, SMartbe ensures the administrative and legal coverage of its members, both when they are engaged in the production of cultural goods and services and when they are off-project. SMartbe has been developing innovative services for artists and creative professionals for over two decades. Moreover, it defends the interests of its members as special types of workers and makes sure that their voice is heard in policy discussions related to their employment and rights as well as to issues widely related to culture. SMartbe is well known for the battles against the precarisation of cultural and creative workers in Belgium. SMartbe is present at the European level both through replying to open consultations and collaborating with other European institutions such as the European Economic and Social Committee. It also has a strong presence in European networks (e.g. Culture Action Europe) and research projects (e.g. CulturalBase Social Platform).[2]

In the 18 years covered by the research included in this book (1998–2015), the growth of SMartbe has been impressive: in 2012, SMartbe had 173 employees (far from the original five employees), 37,000 members and a turnover of €130 million. The evolution of the membership base is illustrated in Graph 5.1. What originated as a small organisation anchored to the social economy of Brussels rapidly spread to other Belgian cities. By 2015, it had 10 offices, two in Brussels and eight across Belgium (Antwerp, Charleroi, Gent, Kortrijk, Liege, Mons, Namur and Tournai). Ultimately, considering the social aims of the organisation (ending precarity and ensuring that professionals in the creative sector make a living out of their professional activity), the results are undeniable: in 2011, the average funding managed via an online management system was €25,000 per year. In addition, at a more systemic level, artistic services amounted to the equivalent of 600 full-time jobs per year (i.e. 120,000 work-days) (Dujardin and Rajabaly, 2010).

The SMart model was created as a response to a specific context: the Belgian labour market of the 1990s. Even though SMart was not technically an organisation producing cultural art, it was called upon to play a crucial role in articulating the sector, thanks to the innovation it introduced both in the labour and cultural fields. As a matter of fact, its growth can only be explained by the progressive enlargement of SMartbe's target audiences wherein it, although initially focused on 'creative professionals', is currently moving on to include any project-based worker (Xhauflair et al., 2015). In parallel with such accelerated growth, SMart has always faced criticism from other players in the labour market who saw traditional negotiation schemes and field boundaries threatened; such negative reactions, however, have been accompanied by strong diffusion among users going beyond geographic boundaries (Xhauflair et al., 2015).

Indeed, one of the strategies deployed by SMart to minimise uncertainty in the process of spanning boundaries was 'the allocation of numerous

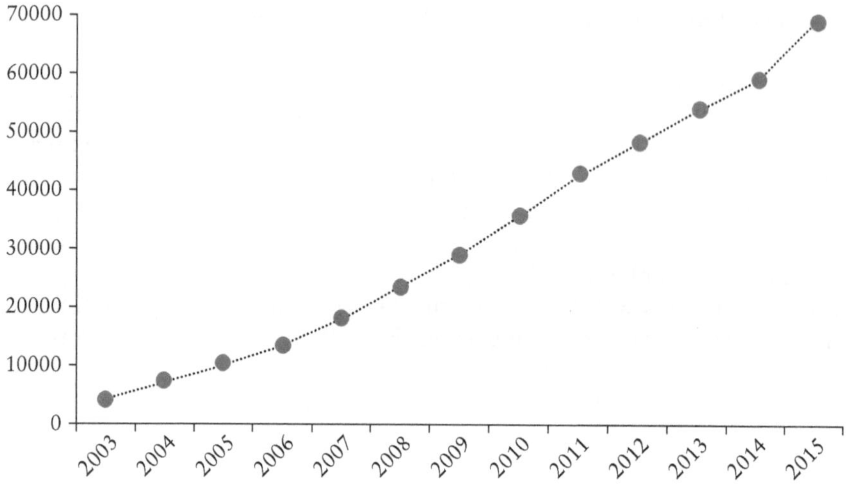

Graph 5.1 Membership evolution of SMartbe (2003–2015).

personnel to boundary spanning roles' (Hirsch, 1972: 650). Although Paul Hirsch (1972) focused on the book, film and music industries with specific raw material (actors, singers, composers, etc.), he also associated this type of behaviour with entrepreneurial organisations in culture industries.

SMartbe gradually underwent a boundary-spanning and audience-enlarging process that had an impact on the Belgian institutional landscape and regulatory framework related to employment (Xhauflair et al., 2015). Through an incremental expansion of these boundaries, SMartbe became a 'cross-boundary organisation', active both in the labour market as an employer of thousands of cultural and creative workers and in the cultural sector through increasingly assuming functions of production and mediation via the commissioning of, and making direct investment in, culture and the arts.

5.1.2 The Operational Model of SMartbe

As already mentioned, SMartbe focused on the operational aspects of the organisation during the initial year, ensuring efficient implementation of services and satisfaction for the members. The promotion of 'associative spirit' was not a priority, although once the organisation was established from a management and business perspective, that would become one of the main priorities.

Besides the basic administrative and information services, additional services continued to be developed, including training, leasing, microcredit, legal assistance, training, a research unit, crowdfunding, art collection, insurance and so on. As indicated, only those elements of the operational model of SMart of relevance to replication and adaptation (the focus of this book) were considered, namely the services offered (core and accessory) and the technology that permits increasing efficiency and accessibility to members (which is referred to internally as 'the tool').

The operational model of SMart can be identified through 10 services – five core services and five accessory ones – as described below:

1. *Contract and/or activity management:* SMart developed an ICT management system called 'Activity' to allow creative professionals to manage and produce individual or group projects.[3] The developers of the system – Productions Associées, a sub-division of SMartbe – perfectly understood the project-based nature of the initiatives and developed the system accordingly: it is currently used by over 10,000 members of SMart and is being adopted by other countries despite the intensive adaptation required. 'Activity' has to ensure that projects are managed with respect to all legal requirements and in a secure manner. Within the system, users can enjoy the 'employee' status, thereby activating a number of social and fiscal benefits usually unavailable to casual workers. SMart explains the functioning of 'Activity' as follows:

    > From a practical standpoint, the 'Activity' management system enables the professionals who use it to deposit funds into a budget that is earmarked for their project – through the invoicing of clients, funding contributions, and the invoicing of intellectual property rights licences. This budget can then be used to finance employment contracts, reimburse professional expenses or to pay for rights licences.[4]

    Users of 'Activity' are divided into 'coordinators', 'project backers' (who manage the budget for a specific project) and 'participants' (who participate as members of a collective project). Other important actors in the system are the 'clients' (who commission the project and to whom coordinators will be invoicing) and other actors such as sub-contractors and professional agents.[5] Different forms of money flows (in or out of the budget within 'Activity') exist depending on the fiscal and legal regulations of each country (e.g. submitting expenses and invoicing and paying intellectual property rights, subsidies and grants). The ultimate goal of this system is to set creative professionals free from administrative tasks so they can focus on their creative activities. Figure 5.1 visually summarises the functioning of 'Activity'.

    SMartbe presented the idea of a 'shared production house' to explain how it works for newcomers, proposing an easy alternative to setting up an organisation for any discipline with significant savings in terms of legal and financial hurdles. The members' projects are treated as

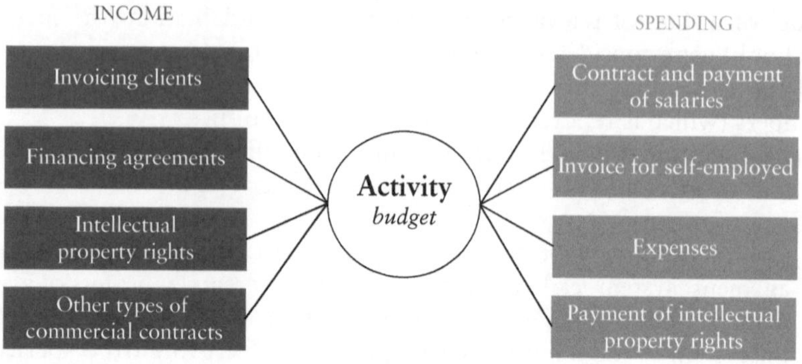

Figure 5.1 SMartbe 'Activity' system.

small businesses within SMart, thus simplifying bookkeeping, thanks to 'Activity' that allows access to the various additional services (mutual guarantee fund, leasing of equipment, insurance, etc.). The ultimate goal is to secure the career paths of cultural and creative workers facing casual and one-off work opportunities.

Ideally, the tool represents a real added value in terms of task simplification, which leaves more time available for SMart workers, members and users to develop other dimensions of the project. Unfortunately, however, this tool was only available to non-Belgian SMart national organisations in France and Germany by the end of 2015, which contributed to a slowdown in its adaptation in the rest of European countries.

2. *Information and advice:* Knowledge and expertise is recognised by SMart as one of the pillars of their model. This wealth is transferred to target users and current members on a regular basis in the form of information sessions, personal appointments and information sheets focusing on specific topics. This dissemination focuses on both internal (making current and potential members acquainted with the tools and actions of the organisation, stimulating member interactions, etc.) and external topics (work and social conditions in the sector, the status of the sector at local, national and European levels, etc.). In addition, SMart created its own research unit (*Bureau d'études*) in 2007 to capture the richness of data and knowledge created by the organisation and its members as well as their interactions with other social actors in the field of culture. The research unit, which was composed of both in-house and external researchers, published a yearly study as well as sectoral studies and statistical analyses about its membership. This research unit also monitored the evolution of the social and labour fields to track the changes affecting the creative sector. In 2012 an additional branch was added

with the aim of publishing and disseminating analyses dealing with the various activities of SMart. Furthermore, SMartbe complemented its research and monitoring function through partnerships with numerous university research centres (e.g. the Center for Social Economy at the University of Liege) and think tanks (e.g. *Pour la Solidarité*), with whom they co-organised seminars and published working papers.

3. *Guarantee funds:* The main fund of SMart is called the 'mutual guarantee fund', which ensures the payment of salary even if the client has not paid. This pay day is set differently in each country; for instance, in Belgium it is seven working days after the assignment is finished, while in Spain it is on a specific day every month. Pooling of resources – a pillar of the organisation's philosophy – allows for all members to contribute to this fund in order to spread risks: a varying fee ranging from 2% in Belgium to 1% in Spain is charged on all amounts invoiced through SMart to support the mutual guarantee fund. The idea is that this fund can be integrated into the larger European SMart platform to provide financial services to members across Europe. A second type of fund exists in some countries, called the 'social fund'. The objective of this fund is to create a pot of money that members can decide where to invest as long as it meets the mission of SMart.
4. *Debt collection:* SMartbe identified that one of the main barriers to the development of the cultural and creative sector is delayed payment and the efforts required from overburdened professionals to chase their clients to get paid. SMartbe created a debt collection unit that makes sure clients fulfil their payment obligations, thereby reducing the precariousness of casual workers and ensuring cash flow for the members. Debt collection is done by trained people who are known to the clients, with an aim of not jeopardising the potential for future work for their members. In combination with the mutual guarantee fund, these two services ensure that members are protected against debt after having performed a service.
5. *Insurance:* Being a creative worker entails a number of risks, which are covered by the insurance under law (work accidents, civil liability, etc.). In addition, several types of insurances are offered exclusively to SMart members, usually related to their professional activities (e.g. theft abroad, travel insurance, shipping insurance, etc.).

Along with these five core services, other 'additional services' offered by SMart include:

1. *Financial services:* Several tools have been developed ranging from leasing of equipment and vehicles to specific financial tools: microfinance, advances of subsidies, fund for career development, small loans and more innovative ones such as crowdfunding. For instance, Push was a SMart-powered crowdfunding platform for financing, supporting

and communicating artistic projects. Based on mutualistic and non-profit principles, Push aimed at funding artistic projects, thanks to the coaching and support of the SMart community. Another innovative service was a scholarship scheme that ensured excellence was nurtured and that 'hard to finance' projects got the required funding.

2. *Online community network:* SMartAgora aims to create and strengthen the links and interactions among creative professionals. It was conceived as a community-based environment where additional resources and advice could be found in order to support the creation of projects.
3. *Co-working space:* An affordable working space is available for the members of SMart in some countries. This opportunity is developed either independently, in partnership with other organisations or even with public administrations.
4. *Art collection:* Available only in Belgium for now, this service encourages the formation of a permanent SMart visual art collection, with pieces from SMart members across Europe. In addition to creating an internal market, this collection could also tour the members' spaces and even be loaned to other cultural institutions in order to generate revenue to sustain the mission of SMartbe and its members.
5. *Professional training:* In addition to the information sessions offered by the advisors, members also have access to training programmes aimed at increasing their entrepreneurial skills. These training programmes were offered after identifying the need in SMartbe members who have received little training beyond their own discipline.[6] An innovative service developed to encourage the mobility of Belgian cultural and creative workers to other countries is called 'Mobility services'. It provides information and advice on going abroad to work (work permits and rights of stay, visa, intellectual property rights, etc.). Concrete actions include ensuring that the members' contracts are secure and in accordance with the national law when mediating with foreign contractors. One example of this type of training is the *peer-to-peer sessions* organised to transfer knowledge among SMart members with complementary professional profiles.

As can be seen in the list of services offered, SMart relies heavily on ICT to deliver some of them. Moreover, they have adapted new-generation technology tools to their needs, such as mobile devices and applications, virtual meeting tools and social networking. According to HBR (2012: 3), these 'leading users are achieving higher levels of innovation, lower costs, faster time to market, and increased productivity/efficiency'. Although this article applies only to traditional for-profit enterprises, technology has the potential of transforming business models such as SMart into what they term 'next-generation enterprises'.

Having said this, the personalisation of services is one of the added values of the SMart model. Each member is assigned a personal 'advisor' who follows the former's activity on a day-to-day basis and provides guidance when needed. These advisors ensure that specific situations are known and that there is a sustained follow-up. Such closeness is illustrated physically via multiple offices and activities to meet face to face but also by the development of online tools to create communities. The idea of 'proximity services', promoted by the social and solidarity economy, is therefore at the heart of what SMart does.

5.1.3 Enterprising Communities: SMartbe and the Social Economy

As already indicated, the basic principles behind SMart are mutualisation and non-profit behaviour. The pooling of risks and benefits that forms the basis of this mutualisation is a very old principle in many cultures, but one which has been reduced in the Western European tradition to mutual societies in the health sector and expressions related to 'debt mutualisation' that have arisen in the context of recent financial and economic crises.[7] However, mutualisation practices abound in the informal sector, which proves that it is a well-tested way of getting by and supporting each other's needs (Laville, 2011). Indeed, mutualisation does not imply a 'detached' form of solidarity, but a responsible, informed and participatory solidarity.

In the specific case of the SMart model, both emerging and established artists and creators know that, while 'profitable' periods fluctuate, everyday financial needs do not. Only by pooling what is collected at harvest time in preparation for potential moments of scarcity can these creators cope serenely with making a living. In this sense, there is a clear call to consciousness and action for any person joining SMart, insofar as someone who chooses to pool risks and benefits with others has to do so in a fully conscious, informed, responsive and active way while s/he continues to grow as a professional. And yet, one of the biggest obstacles to explaining the concept of SMartib or SMarthu to Spanish and Hungarian people who have never heard of this model before is precisely the incredulity expressed in front of the principle of mutuality as collected during the fieldwork.

A non-profit maximisation behaviour refers to the absence of any profit-driven logic in the mission and purpose of the organisation, therefore giving a major role to the well-being of members and the community at large. This does not mean that SMart seeks to be unprofitable or uncompetitive in its market. The main difference is that any generated profits are reinvested into the cooperative in order to provide more and better services to cooperative members. In SMartbe, as well as across the rest of the countries analysed here, this commitment to the well-being of members is illustrated by two concrete examples: firstly, the continuous high level of personalised care provided to members by the advisors, which is sustained as the membership base grows with the incorporation of new advisors; and secondly, the creation of a social fund managed by members themselves with regard to how it is invested.

In this context, SMartbe is embedded in the social and solidarity economy, which roots its principles and dynamics in the logic of solidarity and reciprocity. Identification with the social economy is actively promoted by SMart, both at the national and the European levels. At the national level, SMartbe has always presented itself as an organisation from the social economy. Such identification has been stated via the documents and discourse presenting SMartbe as well as by belonging to numerous cross-sectoral and sectoral federations from the social and solidarity economy. As already mentioned, it also partners with research organisations working in the social and solidarity economy, both at the national and European levels.

As explained in Chapter 3, the example of social innovation diffusion that SMart constitutes takes the form of institutional work, specifically via the institutional arrangement of a social enterprise (according to national legal contexts) and in dialogue with public administrations, the traditional private sector and other civil society actors. Attending to research developments in social economy and third sector studies, SMartbe could be considered as a social enterprise insofar as it engages in economic activity for a social purpose and is managed in a transparent and participatory way. Indeed, it combines social and economic goals and has engaged in a replication process that tests the robustness of its operational model beyond sectoral and geographic boundaries (see the next section 5.2). SMartbe constitutes an innovative type of community enterprise due to the local roots and legitimisation, the limit to the distribution of economic surplus and the aim to benefit the cultural community (and thus society) at large. Lastly, due to the existence of a clearly articulated political agenda supported by concrete actions, ultimately aiming to increase emancipation for the precarious type of the average worker's employment, SMart can be considered an organisation tied to the social and solidarity economy.

5.2 Scaling Up the SMart Model

After more than 20 years of existence and having overcome both internal and external challenges, SMart had proven its validity by increasing the well-being and performance of creators and artists, principally through reducing uncertainties related to their intermittency status. The expansion of fields of activity that preceded the geographic expansion of SMartbe is worth noting, explained below.

5.2.1 Description and Planning of the Replication Process

The strategies of social enterprise replication proposed by the BENISI project (diffusion of knowledge; capacity-building; affiliation, joint venturing and franchising; and creation of new sites) are very useful in describing SMart's expansion process. However, it is worth noting that these four strategies cut across each other in the case of SMart, and so they should be considered as an analytical tool and not a clear-cut categorisation of organisational behaviour. The impressive expansion of SMartbe began with the capacity-building dimension offered to its members, leading to its more complex geographic growth across countries. Indeed, the initial in-country geographic expansion involved the opening-up of nine offices in nine different cities. In addition, the expansion of activity field categories (from artists, to creative workers, to project-based workers) provided a unique opportunity to refine the original core operating model, test the viability of added services and adapt the original core operating model to new contexts. The fact that Belgium is characterised by marked cultural differences between the Flemish and the Wallonian regions was an added value to this refining, testing and adaptation of the national expansion strategy.

The SMart model rapidly got the attention of partners and cultural actors in neighbouring countries, starting with France.[8] In less than five years (2011–2014), an adaptation of the model was either under development or already implemented in 12 European countries. The expansion process was not an easy one, given the numerous administrative, cultural, social and political contexts present in Europe. Indeed, three out of those initially interested 12 countries (Denmark, Estonia and the UK) stopped their adaptation at different stages for different reasons. During an interview held with one of the leading managers of SMartbe, it was highlighted that waiting for the model to become fully implemented and working in a core group of three countries would have been better than moving on with what can be perceived as a rushed decision. According to the interviewee, starting off with such a small number of tested cases (technically one-and-a-half) involved an 'unfinished model' that was to be not only adapted but also somewhat completed in the course of its implementation in new countries.

Despite this set of *a posteriori* reflections, at the time, the initial success of the source organisation and the promising situation in France were enough to start SMart on a replication path that combined the two trajectories involving partnering with others: dissemination of knowledge and affiliation strategies. The rationale was to make SMart available in other countries but drawing on the strengths, local expertise and contacts of local teams, which would act as a collective, core social entrepreneur driving the implementation. As we will see, the specific form this took across countries varied greatly.

SMart mobilised the strategy known as *dissemination of knowledge*, which allowed them to tap its experience and know-how while connecting with individuals and groups already active in the cultural field. In addition to the formal steps described below, these individuals and groups had to share at least three principles with the SMart originators: the identification of the main problem to be solved (precariousness of artists and cultural workers and lack of articulation of the cultural sector), a commitment to the values of the social economy and an involvement in the construction of a European platform.

The *affiliation strategy* refers to processes whereby local adaptation is required but based on partnering with ongoing successful initiatives and sharing the abovementioned three principles. Interestingly, this strategy causes the local partner to subsequently undergo a capacity-building expansion process, allowing it to increase its presence in its own country. Normally, the existing partners may be active in the social economy and interested in expanding to the cultural field, or else they may be active in culture and the arts but ready to commit to an efficient and fair way of finding alternatives for their sector. This strategy is characterised by a high degree of formalisation since organisations are usually standing behind those individuals initiating the discussion.

Two main elements that characterised the initial steps of SMart expansion were the exponential growth of networking potential and the intensive transfer between the originating cluster (SMartbe) and the new clusters of interested people and groups around Europe. Rapidly, the relationship with Belgian originators became a combination of support and monitoring of objectives.

It is noteworthy that the geographic expansion of SMart did not follow an elaborate replication plan linked to a detailed timeline, processes and objectives crafted since the beginning. On the contrary, the expansion grew naturally based on the personal networks established and the shared identification of needs for the sector and the increasing commitment of the originating organisation to the process through the devoting of resources. Although clear-cut phases were not established in the expansion process of SMart, this identification of phases can be done *a posteriori*, namely the 'latent scaling-up' and the 'formal scaling-up' phases. The first one began around 2002 and drew on the close contacts that existed between the French-speaking Belgian community and France.[9] Indeed, there is a tradition of cross-border movement of workers between Belgium and France resulting in highly permeated cultural communities on both sides of the border as well as in some regulatory adaptations, particularly on the status of workers.

The second phase in the scaling-up of SMart, which we have termed 'formal scaling-up', began around 2006 and is identified by an internal formalisation process. This resulted in a standardised replication procedure and the creation of a department within SMartbe devoted to the development of the European platform, where all contacts and actions concentrate. This Belgium-based EU office reached a unique level of independence within the Belgian organisation as well as acted as a facilitator of exchanges and best practices among countries and as a finder of opportunities in other countries.

The evolution of the Belgian case illustrates that the more services SMart developed, the more the cultural and artistic sector seemed to thrive in a given country.[10] The French case constituted a special testing ground for what was to come in terms of a planned replication strategy across Europe. Indeed, as already mentioned, contacts had always existed between Belgium and France given the geographic closeness and border labour issues shared, but they intensified in 2002. An initial unit was set up to create links with other partners active in the complex French cultural landscape, establish connections with public administration representatives, adapt both the technical tool ('Activity') and the core services (particularly contracts and social security management) and identify local sources of financing.

The list of neighbouring countries interested in exploring the possibility of implementing the SMart model in their own contexts reached a peak of 12 in January 2014: Austria, Denmark, Germany, Estonia, France, Hungary, Italy, Poland, the Netherlands, Spain, Sweden and the UK. Moreover, expressions of interest in the form of visits to SMartbe and requests for information were received from Canada in 2012 and Mexico in 2013.

In 2011, a document describing the various phases (the 'Roadmap') was produced by the international development department together with a number of documents to accompany the implementation process in new countries. By developing a standardised process for replication in new countries, SMart formally brought the scaling-up process into its organisation. The process acknowledged the need to gather information about several elements, evaluate this information against concrete indicators and make decisions based on a comparison between the social impact sought and the conduciveness of the contexts, which include resource availability. In this context, newcomers entered a formal process leading to their acceptance into the 'SMarteu platform' (discussed more in the next section 5.2.2). The three phases of the process are summarised in Figure 5.2.

The developmental and adaptation process includes going from 'point 0' to a 'break-even point', which means that the organisation in the new country has proven its financial stability and robustness in the field. If a country reaches this point, the adaptation can be considered successful. The process takes an average of three to four years and consists of the following phases:

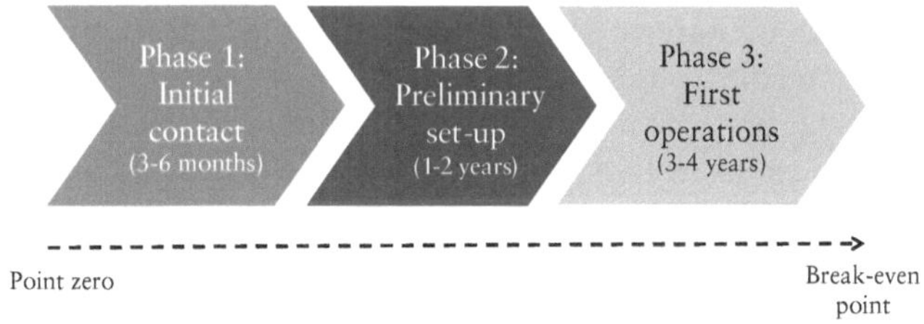

Figure 5.2 Phases and duration of the SMart scaling-up process.

5.2.1.1 Phase 1: Initial Contact

This phase includes initial intensive discussions between Belgian representatives and the local leaders interested in developing SMart in their country via face-to-face and virtual meetings. Competences of the local team are assessed, and local partners are identified and mobilised in order to ensure that the various types of capital (financial, social, human) are present. This phase requires the local partner to go through the following formal steps:

- Participating in a two-day intensive training program in the Belgian central office to meet the key people and on-site central structure. All the documents and workflows are explained and experiences from other European countries are shared.
- Filling out the Territorial Checklist, which describes the different roles and profiles that have been identified as fundamental to allow a SMart project to develop in a consistent and coherent way. The aim of this overview document is to clarify some questions territorial partners may have when setting up a team.
- Completing a Local Information Questionnaire (LIQ) aimed at collecting information about the territorial context with a twofold objective: to describe the specifications for the adaptation of the ICT tools and to learn about the sociopolitical context. The LIQ is a crucial document with two main sections: the Business Process Needs and the Territorial Context. The former includes the production of services and activities (organisation and management of workflows), the management of contracts and invoices with third-party payers (members' clients) and the financial services. The latter focuses on gathering data about the public and private sectors, forms of business entities operating in the sectors, artistic activity management workflow and ICT management.[11]
- Conducting some basic market research via an initial mapping of the sector and some focus groups with local stakeholders. The goal of focus groups is, on the one hand, to receive feedback on and inputs for the development process and, on the other hand, to mobilise new supporters and spread the word about the initiative. The initiators must be personally involved in the invitation, running and assessment of focus groups in order to fully benefit from them.
- Setting up the local team, which includes a minimum group formed by the leader, some administrative support, a legal advisor, an accountant and other types of advisors.

Table 5.1 describes the crucial elements, sub-elements, indicators and milestones involved in this phase.

Table 5.1 Overview of SMart scaling-up phase 1 (initial contacts)

Average duration	*3–6 months*	
Elements	*A start-up team*	*Context definition/market research*
Sub-elements	Initiator(s) and business developer (*can be the same*) Two-day training Checklist	LIQ Initial mapping Focus groups
Indicators	Initial partners: Have networks Understand creative workers' environment Have business knowledge	Quality of the content Self-produced or sub-contracted Attendance rate
Milestones	Initiator(s) participate in two-day training	Market research is completed

5.2.1.2 Phase 2: Preliminary Setup

Based on the initial phase, a decision is taken on whether or not to launch the development of SMart in a given country (see Table 5.2). This decision is also initial and so pre-operational (i.e. nothing has been formally launched yet), but it includes laying the blueprint for the organisation and running of activities. Bilateral discussions continue and increase, as the partners may be invited to meetings of the European platform to get to know other countries' actors. Therefore, it is a phase that involves crucial decision-making, negotiation, networking and strategising. The financial risk associated with these two initial phases is overcome by the availability of seed funding from SMartbe, which may cover all the initial operating costs provided the minimum requirements are being met in a timely manner.

5.2.1.3 Phase 3: First Operations

Based on the successful implementation of the two initial phases, the first operations are launched. Several options are offered to the partners in terms of starting to offer their services; allowing to use an adapted version of the 'Activity' tool as in Belgium and France while workflows that may be different are identified; and collecting all the required information to guide the adaptation of workflows in the territorial context (practical, legal, administrative, etc.). This phase includes a detailed, ongoing evaluation with a yearly follow-up of the accounting, administration and services levels. The end point of this phase (and the entire process) is a break-even analysis, which determines the moment in which the generated revenue equals the costs associated with generating it. Several indicators are monitored throughout the period with the aim of reaching a financial situation where

Table 5.2 Overview of SMart scaling-up phase 2 (preliminary setup)

Average duration	*1–2 years*				
Elements	*A solid team*	*Services identification*	*Creation of a legal structure*	*Management, communication and insurance packages*	*Outreach launch and advisor setup*
Sub- elements	General manager/financial officer Advisor/office manager Legal advisor	SMart fee for members Information document on services	Definition of types of status and organisational structure Seed loan from SMartbe	Solid strategy-making potential	Website and communication materials are ready Advisor(s) ready to work
Indicators	Competences: – *Manager* (evaluates effectiveness, has good links to authorities, understands the services, is cost-efficient, strives for results) – *Advisor* (dynamic, motivated, contributes to new solutions, knows cultural sector, has access to networks) – *Legal advisor* (available to users and the organisation)	Ability to overcome legal and political obstacles	Legal status belongs to the social economy Seed loan/total costs	Whether there is enough in-house knowledge Whether the team defines a strategy with limited resources	Whether there is enough in-house knowledge Whether there is collaboration with the SMarteu communication department Deep knowledge of the advisor position Whether they do their job manually or using the tool
Milestones	Core team is set up	A list of services is available	A new social enterprise is set up	A clear message is agreed upon	Advisors receive users A website exists

Table 5.3 Overview of SMart scaling-up phase 3 (first operations)

Average duration	*3–4 years*			
Elements	*First operations, monitoring of users, alternative funding, partnerships*	*Debt collection*	*Focus on quality and member diversity*	*Focus on territorial and service expansion*
Sub-elements	Initial action plan Quality assessment		Satisfaction survey for members	Evaluation (break-even analysis) and diagnostic
Indicators	Total invoiced amount Number of active users Number of users invoicing more than once Number and types of partnerships established/initiated New funding/seed loan Office location Number of personal appointments per advisor	Debt/total sales	Turnover allows for 1 Full Time employee (FTE) Number of information sessions Number of represented cultural fields	New offices are opened New services are offered Estimated time to reach financial break-even point
Milestones	A stable operations chain is in place	Accumulated debt is minimised	Positive evaluations from members are collected	Break-even point is reached

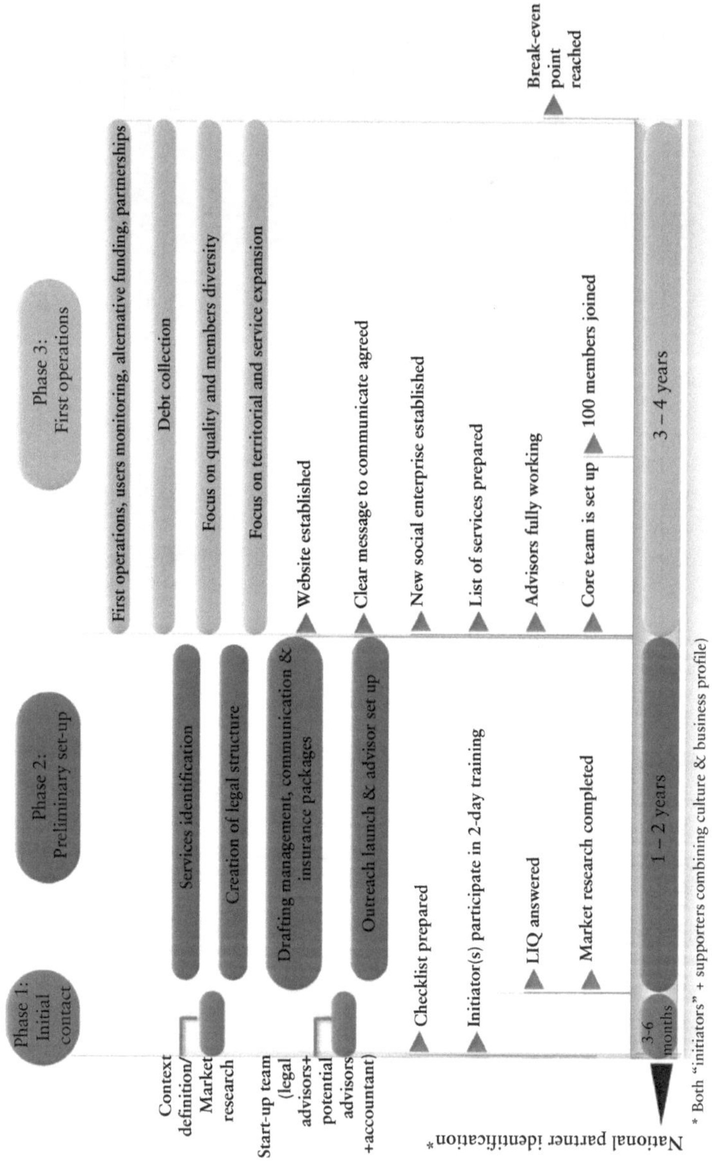

Graph 5.2 SMart scaling-up process.

gains equal losses (including the return of the seed grant). After the break-even analysis, a diagnostic is produced: if the organisation has reached this break-even situation, it is considered a fully independent organisation having taken its first step towards financial stability. On the contrary, if it fails to break-even, several corrective actions are designed and implemented to redress the situation. Phase 3 is visually summarised in Table 5.3.

Many factors influence the implementation of the model across countries and a variety of elements came into play in the adaptation process. In terms of organisational engineering and scope, SMartbe initially included an association and a foundation, beginning the transformation into a cooperative in 2017, whereas in other countries, different forms have been selected (e.g. in Spain a new type of cooperative was selected). SMartbe began as a mere administrative intermediary for the cultural and creative industries, with mutualistic services added gradually, whereas in Spain, SMartib provided a real organisational umbrella for creative professionals.

Graph 5.2 summarises the scaling-up process of SMart visually, including the main milestones, tasks and phases.

5.2.2 Setting Up a European Platform

An important external driver behind the scaling-up of SMart was provided by the European context of cultural production (see Chapter 1). The founders of SMartbe were convinced that solutions could be designed to allow artists and creative professionals to work on their projects without being overwhelmed by administrative burdens and the worry of unpredictable cash flow. Since the beginning, technology was a key ally in the creation of value for the organisation. An internet-based portal allowed these cultural workers to manage their professional activities with a small portion of receipts going to the financing of the structure and another small portion going to the creation of a 'social and guarantee fund'. The heavy ICT component of SMart is further complemented by the proximity component, as already explained.

As SMart was taking hold in various countries, an informal European platform named SMarteu was launched in order to articulate the voices coming from various national entities, facilitate communication among partners and identify future large-scale initiatives and partners worth exploring. Particularly, SMarteu has been very active in debates around culture at the European level using mainly four strategies: a formal involvement in European and international networks;[12] an intensive collaboration with think tanks and policymakers; a department devoted to research to document the evolution of the organisation and numerous publications aimed at SMart members, policymakers and the general public; and a second department, launched in 2011, responsible for the international development of the model based on the success of the replication in France (SMartfr).

Table 5.4 SMarteu preparatory discussion groups and partner meetings

Meeting name	*Date*	*Place*
Preparatory discussion group 1	December 2010	Brussels
Preparatory discussion group 1 bis	June 2011	Brussels
Partners' meeting 1	February 2012	Brussels
Partners' meeting 2	June 2012	Brussels
Partners' meeting 3	October 2012	Brussels
Partners' meeting 4	December 2013	Brussels
Partners' meeting 5	March 2015	Berlin
Partners' meeting 6	June 2015	Vienna
Partners' meeting 7	October 2015	Milano

A basic set of goals were identified and crystallised in 2011 when enough initial contacts turned into concrete partnerships, with organisations engaging in the first or second phases of the scaling-up process (SMart, 2012). The lack of legal status did not prevent the various national organisations from forming a platform that was led and animated by SMartbe in the beginning but which gradually began to hold its own meetings with its own produced agendas. These meetings, as well as the preparatory discussion groups organised two years earlier, are presented in Table 5.4. Additional partner meetings have been organised since, but not included in the table as they fall outside the period covered by this book.

The goals and means to achieve the transformation sought by SMarteu are well explained in their website (launched in 2012), which, in the absence of a set of bylaws, acts as a declaration of intentions.[13] Written in inspiring language, the ultimate goal of SMarteu is to end precariousness and support artists all over Europe by focusing on their autonomy ('with the help of simple tools and a wide range of services'), the infrastructure required to enact international mobility (using information and knowledge) and economies of scale ('to offer more and improved services while avoiding rising costs'). The official goals that emanate from these published statements are:

1. To deliver solutions adapted to the local needs by creating economies of scale at the EU level.
2. To increase the mobility of artists and other creative professionals across Europe.[14]

However, during the course of the present research, additional goals have been identified from interviews and focus groups:

- To create a European/international platform (possibly a federation) to lobby in EU and international fora, influence cultural policy and support national and regional demands from the sector.

- To facilitate funding access to creative professionals for launching their project, regardless of where they are located.
- To articulate a common agenda and common strategies for the sector.
- To increase the market for creative professionals in Europe by expanding the demand base.

Fulfilling these goals requires going beyond national borders; therefore, SMarteu rapidly identified the formal structure required to do so which, in addition to a legal status, includes the following elements (text extracted from the now extinct SMarteu website):

- A European think tank to bring together those involved in the creative economy, to examine issues and share expertise. Artists, creative professionals, researchers, representatives of European and national public institutions, consultants, and all those who strive to find solutions for the development of a project in the creative sector are brought together. They participate in building, debating, and rethinking this common project.
- A European association for creative professionals. Following the principles of social economy, the goal of the association is to enable all members, regardless of which country they are based in, to be involved in the European project and to participate in democratic governance.
- A federation of social entrepreneurs that ensures the harmonisation of basic principles throughout the countries of the members. It allows the values of the social economy to be clarified and implemented while embracing the diversity of the partners.

The associative dimension involved in the process is therefore present both at the legal level suggested (association and federation, which are typical of the social economy) and at the participation level of stakeholders working for them.

A minimum structure was granted to the European group, namely a managing board and a number of periodic meetings paving the way to the group's formalisation. The managing board was composed of one country representative plus three staff members from SMartbe (one of the two founders and two members of the SMarteu department, at the time of closing this research). However, formal decision-making within SMarteu continued to be informally based on consultation and exchange between the national level and the central SMartbe office (particularly the 'international development' department). In fact, this dialectical relationship between the different national partners and the central Belgian team was effective in terms of meeting the objectives jointly in a timely manner.

The actors involved seemed to recognise from the beginning the fact that adapting to a new national context requires both specific knowledge and contacts in the field, on the one hand, and deep knowledge and experience about the model to be adapted as well as a broader view of the larger context, on the other hand. Within that acknowledgement laid two important recognitions – that the national actors involved were (or had the potential to be) the most knowledgeable, the best connected and the best suited to fulfil the social mission of SMart in their country, and that SMartbe (and specifically the SMarteu office) had the best knowledge about the operational model, the greatest expertise in replicating it and the finest general view.

However, with the financing of the two initial scaling-up phases being ensured by a seed grant from SMartbe, autonomy and freedom may have been jeopardised. Nevertheless, while such a strong position was recognised as having exerted a weight on the decision-making process, gradually the 'financial dependency relationship' evolved into a 'collaboration relationship', which brought a higher level of independence into the decision-making process, but also more responsibility (in the sense of avoiding mission drift and ensuring country and European mission alignment) as well as financial stability of the organisation.

In the end, decisions continued to be made based on personal perceptions of trust and potential as well as on existing contacts with key players and supporters within new countries. This informality extended to the way members of the SMarteu group interacted as well as to its mandate. An important milestone in the process of setting up the SMarteu platform was that some members of the group felt gradually more empowered to act as leaders and began to organise meetings and prepare the agendas in parallel to the efforts conducted by the SMarteu office in Belgium.

After more than four years of de facto existence as SMart actors across European member states, by the end of the period covered by this research, SMarteu still was not a legal entity.[15] Part of the reason was the lack of an ideal type of legal status that SMart would require in order to be efficient at a local level. Finally, the group began its process of formalisation in October 2015 during the course of meeting the members of SMarteu in Berlin. During that meeting, the idea of signing 'Partnership Agreements' (*Conventions de Partenariats* in French) to formalise the bilateral relationships between SMartbe and each country was introduced and agreed upon.

5.2.2.1 Relationship between SMartbe and the National SMart Offices

The exchanges between the various national offices and the source organisation take place both formally and informally. The formal way of interacting consists of first assessing and then monitoring the evolution of the national office with respect to the agreed-upon objectives. As for the informal exchanges, they take place through a variety of channels and are not necessarily related to monitoring. I will now focus on the first category of exchanges as several documents need to be created for the different phases of the replication process (see Table 5.5).

Table 5.5 List of annexes accompanying the agreement

Category of documents		*Update frequency (months)*
The partner	ANNEX 1: Identification of the parties (social purpose, bank account, etc.)	12
Development strategy	ANNEX 2:	
	Annual action plan	12
	Annual budget	12
	Tri-annual programme	36
Monitoring and evaluation	ANNEX 3: Indicators for monitoring	12
Operational procedures	ANNEX 4: Dashboard of indicators Services description Manual of procedures Communication	3–6
Financial procedures	ANNEX 5: Payment requests (structure) Payment requests (cash flow) Financial situation (bank, cash, forecast)	1

When a group of people expresses interest to a representative of the mother organisation (phase 1), a number of documents are prepared. Then, once the preliminary check-up phase kicks in, another set of documents is produced by the candidate country. Once a positive evaluation has been produced, the preparation for a partnership agreement begins. In addition to the core agreement document, a number of annexes are produced to monitor the evolution of the organisation for the period covered by the agreement (except for Annex 1, which is a description of the organisation). The monitoring activity focuses on four main areas: development strategy, monitoring and evaluation, operational procedures and financial procedures.

The tone used in the documents supports the collaborative attitude and the institutional discourse of SMarteu. For instance, in the document 'Indicators for Monitoring' (called 'Annex 3'), the indicators are 'meant to serve the development process (not the other way around)'. In order to ensure that tools are at the service for an organic development of the institution, and not the other way around, the following piece of advice is provided: 'Freedom of choice, as long as they are SMart.'

There are two types of indicators: standardised (allowing the comparison of situations between countries) and 'sur mesure' (decided on a country-by-country basis). The second type is extremely important from an organisational assessment standpoint, as it includes the objectives, the outputs and the way in which performance is defined for a given national SMart.

5.2.2.2 Financing the Launch of SMart in a New Country

The implementation of the various phases of SMart is left to the national partners. However, after that, the need to diversify the sources of income as much as possible is stressed. This approach is consistent with the multi-resource nature of social enterprises (Defourny and Nyssens, 2010; Mendell and Nogales, 2009) and ensures the diversification of risks in an unknown context. As a matter of fact, the access to finance from SMartbe is non-exclusive; indeed, it should be considered as a seed capital that will cover basic day-to-day operations and leverage different sources of finance, ranging from the public to the private sectors in addition to the revenue-making services offered by the organisation. Plenty of leeway to deal with financial planning is offered to the national partner, although a clear message is given about the need for a transparent and efficient financial management.

Regarding the types of funding to be mobilised, clear guidelines are offered in order to allow for cross-country comparison:

Level 1: Structure (referred to as 'STR-Structure' in the internal documents). This level corresponds to the initial development phase. At this stage, the level of development of services does not allow for generating any income. Outgoing cash flows are typically related to the feasibility study (consultants' fees) or to the running costs (wages and consumables) for availing support services.

Level 2: Activities (referred to as 'USR-Users' in the internal documents). This level corresponds to the development phase where services provided to users start to generate income streams.

Level 3: Payback. Specific financial procedures are required at this level regarding the use of the profit generated, which includes generally the compensation for the additional capital invested by SMartbe into the business development of national partners. This level refers to the eventuality that a gross margin is generated by the new activities, which would allow covering the costs connected to the depreciation of SMartbe's immobilised production asset.

These three levels of financial procedures (summarised in Table 5.6) coexist throughout the different stages of development as initial needs tend to diversify.

Table 5.6 Levels of financing procedures related to the creation of a SMart national office

Procedure level	Structure	Users	Payback
Stage of development	Feasibility	Start-up	Growth
Type of financing needs	Costs of the core structure	Cash flow connected to services	Threshold of profit

Source: SMarteu.

5.2.2.3 Technical Resources Involved in the Launch of SMart in a New Country

Considering the complexity in the operating model of SMart, the technical resources needed to launch SMart in a new country are as much critical as the financial or human resources. They facilitate the administration and financial organisation on the part of the partner as well as the implementation of follow-up and support procedures, allowing the development of new services on the part of SMartbe. Indeed, upon assessing the evolution of the national office, SMartbe is able to offer guidance, technical support and access to information. This up-to-date information is also deemed relevant for the search of complementary financial sources, namely SMartbe which can support the identification of financing opportunities and assist in the preparation process of funding applications. Moreover, this updated information can also support the internal production of a manual of operational and financial workflow to be shared with members of SMarteu as a useful administrative tool.

Regarding ICT resources, the crucial elements to be considered are:

1. *Internal (back office) software*, including the software packages used and their functionalities.
2. The *user interface*, which refers to the 'Tool' that is provided to all partners of SMartbe. However, its implementation has been uneven across countries. By the end of 2015, only SMartfr had implemented it. The development of this Tool is partially financed by SMartbe and adopted by national partners once modifications based on national contexts have been incorporated.
3. National *websites* are hosted by SMartbe under its umbrella site that offers a content framework for partners to follow (eventually it will allow access to the user interface once it becomes available to all countries). The use and content of the website is described in each partner's communication plan.

The national partner and SMartbe jointly identify and define these resources, and yearly updates on their evolution are provided.

5.3 Assessing the Impact of SMart and Its Scaling-Up Strategy

Scaling up beyond geographical borders is more complex than doing so within the same country, and so it should always be attempted after scaling-up has been completed locally (Weber, 2016). In the case of SMartbe, this was indeed the case in terms of both boundary expansion and geographic enlargement within Belgium (Xhauflair et al., 2015). The third step was to engage in trans-border expansion with the creation of SMartfr, which offered a unique laboratory to test the model and the adaptation needed.

The subsequent steps towards the scaling-up in other countries were implemented in a reactive manner (based on the proposal from other countries' partners) rather than proactively (ensuring that the identified requirements for each scaling-up attempt were in place).

This process of cross-border expansion was commented upon during the interview with one of the key decision-makers within SMartbe. Indeed, according to the interviewee, a more efficient strategy would have been to wait and consolidate SMart in a third country (after SMartfr) to be able to stabilise and define the model in order to operationalise its replication and adaptation. Moreover, the resources required to launch SMart in eight different countries while maintaining its successful operations in the source country went beyond what any individual organisation could provide. Indeed, a 'culture of partnerships and collaboration' has to be promoted if SMart is to be successful in this multiplication of requests from several 'centres of action'. The challenge for SMartbe, therefore, stemmed from leaving behind the 'do-it-yourself and independence culture' that had characterised it for everything related to its internal management, in the quest for its essential resources.

5.3.1 State of Scaling-Up Process per Country

Before I begin to analyse the factors of the scaling-up process in the next sub-section 5.3.3, it is important to know the status regarding the scaling-up phases as of December 2015 – the end of the timeframe in the present study. In order to assess the evolution of the scaling-up process, I will look at two indicative sets of information: the status of the scaling-up process, and the

Table 5.7 State of the scaling-up process by December 2015

Countries		*Start date of the process/first contact*	*Phase reached by December 2015*
First wave of countries	Austria	2011	2. Preliminary setup
	Germany	2011	2. Preliminary setup
	Spain	2011	3. First operations
	Sweden	2011	3. First operations
	UK	2010	*Interrupted*
Second wave of countries	Denmark	2012	*Interrupted*
	Italy	2011	3. First operations
	The Netherlands	2012	2. Preliminary setup
	Hungary	2012*	2. Preliminary setup
	Estonia	2012*	1. Initial contact
	Poland	2012	1. Initial contact

* Participation in partners' meeting.

Table 5.8 Core and additional services across SMart country offices

	AT	*BE*	*DE*	*FR*	*HU*	*IB*	*IT*	*NL*	*SE*
Service fee	7.5	6.5%	7.0% 5.0%	8.5% 6.5%	8.5%	7.5%	8.5%	6.5%	6.5%
Core activities									
Activity management	■	■	■	■	■	■	■	■	■
Contract management	■	■	□	■	□	■	■	■	■
Debt collection	■	■	■	■	□	■	■	■	■
Guarantee fund	■	■	□	■	□	■	■	■	■
Insurances	■	■	□	■	□	■	■	□	■
Events and encounters between users	■	■	■	■	■	■	■	■	□
Additional services									
Financial services (micro-loans, leasing)		■		■			□		
Financial support (grants)		■		■					□
Research unit (for users)	■				□				
Research for internal SMarteu use and external partnerships	■	■	■	■	□		■		
Co-working spaces/studio spaces		■		■	□			□	■
Externalised services									
Legal advice (external)	■	■	■	■			■	■	■
Training		■	■	■			■		■
Centralised purchase (e.g. vehicle rental)			■		■				
Others (specify)	Mobility portal & advice		Mobility help desk					Tax together	SMart Space

■ Realised (2015) □ Projected (2016)

Source: SMarteu.

level of implementation of the core and additional services across the countries (see Table 5.7). Regarding the first set, we see almost all of the countries where SMart was operational.

Information in the second set, stemming from the process of consolidation of SMart across European countries, shows the level of implementation (after the required adaptation) of the core and additional services. This is something the central office of SMart watches quite closely and is summarised in Table 5.8.

5.3.2 *Overview of Scaling-Up Process in Three Select Country Cases*

I focus on the following three indicators to compare the scaling-up process across the three countries, namely Austria, Spain and Hungary:

1. *Speed of implementation:* By looking at how long the adaptation has taken in each country, one can get an idea of how arduous the process was. Table 5.9 summarises this information across the countries.
2. *Number of users/members:* By tracking the evolution of membership in each country office (see Table 5.10), it is possible to check the attractiveness of the model to the local target groups. Unfortunately, given the limited timespan of the current research, for Austria and Hungary there is only one full year of data to draw from, which may be insufficient for making a longitudinal comparison.
3. *Turnover and surplus:* As an important financial indicator, the annual turnover allows us to understand the volume of activities generated by a national office (see Table 5.11 for a summary of this information across the three countries). The surplus allows an understanding of, firstly, whether the organisation managed to generate enough income to cover the operating expenses and, secondly, whether new resources were available to ensure the improvement of existing services or the development of new ones. However, financial indicators may be misleading when considered for such a short timeframe, as in the case of Hungary or Austria; on the one hand, a high turnover does not per se imply long-term financial sustainability; on the other hand, a low turnover needs to be followed up along a timeframe that reflects the evolution pattern. In all, it is generally accepted that a high turnover represents higher possibilities for the newly created country office to survive than the one having a lower turnover.

5.3.3 *Quantitative Analysis of the Factors Involved in the European Scaling-Up*

A Likert-type questionnaire was distributed among the initiators and staff at SMart. The goal was to capture attitudes towards the adaptation and replication process of SMart across countries. The model used was the one

Table 5.9 Duration of the implementation process of SMart in the three countries

	Phase 1: Initial contact (3–6 months)	*Phase 2: Preliminary setup (1–2 years)*	*Phase 3: First operations (3–4 years)*
AT	First contact: March 2011* Formal creation: 2014	*Completed by the end of 2016 (including full repayment of the loan to SMartbe)*	*Full-fledged operations: 2017* *Break-even point ('point 0'): 2019*
ES	First contact: January 2011* Formal creation: 2013	Completed by the end of 2013 (including full repayment of the loan to SMartbe)	*Full-fledged operations: 2013* *Break-even point ('point 0'): 2019*
HU	First contact: December 2012* Formal creation: March 2014 (full operations: November 2014)	Completed by early 2016 (not including full repayment of the loan to SMartbe)	*Full-fledged operations: 2018* *Break-even point ('point 0'): 2020*

*Effective dates vs. *planned dates* (in italics).

Table 5.10 Evolution of membership in the three countries

Country	*Indicator*	*2013*	*2014*	*2015*	*2016*
AT	Members/users	–	–	80	132
	Growth	–	–	80%	60%
ES	Members/users	64	800	1.439	2.871
	Growth	–	1250%	80%	100%
HU	Members/users	–	–	170	280
	Growth	–	–	170%	65%

Table 5.11 Annual turnover in the three-country studies (since year of establishment)

	2013	*2014*	*2015*	*2016**
AT	–	–	61,400 €	160,450 €
ES	114,459 €	2,270,601 €	4,925,169 €	9,000,000 €
HU	–	–	5,000 €	42,500 €

* 'Projected', since the date range of the research ended in 2015.

developed by Professor Weber and her colleagues specifically for social enterprises in 2014 and updated in 2016. The revision of the model entailed the inclusion of two prerequisites and the reduction of success factors from seven to six (Weber 2014, 2016). The definitions of the items were based on Weber's original (2014) text, and the factors that would effectively capture

Table 5.12 Measured success factors for scaling-up as included in Weber (2014)

Success factor	*Questions*	*Number of items*
Commitment of the individuals driving the scaling process	1.1–1.8	8
Competence of the management	2.1–2.12	12
Entire or partial replicability of the operational model	3.1–3.12	12
Ability to meet social demands	4.1–4.6	6
Ability to obtain necessary resources	5.1–5.12	12
Potential effectiveness of scaling social impact with others	6.1–6.8	8
Adaptability	7.1–7.7	7
	Total	**65**

the specificity of the SMart scaling-up attempts were identified as reported in Table 5.12.

A basic statistical analysis of the survey data was performed across the countries that replied, in order to analyse the initiators' and staff's perceptions of the ways in which the scaling-up process had taken place in their countries. Out of the 45 participants contacted (five representatives – founder, manager, advisor, council member and supporter – each from nine different countries), I received 31 responses (68%), which form the population for the analysis (N = 31).

Given the nature of the variables (ordinal) and the decision made during questionnaire design, descriptive analyses were run in order to assign minimum and maximum values to factors as well as the means and standard deviations. The survey aimed to capture the perceptions of the five categories of stakeholders about the relevance of the seven factors in the Weber (2014) model for the scaling-up of SMart in their own country. To this end, the means and standard deviations were the focus, as shown in Table 5.13.

The mean is a measure of central tendency that allows researchers to see the average value per factor. Since the data is ordinal and indicates values from 1 (fully disagree) to 7 (fully agree), one can see that the factors were identified as highly relevant with all of them scoring above 4. For instance, of the factors included (all of them explained below), 'ability to meet social demands' scored the highest (5.44) across all seven countries, which is consistent with the concern strongly felt across European countries (the precariousness of creative workers). On the contrary, the 'adaptability of the operating model' scored the lowest (4.12), although having a relatively high score overall.

As for the standard deviation (SD), it is a measure of dispersion that tells us how the responses spread out around the mean. Usually a high standard deviation indicates very different item scores across countries, which is not the case in this research. In this sense, the factor that shows the highest level

Table 5.13 Results for the seven factors of the scaling-up process (N = 31)

Scaling-up factor	*Brief description*	*Mean*	*Standard deviation*
Commitment of the individuals driving the scaling process	Level of commitment of the key people (initiators) involved in the process of adaptation	4.63	0.96
Competence of the management	The ability of the leaders to ensure day-to-day operations while thinking strategically	5.23	1.11
Entire or partial replicability of the operational model	The ability of an organisation to reproduce not only its products and services but also, where appropriate, its structures and processes	4.43	1.04
Ability to meet social demands	The ability to scale up the creation of social value most effectively both in quantitative and qualitative terms	5.44	0.77
Ability to obtain necessary resources	The ability to generate the resources needed across the various phases of scaling-up via internal human capital or external supporters, partners and networks	4.74	0.62
Potential effectiveness of scaling social impact with others	The role of partners in the adaptation process both between the source enterprise (SMartbe) and the national SMart, and between the national SMart and other local partners	4.87	0.99
Adaptability of the model	To what degree is the model adaptable and what some of the obstacles are to its adaptability	4.12	0.68

of homogeneity across countries is the 'ability to obtain necessary resources' (factor 5) with the lowest standard deviation result (0.62). However, when referring to its importance relative to the other factors, it stands at fourth position, with a rating of 4.74, after the 'ability to meet social demands' (factor 4), the 'competence of the management' (factor 2) and the 'potential effectiveness of scaling social impact with others' (factor 6).

In order to look at how different items within each factor behaved, I ran a descriptive statistical analysis of each of the seven factors across the seven countries. I included two additional values – the minimum and maximum scores – with a view to appreciate the range of responses mobilised for each factor. The description of each of the factors is included in the following seven sub-sections: one table summarises this statistical description and these values are shown graphically using a spider graph for each of the factors.

By conducting this survey I aimed at running the Weber model in the transnational scale-up effort of a successful CASE with an view to validating it in a new field and eventually strengthening it.

5.3.3.1 Factor 1: Commitment of the Individuals Driving the Scaling-Up Process

The statistical analysis included in Table 5.14 shows that what was perceived to be critical with a rating of over 6 is the involvement of individuals from within the organisation: the initiators, the source organisation (SMartbe), the management and the staff. On the contrary, the commitment of external stakeholders (local and national governments and other social economy organisations) received a significantly lower rating. This reflects in Graph 5.3 where the line referring to internal actors (on the right) appears to fill a wider area, while the other lines come closer to the centre (value = 0). In particular, the commitment of the manager was perceived to be the most important sub-factor (6.22). The rating assigned to volunteers varied across countries depending on whether their participation in SMart is formally recognised by the country or not.

This research hypothesises about the relevance of a social and solidarity economy environment to achieve successful scale of social enterprises. It includes the following two hypotheses. Firstly, the higher the recognition by public administration of the social and solidarity economy, the higher the tradition of collaboration among them and the higher the possibility of creating a supportive environment for adapting the CASE. Secondly, the higher the level of collaboration among social enterprises in the social and solidarity economy, the higher the possibility of replicating a successful CASE model.

In this sense, the high 4.93 rating given to item 8 of factor 1 ('Other social economy organisations are highly committed with the implementation of SMartX') seems to confirm these hypotheses. In any case, its rating was substantially higher than that given to the commitment of local government (3.46) or to the national administration (3.29).

A score worth mentioning about factor 1 is the high standard deviation of the item related to volunteers (1.5), which is in fact the second highest across the 65 items studied (2.24). The high variability in the score can be explained by the differences in the understanding of 'volunteers' across

Table 5.14 Descriptive statistics for factor 1 (N = 31)

Commitment of the individuals driving the scaling process	*Minimum*	*Maximum*	*Mean*	*Std. Deviation*
1.1 Initiators	1.0	7.0	6.06	1.39
1.2 SMartbe	2.0	7.0	6.07	1.31
1.3 Management	1.0	7.0	6.22	1.31
1.4 Staff	2.0	7.0	6.07	1.34
1.5 Volunteers	1.0	7.0	5.50	2.24
1.6 Local government	1.0	6.0	3.46	1.70
1.7 National admin	1.0	6.0	3.29	1.49
1.8 Social Economy (SE) organisations	1.0	7.0	4.93	1.55

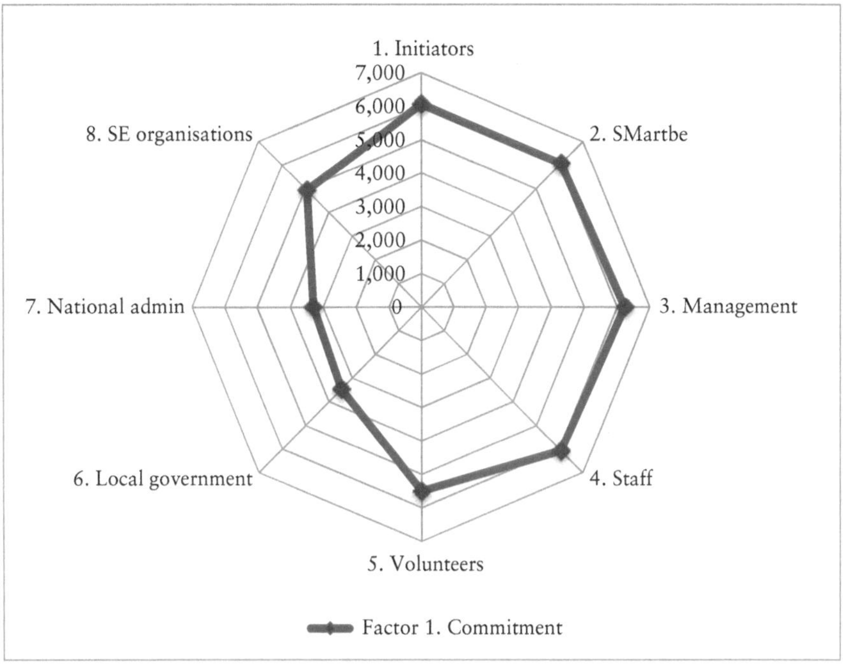

Graph 5.3 Rating of scaling-up factor 1 across countries.

countries. For instance, in countries with a strong cooperative tradition (Austria or Spain), the perceived importance of the item can be much lower than in countries with an associative tradition (Belgium or France) where the notion of volunteers is present both formally (in the bylaws) and practically (they constitute a crucial resource for organisations). The issue of whether (or under what circumstances) national SMart offices should be encouraged to mobilise volunteers, however, is not clearly addressed in the official documents, so it is left to the discretion of the leaders of the process.

5.3.3.2 Factor 2: Competence of the Management

The competency of the management in driving the scaling-up and adaptation process in a new country is the second factor in the proposed model, whose relevance has been also explained theoretically. The statistical analysis offered in Table 5.15 also seems to confirm this importance (the highest rated item in factor 1 corresponds to item 1.3 – the commitment of managers).

It is worth noting that three main blocks can be distinguished in factor 2: resource finding (items 2.1–2.3), managerial capacity (items 2.7–2.10) and leadership vis-à-vis external partners (items 2.4, 2.11, 2.12). The ability

Table 5.15 Descriptive statistics for factor 2 (N = 31)

Competence of the management	*Minimum*	*Maximum*	*Mean*	*Std. Deviation*
2.1 Develop strategy	3.0	7.0	5.61	1.33
2.2 Network and legal resources	2.0	7.0	5.50	1.33
2.3 Financial resources	2.0	7.0	5.60	1.43
2.4 Peer-to-peer support	3.0	7.0	5.23	1.41
2.5 Business coaching	1.0	7.0	4.93	1.50
2.6 Academic expertise	1.0	7.0	4.79	1.59
2.7 Activate governance	2.0	7.0	5.13	1.41
2.8 Manage stakeholders	2.0	7.0	5.17	1.44
2.9 Manage staff	2.0	7.0	5.27	1.51
2.10 Manage finance	2.0	7.0	5.80	1.30
2.11 Position within SE	3.0	7.0	5.83	1.23
2.12 Pride belonging to SE	3.0	7.0	5.89	1.11

to mobilise business coaching (item 2.5) and academic expertise (item 2.6) was perceived to be the least relevant, having ratings below 5, while the items associated with leadership (item 2.4 related to mobilising peer-to-peer support, and items 2.11 and 2.12 related to mobilising social and solidarity economy community) were perceived to be more relevant.

When looking at Graph 5.4 it is clear that all competences were considered to be important, especially the ones related, firstly, to strategic planning and implementation capacities of managers (item 2.1 = 5.61) and, secondly, to financial resources finding, namely the ability to access necessary financial resources (item 2.3 = 5.6) and manage all financial matters (item 2.10 = 5.8).

As already explained, a unique competence overlooked in the model was being able to interact and position the social enterprise in the wider social and solidarity economy. I added two items in factor 2 to measure how important this competence was to the respondents. Both items, indeed, received the highest score across all 12 items included in this factor: the 'ability to position the national SMart within the social economy' received the second highest score (5.83). The highest score was given to the 'ability to nurture a feeling of membership and pride in belonging to the social economy' (5.89). A conclusion that can be drawn is that by attributing a high value to these competences, respondents consider alignment with the social and solidarity economy a plus in adapting the model to their own country.

Incidentally, the importance of academic expertise in the scaling-up process received the lowest rating across the factors (item 2.6 = 4.79), although it is accompanied by the lowest homogeneity in responses (SD = 1.59). In order to find an explanation for this heterogeneity, it is necessary to look into the responses per country and category of respondents: managers in Austria and Spain and 'council members' in Italy and Spain assigned ratings equal to or below 2 to this item.

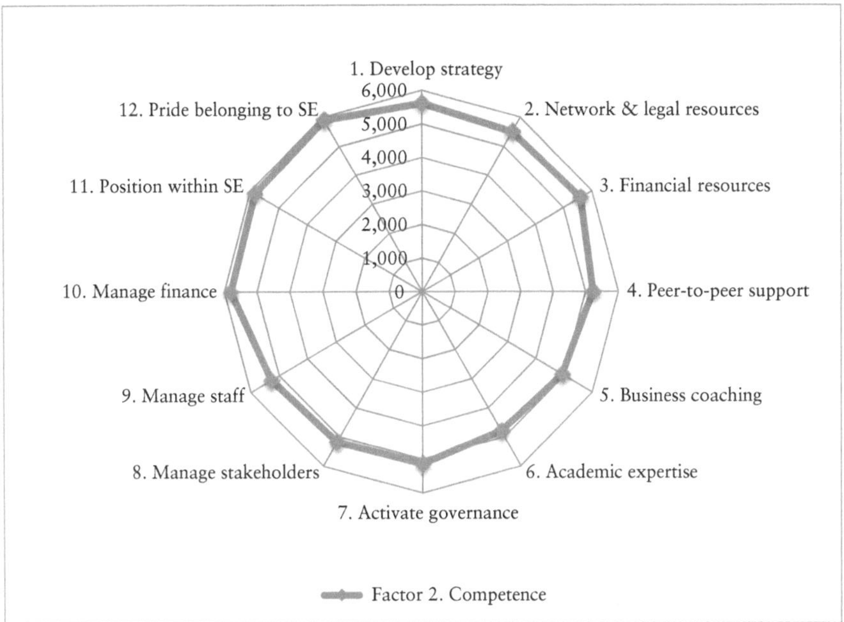

Graph 5.4 Rating of scaling-up factor 2 across countries.

In all, the analysis of this factor seems to confirm that, while having a viable and replicable model is a key for a successful transnational scale-up effort, it is really *people* who need to work out well at the end of the day. People driving the process need to be able to find financial resources; manage the organisation effectively while ensuring that participatory governance is in place; and demonstrate high levels of leadership, particularly with regard to external partners, including other social and solidarity economy actors. As explained in previous chapters, this connects with the way social value is created by social enterprises: while *what* is produced matters (depending on the market orientation of each social enterprise), the critical aspects are *how* and *with whom* they are produced.

5.3.3.3 Factor 3: Entire or Partial Replicability of the Operational Model

Replicability is at the core of any scaling-up attempt, and so factor 3 aims to capture whether the SMart model can be reproduced transnationally or whether an intensive adaptation is required (see Table 5.16). The 12 items that compose factor 3 refer to the level of complexity in replicating the SMart model, but also link to the social mission of the organisation. Three blocks can be identified: firstly, six items that refer to the replicability level of the core elements; secondly, two items that connect these replicable elements

Table 5.16 Descriptive statistics for factor 3 (N = 31)

Replicability of the model	*Minimum*	*Maximum*	*Mean*	*Std. Deviation*
3.1 Core model	2.0	7.0	4.72	1.51
3.2 Contract via online tool	1.0	7.0	4.52	2.16
3.3 Info and advice service	1.0	7.0	6.17	1.42
3.4 Debt collection	1.0	7.0	5.29	1.43
3.5 Guarantee fund	1.0	7.0	5.38	1.57
3.6 Insurances	2.0	7.0	5.04	1.40
3.7 Social impact achieved	3.0	7.0	5.21	1.29
3.8 Supporting culture	4.0	7.0	5.82	1.09
3.9 Fail: lack of network	1.0	7.0	3.72	2.31
3.10 Fail: lack of finance	1.0	7.0	4.27	1.91
3.11 Fail: lack of peer2peer	1.0	7.0	3.25	1.80
3.12 Fail: Lack of business coach	1.0	7.0	3.41	1.93

to the social value created; and thirdly, four items that try to identify possible elements (network and legal resources, financial resources, peer-to-peer support and business coaching and support) that could explain the failure to replicate those elements.

Overall, the replicability of the SMart model was perceived to be achievable (item 3.1 = 4.72). The five core services of the SMart model were rated in the following order regarding their complexity:

1. Information and advice (item 3.3 = 6.17)
2. Guarantee fund (item 3.5 = 5.38)
3. Debt collection (item 3.4 = 5.29)
4. Insurances (item 3.6 = 5.04)
5. Contract and/or activity management, ideally via online tools (item 3.2 = 4.52)

This rating should be interpreted on the basis of the complexity of reproducing each element in each of the countries (see Graph 5.5). Where standardisation and implementation depended on the local SMart team, such as for developing and conducting information and advice sessions, their replicability was perceived to be high. Indeed, item 3.3 (information and advice) was rated the first in terms of easiness to reproduce. Similarly, for the model elements to be fully tailored to each country context, efforts at the local level were perceived to be relevant. In this context, the possibilities of providing a guarantee fund, debt collection mechanisms and various types of insurances to members were rated as quite replicable.

Lastly, the management of contract and/or activity was perceived as being the most complex to implement (item 3.2 = 4.52), but the variability in terms of responses was very high (standard deviation = 2.16). The fact that the question in the survey included explicitly 'via online tool' reflects how

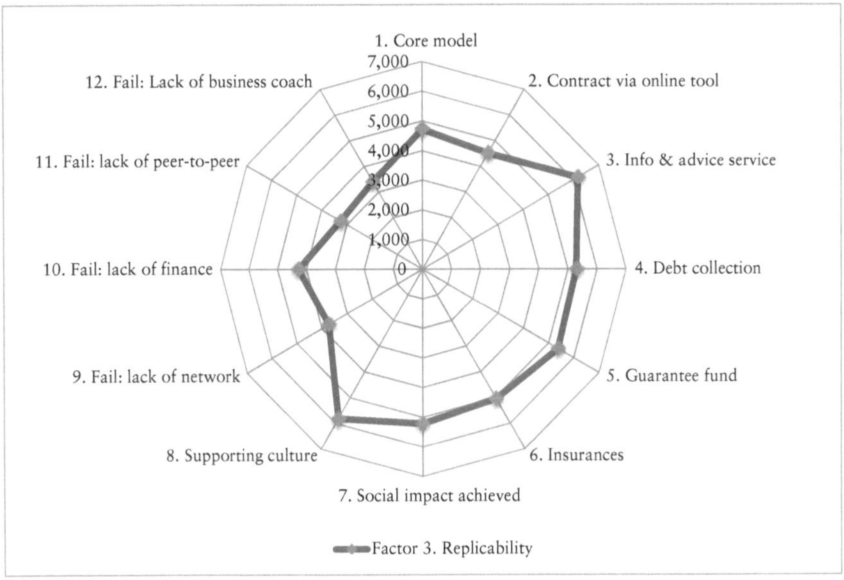

Graph 5.5 Rating of scaling-up factor 3 across countries.

unevenly the online tool has been implemented across countries. Indeed, such a high heterogeneity in responses can be explained by looking at the responses per country: in countries where the online tool was readily available (Belgium and France) or was about to be implemented (Spain and Germany), the ratings were higher, whereas in countries where the tool was still not available, the perceptions were much lower (Austria, Italy and Hungary). Not surprisingly, it was noted that standardisation and IT-based solutions can facilitate scaling processes (von Krogh and Cusumano, 2001). However, even if the rating of item 3.2 is affected by the uneven implementation of the online tool in the countries surveyed, it must be noted that the tasks and processes associated with this service demand an intensive adaptation on the part of the national teams.

Two items worth mentioning are items 3.7 and 3.8 which capture, respectively, the 'ability of the replicated parts of the model to achieve the social impact desired by SMart' and the 'ability to support culture throughout Europe'. The ratings assigned by the respondents agree with the statements proposed, and so the elements that achieve replicability appear to contribute to the mission of SMart (item 3.7 = 5.21; item 3.8 = 5.82).

The last block of items (3.9–3.12), which sought to identify the possible sources of failure in the replication of operational elements, received the following ratings: 'lack of network and legal resources' (item 3.9 = 3.72), 'lack of financial resources' (item 3.10 = 4.27), with 'lack of peer-to-peer support from others working in similar fields' having the lowest rating (item 3.11 = 3.25) and 'lack of business coaching and support' perceived to be having little impact in the failure of the scale attempt (item 3.12 = 3.41). In short, the lack of financial resources is most endangering to the viability of scale-up efforts of the SMart model across Europe.

5.3.3.4 Factor 4: Ability to Meet Social Demands

This factor captures the social value creation of SMart: it describes its mission by means of addressing an identified social need of a group of people. Via its concrete social value proposition, SMart proposes to its target audiences a unique combination of services covering a vast array of needs related to the creative and cultural sector. The analysis of data summarised in Table 5.17 suggests that what respondents valued the most was the innovative character of the services proposed (item 4.3 = 6.35), followed by the fact that SMart clearly addresses a specific social need shared by a group of professionals (item 4.1 = 6.23) and that it does so effectively (item 4.2 = 6.13).

With regard to the most common risk factors in scaling-up, economic challenges (item 4.5 = 4.7) represent quite an important risk, even more so than operational challenges (item 4.4 = 5.23). In this sense, it is worth mentioning that the Weber model was further refined in 2016 and one of its key revisions was precisely the inclusion of heavy transfer costs and the ability of managers to ensure the availability of funds to cover them (Weber, 2016).

Graph 5.6 clearly shows that SMart excels in what is known as 'customer orientation' in traditional management science literature. Considering that SMart is a social enterprise and that creating social value to its members while serving the general interest lay at the core of its mission, it is not surprising to see that the three items (3.1–3.3) measuring the perception of how well it creates social value are quite relevant.

On the contrary, the perception of how well the target group has benefitted de facto from the services offered (item 4.6 = 4.72) received the lowest rating. Document reviews, exchanges with key informants and interviews confirm that, except in countries like France and Spain, a major effort is to

Table 5.17 Descriptive statistics for factor 4 (N = 31)

Ability to meet social demands	*Minimum*	*Maximum*	*Mean*	*Std. Deviation*
4.1 Clearly addresses a need	1.0	7.0	6.23	1.31
4.2 Clearly alleviates the need	3.0	7.0	6.13	0.99
4.3 New/revamped services	1.0	7.0	6.35	1.23
4.4 No operational challenges	2.0	7.0	5.23	1.28
4.5 No economic challenges	3.0	7.0	4.76	1.24
4.6 Target benefits from service	2.0	7.0	4.72	1.25

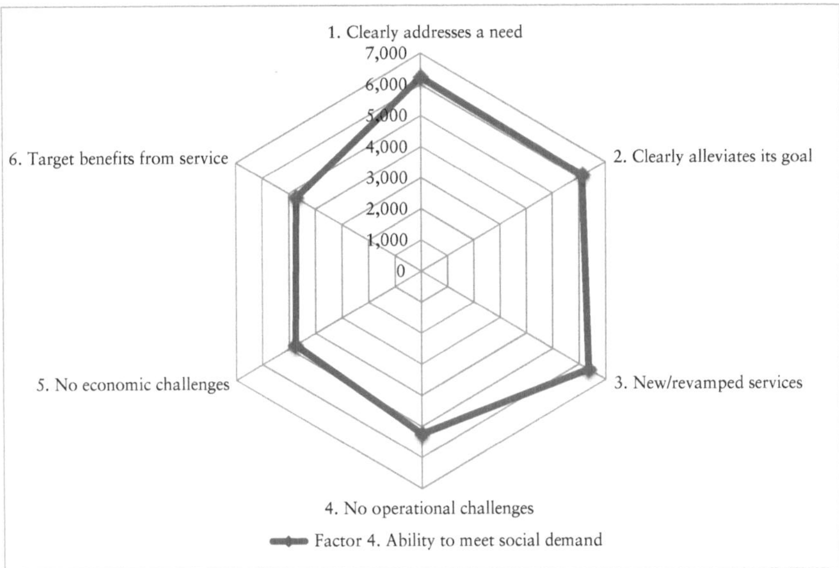

Graph 5.6 Rating of scaling-up factor 4 across countries.

be put in to attract new users and members either based on a purely economic value proposition ('it will cost you less to work under the SMart umbrella') or a purely social value proposition ('you will be able to achieve more as a community and work under better conditions') or both. Wide outreach efforts to attract new members are likely to be undertaken once the core services have been implemented and tested, and when a critical mass of members has been attained with a view on activating the most effective means of promotion for SMart: word of mouth and real-life testimonials.

5.3.3.5 Factor 5: Ability to Obtain Necessary Resources

The descriptive statistics associated to the various items included in factor 5 are summarised in Table 5.18. The highest rated item in factor 5 is directly connected to the fact that culture workers can save time, money and administrative hassle through the SMart services (item 5.4 = 6.23).

Graph 5.7 illustrates the high ratings the items related to social capital received versus the lower ratings of items related to financial resources. Indeed, the three items related to engaging with others (including political and social economy networks) received ratings above 5 as follows: 'appreciating the added value of partnerships in comparison to acting alone' (item 5.9 = 5.93), 'ensuring right connections with external resource providers in case of need' (item 5.8 = 5.34) and 'communicating with key constituencies

Table 5.18 Descriptive statistics for factor 5 (N = 31)

Ability to obtain necessary resources	*Minimum*	*Maximum*	*Mean*	*Std. Deviation*
5.1 Staff with skills	2.0	7.0	5.26	1.29
5.2 Revenue stream created	2.0	7.0	5.10	1.27
5.3 Financial streams	2.0	7.0	4.47	1.28
5.4 Concept proven	3.0	7.0	6.23	1.17
5.5 Public funds secured	1.0	7.0	3.37	1.63
5.6 Communication to target users	2.0	7.0	5.10	1.27
5.7 Informed our customers	3.0	7.0	5.40	1.22
5.8 Connections for resources	4.0	7.0	5.34	1.14
5.9 Partnerships have helped	3.0	7.0	5.93	1.15
5.10 Legal support	1.0	7.0	3.61	1.87
5.11 In the political agenda	1.0	7.0	4.33	1.60
5.12 SE actors' support	1.0	7.0	4.83	1.53

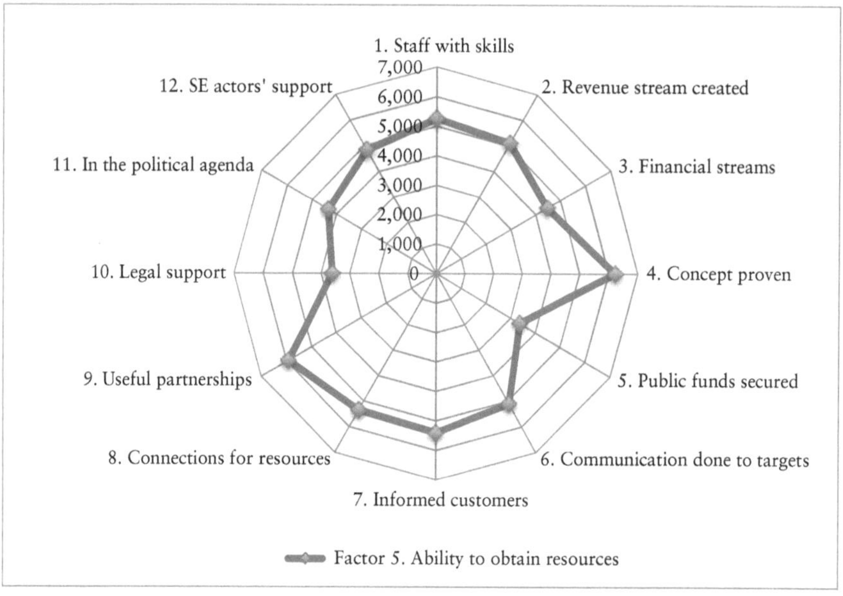

Graph 5.7 Rating of scaling-up factor 5 across countries.

and stakeholders' (item 5.6 = 5.10). There are some differences worth emphasising among the types of effort to obtain support and buy-in from others. On the one hand, the item that expresses the perceived value assigned to creating networks with political bodies and actors (item 5.10, 'getting government agencies and officials to create laws, rules, and regulations that support the adaptation effort of the SMart model'), receives the lowest rating (3.61). Similarly, perceptions of 'how effective national SMart offices are able to place their cause high in the political agenda' were medium (item 5.11 = 4.33). On the other hand, perceptions about getting other social economy actors to provide support for the scaling-up efforts were the highest of the three (item 5.12 = 4.83).

Lastly, items related to financial resources received varied ratings: if considering a specific form of revenue stream from services and activities delivered, the perception was quite high (item 5.2 = 5.10). However, this rating decreased when talking about securing financial streams to ensure sustainability (item 5.3 = 4.47) and reached the lowest for the ability to get government agencies and officials to provide financial support (item 5.5 = 3.37).

5.3.3.6 Factor 6: Potential Effectiveness of Scaling Social Impact with Others

In Weber's revised scaling-up factor model, she renamed one factor from 'potential effectiveness of scaling social impact with others' to 'control and dependency' so as to capture the two extremes of scaling-up: total control over the process, or complete dependency on others. In our analysis, the respondents indicated that finding partners and allies and being part of a wider network constituted a crucial factor in the scaling-up effort, as summarised in Table 5.19. This is well reflected across all items (see Graph 5.8): the indirect ones stating that scaling-up on their own is better (item 6.1) and cheaper (item 6.2) received low scores (3.37 and 2.88 respectively) in contrast to the direct ones, which all received ratings over 5.5. The 6.3 rating of item 6.6 is the highest, suggesting that respondents perceived a connection between belonging to networks and increasing the social value created by SMart. Along these lines, the perception that, by doing actions jointly with valid partners results are strengthened, is well rated as well (item 6.4 = 5.7).

Moreover, collaboration was perceived to have a strategic value (item 6.5) as a scaling-up process if conducted with other organisations

Table 5.19 Descriptive statistics for factor 6 (N = 31)

Potential effectiveness of scaling social impact with others	*Minimum*	*Maximum*	*Mean*	*Std. Deviation*
6.1 Success alone	1.0	7.0	3.37	1.99
6.2 Partnering is expensive	1.0	6.0	2.88	1.56
6.3 Soc impact max with others	1.0	7.0	5.69	1.56
6.4 Local part, better results	1.0	7.0	5.70	1.56
6.5 Strategic alliances	2.0	7.0	6.13	1.14
6.6 Connection to networks	1.0	7.0	6.30	1.15
6.7 Supra-national connections	2.0	7.0	5.77	1.31
6.8 Connection to SE networks	2.0	7.0	5.97	1.18

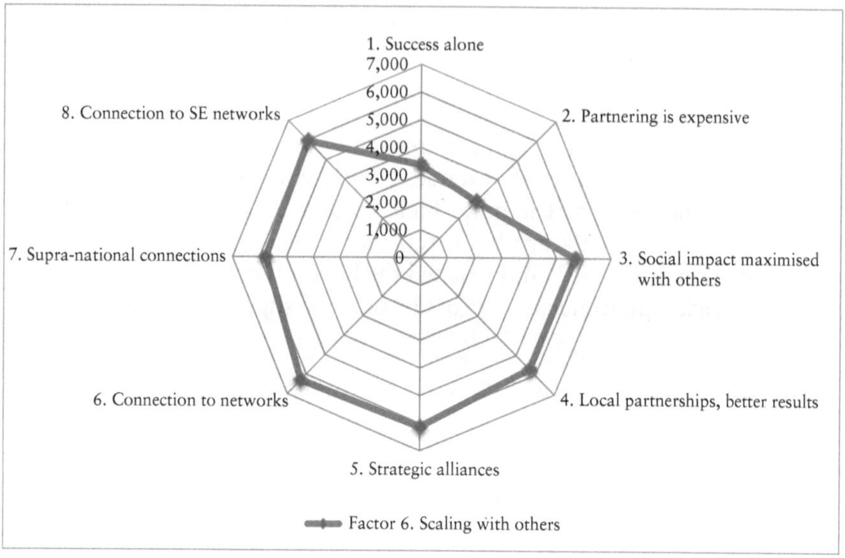

Graph 5.8 Rating of scaling-up factor 6 across countries.

can increase the impact (item 6.3 = 5.69), which was confirmed by the case studies. The last two items capture perceptions about the benefits of belonging to supra-national organisations (item 6.7 = 5.77) and of being connected to the social and solidarity economy. The last item (6.8 = 5.97) was incorporated to confirm the two research hypotheses about the connection to the social and solidarity economy as a success factor in the implementation process. Insofar as this item is concerned, it would suggest that both hypotheses are accepted.

5.3.3.7 Factor 7: Adaptability

When asked about the easiness to adapt the SMart model to their countries, respondents seemed to rate it quite high (see Table 5.20 and Graph 5.9). Indeed, the two items that directly capture this (items 7.1 and 7.4) asked directly whether the model was easy to adapt (item 7.1 = 5.04), while the second one proposed it in a negative manner as a double-check question. To the statement 'the model is too disruptive to be adapted', ratings were very low (item 7.4 = 2.36), thus confirming the conclusion extracted from the previous item.

Going beyond its original field borders entails adapting the original services to new contexts (language, legal, fiscal, etc.) but also expanding the group of people originally targeted. Indeed,

> transnational scaling thus represents – similar to commercial enterprises' internationalisation attempts – a very special challenge for social enterprises, one that should not be underestimated. In such cases the obstacles generally become larger or new ones arise (language barriers, for example), making things even more difficult.
>
> (Weber, 2016: 20)

Two items in factor 7 tried to identify some of these obstacles, namely regulations and policies (item 7.2 = 4.69) and the financial environment (item 7.3 = 3.87). Perceptions about the hindering effects of the local

Table 5.20 Descriptive statistics for factor 7 (N = 31)

Adaptability	*Minimum*	*Maximum*	*Mean*	*Std. Deviation*
7.1 Fully adaptable	2.0	7.0	5.04	1.67
7.2 Legal env needs adaptation	1.0	7.0	4.69	1.77
7.3 Financial env needs adaptation	1.0	6.0	3.86	1.60
7.4 Too disruptive model	1.0	6.0	2.36	1.28
7.5 More impact w/ new targets	1.0	7.0	5.21	1.50
7.6 More impact w/ new serv	1.0	7.0	5.55	1.38
7.7 Cannot expand targets/serv	1.0	7.0	2.68	1.68

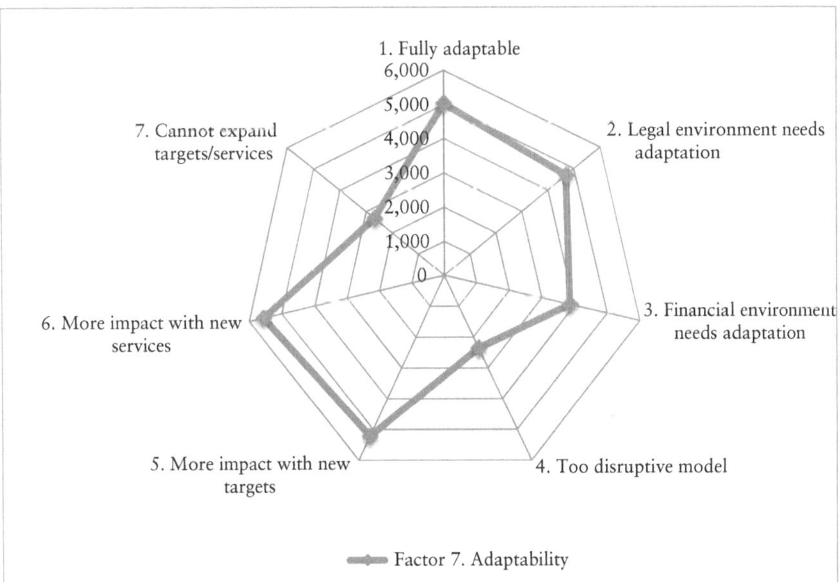

Graph 5.9 Rating of scaling-up factor 7 across countries.

financial environment on the adaptation of the model were rated low, which can be explained by the fact that the overarching financial system and the currency (the Euro) is shared. Such explanation is confirmed by the fact that the only non-Euro SMart country included in the sample (Hungary) actually gave a rating of 6 to this item, as more intensive adaptation is probably needed at the financial level.

The two highest ratings were associated with the immediate results of adapting the model – the expansion of new services and new target groups – thus maximising the creation of social value of SMart. Specifically, perceptions that, by expanding target groups, the mission is further served are rated relatively high (item 7.5 = 5.21), and even more so with the addition of new services (item 7.6 = 5.55) which assumes the creation and maximisation of social value. The rating received by the last item (item 7.7 = 2.68) confirms the member and customer orientation of the SMart country offices: even though financing new activities and reaching out to new groups has may involve additional costs, it is not perceived as jeopardising the sustainability of the office.

5.3.4 National Scaling-Up Processes and Systemic Transformation

The systemic level of transformation reached by the SMart model was due mainly to three factors: the effectiveness of its model, the large representation within the sector and its gradual recognition as a key player in the field of culture. The various levels of social impact generated by Smart are summarised in Table 5.21.The vast representation of the creative and cultural sector achieved by SMart has translated into a large negotiation power vis-à-vis the public administration, governments and other entities influencing policy, schemes and measures affecting the cultural sector. Thus, social innovation is formally recognised as being at the heart of SMarteu as it aims to support and change the creative sector.

Regarding the cross-national expansion of SMart, an interesting parallel can be drawn with the difficulties encountered in the building of the European project in general, as originally conceived by the founders of the European Union. Indeed, while members and new country partners see the value in joining to tackle a need shared with fellow Europeans in other countries, the list of obstacles may be daunting.

It is likely that the negative experiences ended up frustrating and creating costly interruptions in the process (like in the UK or Denmark), which could have been avoided by phasing the adaptation process. Additionally, by having a viable financial model to present to potential funders and supporters (mainly funding from or strategic partnerships with public and private actors), it is likely that key resources would have been more readily available. Having more time at the beginning would have also provided the time needed to assess SMart's ability to achieve transnational scale.

Table 5.21 Various levels of social impact by SMart

	End precariousness	*Support artists*	*Lobbying*	*Policy agenda setting*	*Market expansion*
Macro level	International membership coverage	International mobility	International campaigning and activism	Successful pilot example	International market creation
Meso level	Research and studies	Exchange and learning, entrepreneurial skills	Professional solidarity	Interlocutor role in negotiations	Market expansion
Micro level (the local)	Concrete admin and legal tools	Sense of community	Hearing the voice of artists	Articulation from the bottom-up	Concrete market outlets

Having said this, the overall outcome of the European scaling-up process cannot be said to be negative. It has without doubt put a lot of stress on the source organisation, but it has also put the SMart 'brand' on the European map and provided a European dimension to the actions and plans produced by SMartbe.

Notes

1 In 2017, SMartbe began the process of becoming a cooperative whose new bylaws would incorporate the spirit and values of the original mission. This modification is crucial as it opened a new period within SMart overall, whereby cooperativism would progressively become the value system of reference for SMartbe as well as other offices across Europe. The lastest version of the cooperative bylaws are available (in French) here: https://smartbe.be/wp-content/uploads/2020/06/BE_SmartCoop_AGE-20_Statuts_SmartCoop2020.pdf.

2 Some of the consultations it participated in include the Europe 2020 Strategy over 2010–2014 (available at http://ec.europa.eu/europe2020.pdf/contributions/europe2020consultation_smartbe_20141030_fin.doc). It was also a key player in the EESC event 'The creative and cultural professions in the EU 2020 Strategy' in October 2013 (available at http://smart-eu.org/media/uploads/2013/10/CESE_2013-10-14_prev-Progr-EN_02-10.pdf).

3 Projects are negotiated directly between members and clients (tasks, price, subcontracting, duration, etc.). Once an agreement between the two has been reached, a contract has to be signed in order for the project to be accepted into the SMart system. Upon signing of the contract, the assignment is registered into the project management system before the work begins. SMart takes charge of registering the worker in the social security system, paying the various social contributions to the pertinent administrations and paying the salary.

4 SMartbe (2012) offers a summary of Dujardin, A. and Rajabaly, H. (2010).

5 According to an internal survey from SMart, as of 31 December 2011, there were 6,230 Activities with at least one transaction in their budget since they were set up; they amounted to a total of 42 million euros in 2011. The main reasons for its members to use the 'Activity' tool were the administrative support provided by SMartbe (81%), the alternative to setting up a company or becoming self-employed (72%) and the opportunity to achieve a professional status (61%) (SMart, 2010).

6 Although the Covid-19 pandemic falls outside the scope of the research included in this book, it is worth noting how online sessions held for members continue to increase. For instance, in 2021, SMartib organised 11 webinars devoted to capacity-building and 9 speed-dating sessions to increase knowledge and exchange among members. It also published four posts with specialised contents and over 35 in-depth interviews with members.

7 Interestingly enough, the original sense of 'mutualisation' referred to the conversion of a stock company to a company owned by its workers or customers.

8 As of January 2014, there were national offices of SMart in Belgium, Austria, France, Sweden and Spain, and two years later three more were up and running in Germany, Hungary, Italy and the Netherlands. The situation as of January 2022 includes active offices in Belgium, France, Austria, Germany, Italy, the Netherlands, Spain and Sweden.

9 The French-speaking community of Belgium counts on a number of mechanisms and institutions to support its development in crucial areas such as education, culture, sport, youth, science and research and justice. The most well-known is the Wallonia-Brussels Federation which also promoted exchanges with France in the abovementioned areas.
10 Although this causal connection is still to be proven, it is a priori supported by a number of members in the countries where it exists, which leads to a growing negotiation power vis-à-vis private contractors, public administrations and even a self-promoted market for their members.
11 The research to be done is quite extensive. National LIQs are usually about 60 pages long. They provide an overview on the following: social security, employed and self-employed work, taxes, economic and cultural matters, professional organisations and unions (focusing on artistic sectors), establishing contact points in these areas, the 'status of the artist' (relevant legal framework/measures) and their work flow, private and public organisations working with artists, funding, etc.
12 SMartbe was part of the board of directors of Culture Action Europe from November 2012 to 2017 when it participated regularly in its conferences and meetings. It used to be active in the events of, among others, the Informal European Theatre Meeting (IETM) and the European network on cultural management and policy (ENCATC), but once the scope of the cooperative enlarged, the collaboration with cultural bodies decreased.
13 See www.smart-eu.org (accessed 30 January 2016). However, as explained earlier, the mission of SMartbe underwent a transformation when it became a cooperative and opened its doors to all types of freelance workers, although the focus in the rest of Europe continues to be on culture and the arts.
14 The political-savviness of SMarteu in drafting its goals is reflected in the second one, which is in alignment with EU public policies, therefore making SMarteu an ally for the European Commission in its Single Market Act policy.
15 As of January 2022, SMarteu has not formalised its legal existence although the work around a common agenda and support to national offices continues.

References

Defourny, J. and Nyssens, M. (2010) Social Enterprise in Europe: At the Crossroads of Market, Public Policies and Third Sector, *Policy & Society*, Vol. 29 (3), pp. 231–242.

Dujardin, A. (2014) *Chiffres-Clés. Zoom sur les nouveaux membres utilisateurs en 2012*, Brussels: Bureau d'études de SMart.

Dujardin, A. and Rajabaly, H. (2010) *Être intermittent dans le secteur artistique. Profil socioéconomique des membres de SMartBe, de leurs prestations et de leurs donneurs d'ordre* (*Being a Casual Worker in the Arts Sector: A Socio-Economic Profile of SMartbe's Members, Their Services and Their Commissioning Clients*), Brussels: SMartbe. Available at https://smartbe.be/wp-content/uploads/2015/11/Etre_intermittent-rapport-completFR.pdf [accessed 12 January 2016].

Eisenhardt, K. M. (1989) Building Theories from Case Study Research, *Academy of Management Review*, Vol. 14 (4), pp. 532–550.

Harvard Business Review (2012) *New Operating Models for the Next-Generation Enterprise*, Harvard Business Review Analytic Services Report. Available at https://hbr.org/resources/pdfs/tools/17360_HBR_Cognizant_Report_webview.pdf [accessed 6 November 2015].

Hirsch, P. M. (1972) Processing Fads and Fashions: An Organization-Set Analysis of Cultural Industry Systems, *American Journal of Sociology*, Vol. 77 (4), pp. 639–659.

Laville, J.-L. (ed.) (2011) *Economie solidaire*, Paris: CNRS Éditions.

Mendell, M. and Nogales, R. (2009) "Social Enterprises in OECD Member Countries: What are the Financial Streams? In A, en Noya (ed.), *The Changing Boundaries of Social Enterprises*, Paris: OCDE.

Rodríguez Morató, A. (2012) The Culture Society: A Heuristic for Analyzing Cultural Change in the Global Age. In A. Sales (ed.), *Sociology Today: Social Transformations in a Globalizing World*, 316–338, London: Sage.

Sales, A. (ed.) (2012) *Sociology Today: Social Transformations in a Globalizing World*, London: Sage.

SMartbe (2012) *Developing Your Artistic Projects. The Example of SMartbe Activities*, Brussels: SMartbe.

von Krogh, G. and Cusumano, M. (2001) Three Strategies for Managing Fast Growth, *MIT Sloan Management Review*, Vol. 42 (2), pp. 53–61.

Weber, C., Kröger, A. and Demirtas, C. (2016) *Scaling Social Impact in Europe: Quantitative Analysis of National and Transnational Scaling Strategies of 358 Social Enterprises*, Berlin: Bertelsmann Stiftung. Available at www.bertelsmann-stiftung.de/fileadmin/files/user_upload/BST_ScalingSocialImpactInEurope_final.pdf [accessed 12 December 2016].

Xhauflair, V., Huybrechts, B. and Pichault, F. (2015) *From Art to Project: Cross-Border Diffusion of a Social Innovation on the Labor Market*, Liege: HEC Management School-ULg. Available at https://orbi.uliege.be/bitstream/2268/181172/1/XhauflairHuybrechtsPichault_FromArttoProject.pdf [accessed 15 February 2016].

6 Focus on Three-Country Cases

Austria, Spain and Hungary

6.1 Selection Criteria and Analytical Framework for the Country Studies

6.1.1 Selecting Country Case Studies

Using the Weber model described in the previous chapter, I made a choice according to how countries were ranked in the following six categories (for a description of each category, see Annex):

1. Type of welfare models.
2. Type of models of civil society.
3. Type of models of social enterprise.
4. Variance in terms of the development of social and solidarity economy.
5. Variance in the evolution and shape of the cultural system.
6. New member state status (post original EU-15).

Austria, Hungary and Spain were selected out of those nine countries with a presence of SMart (leaving out Belgium, France, Germany, Italy, the Netherlands and Sweden). A description of the three selected countries follows:

> *Austria*: The model of the cooperative was the clear choice for the people who led the development of SMartat, due to the proven capacity of this legal form to capture the spirit of the SMart model. The Austrian team, however, faced a highly centralised and government-led context where the social economy and culture had not traditionally joined forces to develop the potential of the sector. Therefore, making the choice for SMart constituted a true challenge.
>
> *Hungary*: The country joined the European Union in 2004 and it is the only Member State from the Central and Eastern Europe in which SMart has decided to replicate its model. In terms of the survey analysis, it is the country with by far the least variance among respondents, although we only received responses from three of them. Such an incomplete data set was the result of the specific life cycle of SMarthu: since

DOI: 10.4324/9781003342144-7

its creation in 2013, it does not have a council or board and the roles of founder and manager are combined in the same person. Therefore, despite the two missing categories (management and council representative), we decided to keep the country in the analysis. The founder and current manager of SMarthu was interviewed and several informal conversations with cultural actors from Budapest were held in the last part of the project.

Spain: SMartib is used in the EU platform as a best practice based on its intensive and sustained growth. In addition, Spain represents a country with a high level of unemployment that could benefit from the full implementation of the model. Concomitant with this success story, however, is the issue of ensuring financial sustainability, the engagement and participation of the members, and the personal touch in the interaction between *asesoras* and members.

6.1.2 Institutional Framework Analysis of Country Case Studies

As we have seen, a social enterprise is an institutional arrangement that can be located at the crossroads of the private, public and non-profit sectors, and therefore combines the resources of varied actors to address societal issues. One difficulty in finding a common definition of social enterprise is the different sets of socioeconomic conditions from which social enterprises emerge, as they are embedded in societies that function in diverse ways. In this context, understanding the main elements of the socioeconomic context paves the way for grasping the means by which social enterprises develop in a given country (Kerlin, 2013).

Even though research in this area is limited, important examples such as Kerlin's macro-institutional social enterprise framework (MISE) and the ICSEM project have set the ground for a further understanding of the influences of institutional context in the emergence and consolidation of socially oriented organisations (Doherty et al., 2014; Kerlin, 2013; Defourny and Nyssens, 2016).

For the present research, I mobilised the MISE framework (Kerlin, 2010, 2013) to address this contextual analysis. The framework, visually summarised in Figure 6.1, includes a qualitative, macro-institutional factor analytical grid that describes the institutional and contextual factors at play and has been completed in detail for each of the three countries (Austria, Spain and Hungary).

Kerlin identifies five major areas that describe the national environment:

1. National culture, history and values.
2. Type of economy or stage of economic development.
3. Type of government and development of institutions.
4. Type of civil society sector.
5. International relations and influence.

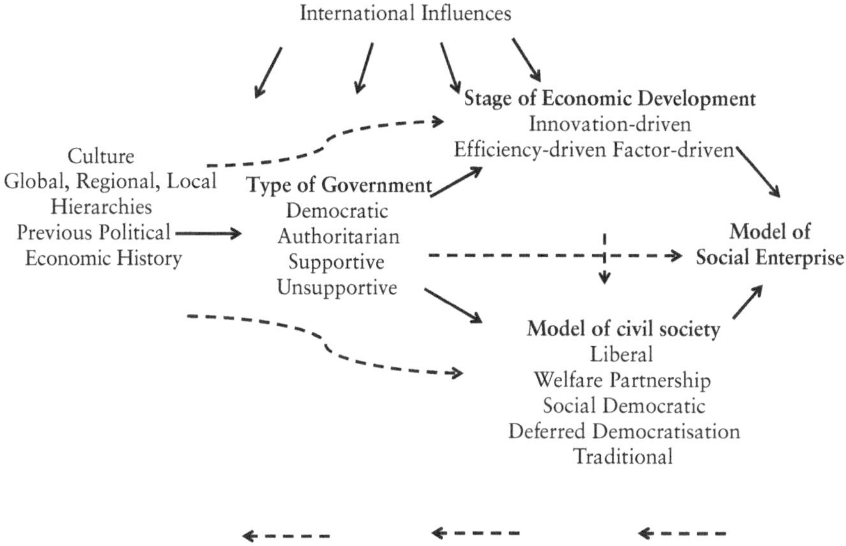

Figure 6.1 Macro-institutional processes and causal paths for models of social enterprises.

Source: Kerlin (2010, 2013).

The benefit of this model relies on its capacity to describe the national contexts of social enterprise emergence but also of some characteristics of social enterprise approaches in those very contexts (Fisac-García et al., 2015). Moreover, it is worth noting the weight given to power relations in the Kerlin model, which helps understanding not only the continuation of a given institutional setting but also the shift to previously subordinate groups (Kerlin, 2013). In terms of indicators, the work of Kerlin and Fisac-García et al. (2015), has been followed to analyse these five areas based on national-level desk research as well as national accounts of experts and interviews.

Given the focus of the present research, a closer look is taken at the field of culture and the development of social economy in Austria, Spain and Hungary, performing a two-step analysis in parallel with Kerlin's five factor, national environment analysis: firstly, a look at the general socioeconomic context and, secondly, at the development of the field of culture and social economy in particular. Based on this input, the national context and approaches to social enterprise are characterised, emphasising the differences and common traits among them with a view to explaining how the macro-institutional factors of the countries may contribute to the emergence of each social enterprise approach. This way of proceeding, which builds explanations while collecting data and analysing them is known as 'explanation building' (Saunders et al., 2009; Yin, 2009).

6.1.3 Socioeconomic Data of the Three Countries

Comparative data was gathered as a way to provide a sense about the situation of the countries with regard to the five elements of the contextual framework (see Table 6.1). Some data will be discussed in more detail in the country-by-country analysis in Chapter 7.

Among these countries, Spain is the largest in terms of population, but it also shows the highest depopulation rate (mostly as a result of emigration and higher death rates), which has reduced entrepreneurial growth and the number of potential workers in the country. On the contrary, Austria shows an increasing growth rate in terms of population, infusing new potential for entrepreneurial creation. Hungary also faces a trend of depopulation, although not as acute as in the Spanish case.

With a view to show some relevant socioeconomic data from the three countries, I recreated part of a table that Kerlin (2013: 13) put together by drawing on information from various sources. The pioneering work of Geert Hofstede's 'Culture's Consequences' and the GLOBE project guided the dimensions to be included in the table (Table 6.2).

Although most analyses were done at a global level (Kerlin, 2013; Salamon et al., 2014; Defourny and Nyssens, 2016), all five elements of the Kerlin's framework in the three selected countries (Austria, Spain and Hungary) will be covered.

Despite the fact that, in all three countries, the term 'social enterprise' was introduced in the last 25 years, they have existed in all a social economy/third sector tradition going well back in time. However, it is noteworthy that authoritarian political projects interrupted such development for long periods in all three of these countries: the Nazi invasion in Austria, plus the Allied occupation (1938–1955); the Nazi invasion and Soviet imposed dictatorship in Hungary (1939–1989); and Franco's dictatorship in Spain (1939–1975).

The next three sections provide an overview of the three selected countries, focusing on how the civil society, third sector and social enterprises developed in each of the countries and then on the cultural field

Table 6.1 Total population, growth and density in selected countries (2013)

Country	*Total population*	*Rate of change in five years (in ‰)*	*Population density (per km²)*
Austria	8,488,511	5.4	102
Hungary	9,906,000	–2.6	107
Spain	46,006,414	–4.1	92

Source: Eurostat database.

Table 6.2 Socioeconomic data per country

	Culture[a]		*Welfare state*		*Governance*		*Economy*	
	In-group collectivism	*Uncertainty avoidance*	*Expenditure in education (% GDP)*[b]	*Expenditure in health (% GDP)*[c]	*Government effectiveness*[d]	*Corruption control*	*Economic development stage*[e]	*GCI ranking*[f]
Austria	4.85	5.16	5.6	8.2	1.6	1.3	Innovation-driven	16
Hungary	5.25	3.12	4.6	5	0.6	0.3	Transition from efficiency to innovation-driven	60
Spain	5.45	3.97	4.8	7	1.1	1	Innovation-driven	36

[a] The Global Leadership and Organizational Behaviour Effectiveness (GLOBE) project, phase 2 – Aggregated Societal Level Data for Society Culture Scales (17 May 2004). Available at http://globe.bus.sfu.ca/data/GLOBE-Phase-2-Aggregated-Societal-Culture-Data.xls. This research uses the project findings for two dimensions: to measure 'In-Group Collectivism' (the degree to which individuals express pride, loyalty and cohesiveness in their organizations or families) and 'Uncertainty Avoidance' (the extent to which a society, organization or group relies on social norms, rules and procedures to alleviate unpredictability of future events). The scale is from 1 to 7, where a higher score indicates higher in-group collectivism in practice and higher uncertainty avoidance. Data is from 2004.

[b] UNESCO Institute of Statistics website (www.uis.unesco.org/Education/EducationStatistics). The definition of 'government expenditure on education as % of GDP (%)' is the 'total general (local, regional and central) government expenditure on education (current, capital, and transfers), expressed as a percentage of GDP. It includes expenditure funded by transfers from international sources to government. Divide total government expenditure for a given level of education (ex. primary, secondary, or all levels combined) by the GDP, and multiply by 100. A higher percentage of GDP spent on education shows a higher government priority for education, but also a higher capacity of the government to raise revenues for public spending, in relation to the size of the country's economy. When interpreting this indicator however, one should keep in mind that in some countries, the private sector and/or households may fund a higher proportion of total funding for education, thus making government expenditure appear lower than in other countries'. Data from 2011.

[c] World Health Organization Global Health Expenditure database (see http://apps.who.int/nha/database for the most recent updates). The definition of 'Health expenditure, public (% of GDP)' is 'public health expenditure consists of recurrent and capital spending from government (central and local) budgets, external borrowings and grants (including donations from international agencies and nongovernmental organizations), and social (or compulsory) health insurance funds'.

[d] World Bank (http://databank.worldbank.org). 'Government Effectiveness: Estimate' captures perceptions of the quality of public services, the quality of the civil service and the degree of its independence from political pressures, the quality of policy formulation and implementation and the credibility of the government's commitment to such policies. The estimate gives the country's score on the aggregate indicator, in units of a standard normal distribution, that is, ranging from approximately –2.5 to 2.5.

[e] Global Competitiveness Report, 2012–2013. It assesses countries' competitiveness along the 12 pillars corresponding to three main stages of economic development: Stage 1: factor-driven; Stage 2: efficiency-driven; and Stage 3: innovation-driven. There are also transition stages as countries move from one stage to the next. Available at www3.weforum.org/docs/WEF_GlobalCompetitivenessReport_2012-13.pdf (accessed 6 August 2016).

[f] Ibid.

6.2 Emergence of Social Enterprises and the Cultural Field in Austria

Austria is currently a federal republic in Central Europe, but had undergone a number of historical events. With a highly mountainous terrain, Austria is landlocked and surrounded by countries with disparate political regimes and stages of economic development.

A leading power in the seventeenth and eighteenth centuries, the Austrian empire (proclaimed in 1804) would become the Austro-Hungarian Empire until its collapse in 1918. Established as a republic first in 1919, the seven-year Nazi occupation imposed a parenthesis on the country's independence, which was regained after World War II in 1945. That year saw the restoration of the Austrian former democratic constitution and ten years later the Second Austrian Republic was formally established. There are two main political movements and long-term ruling parties in Austria: the Social Democratic Party (SPO) and the conservative Christian Democratic Peoples' Party (OVP), although the right-wing Freedom Party (FPO) joined the government in 2000.

The country is divided into nine federal regions (*Bundesländer*), and the largest city is the capital, Vienna. Austria is one of the richest countries in the world: during the years covered in this research, it has seen its per capita GDP almost double (from $27,289.6 in 1998 to $51,148.4 in 2014) and growing steadily.

6.2.1 The Development of Civil Society, Third Sector and Social Enterprises in Austria

In the late nineteenth and early twentieth centuries, several types of organisations (mostly religiously motivated philanthropy, charity organisations, cooperatives, trade unions and interest groups) developed and gathered an important political influence, especially on the setting up of social security and welfare systems. There were two main types of organisations: on the one hand, bottom-up, self-help organisations (such as cooperatives, charitable societies and saving clubs) and, on the other hand, top-down, 'self-help' welfare associations (organisations featuring the expanding social and labour market policy). Both types benefitted from early welfare legislation in Austria (Anastasiadis, 2006b).[1]

As a clear example of the corporatist model of welfare provision, there was a very close connection between these proto-social enterprises and public bodies (Neumayr et al., 2007). Since the nineteenth century, Austria represented a centralised system of wage bargaining with strong involvement of intermediate bodies, larger non-profit associations (NPOs) and cooperatives in social policy formulation. The competences of regions were limited, which strengthened power centralisation. This centralised model resulted in a 'pronounced state-led innovation model', with all the actors whose participation had been guaranteed through processes of industrialisation resisting bottom-up led social innovations, such as initiatives led by social entrepreneurs and community organisations (Esping-Andersen, 1999; Lehner, 2011; Novy and Hammer, 2007).

After World War II, larger NPOs and professional cooperatives dominated the third sector, acting as intermediaries between the state and citizens in the welfare system (Lang and Novy, 2014). As the Keynesian notion of 'social market economy' consolidated, many third sector organisations became either commercial enterprises (e.g. *Konsum*, *Raiffeisen*) or were integrated into the state-financed social and welfare sector.

The rise of 'New Social Movements' in the 1970s created an opportunity to experiment with other organisational forms, although they created links with the traditional cooperative movement via mutual assistance (what has been referred to as 'self-help condition of emergence'; Defourny and Nyssens, 2010). This community-led movement has been considered an expression of dissatisfaction with the centralised welfare model and a request to create new forms of 'welfare-mix' based on the partnership between the state and social enterprises. An example often cited is the experimental labour market. Since the early 1980s, the Austrian Labour Market Service has financed projects and enterprises that address the two major problems caused by long-term unemployment: growing inhibition to take up a new job, and social exclusion. This period was marked by high levels of innovation: indeed, it was in those years that the first social integration enterprises (*Sozialökonomischer Betrieb* – SÖB) and non-profit employment projects/companies (*Gemeinnützige Beschäftigungsprojekte/Gemeinnützige Beschäftigungsgesellschaften* – GBP) were created.

As the notion of 'welfare market' reached Austria, the third sector underwent a turn towards the logic of free market economy. Austria joined the EU in 1995 and had a right-wing conservative-populist government between 2000 and 2006. One of the measures it took was to implement some liberal social policy reforms aimed at reducing subsidies for third sector organisations. This downsizing of the welfare state has prompted traditional NPOs and cooperatives to seek resources from the market, adopting a behaviour that is similar to that of social enterprises. In the case of cooperatives, this economisation process resulted in a membership and community influence reduction (Lang and Anastasiadis, 2016).

Therefore, the Austrian social democratic model of civil society, as described by Salamon and Solokowski (2014), is characterised by:

- A lack of autonomy and openness to state influence and public support. Furthermore, the state-led welfare model in Austria has always had a tendency to incorporate bottom-up social movements.
- Corporatist clientelism and nepotism, which still requires belonging to the right political party in order to have access to the necessary resources (Lang and Novy, 2014).

The term social economy is characterised by a high degree of heterogeneity and complexity concerning organisational and legal forms at the European level (CIRIEC, 2007). In Austria, social economy (*Sozialwirtschaft*) covers all the organisations offering social services in a professional way. The Austrian understanding of the third sector is very close to the European definition, which involves classical NPOs as well as cooperatives, foundations and associations delivering services to (and working with) the community. The most widely used notion is the non-profit sector, although it remains a heterogeneous concept, with the only common trait being non-profit distribution (Lang and Anastasiadis, 2016).[2]

Regarding specific legal forms, cooperatives have a long tradition in Austria as an independent sector with clear institutionalisation paths in various activity fields such as housing, agriculture, banking and, to a much lesser extent, producer cooperatives (Lang and Anastasiadis, 2016). Cooperatives have strong connections to the two main parties, and their powerful umbrella bodies have been an integral part of the corporatist system of the Austrian state.

As for social enterprises, the term is not very frequently used in the Austrian context, where German versions are more common.[3] Slowly a social enterprise practice discourse is emerging supported by research and training as well as the work of international networks (e.g. Ashoka, Impact HUB Vienna, 'Architects of the Future') and networking and exchange initiatives (e.g. Social City Wien or Emersense). In Austria, a majority of social enterprises exist 'under the radar' using legal forms such as associations, limited liability companies (GmBHs) and not-for-profit limited liability companies (gGmBHs).

Traditional social economy networks such as BDV Austria (*Bundesdachverband für soziale Unternehmen*) and *Sozialwirtschaft Österreich*, which respectively represent WISE and social services providers, do not use the term social enterprises widely. Similarly, the majority of Austrian policymakers continue to consider social enterprises only as a work integration strategy that limits the potential of this institutional arrangement (Anastasiadis, 2017). Austrian social enterprises incorporate the attributes of Kerlin's 'enmeshed focused' model (2013), characterised by a small variety of social enterprises and a varying level of dependence from public financing sources. The innovation-driven stage of the economy generates the required resources for the corporatist welfare state and government policies. Other economic actors tend to support innovation and entrepreneurship, although the space for promoting alternative economies and models is not readily available.

6.2.2 *The Austrian Cultural Field*

The Austrian[4] post-war attitude towards culture has been characterised as prestige-oriented, favouring support for official cultural institutions such as theatres and festivals. The Nazi invasion meant that many artists and creators fled and were not invited back. The 1960s and 1970s, with their increased politicisation and radicalisation, are identified as turning points in the acknowledgement of the cultural vanguard, which became political tools for the preparation of the upcoming changes. Under the Social Democratic government of Kreisky, cultural policy was regarded as a variation of social policy, and culture was conceived as encompassing all areas of life.

The Federal Ministry of Education and the Arts adopted a package of cultural policy measures in 1975, which aimed at improving the cultural habits and education levels and reducing the educational gap between city dwellers and the rural population. A distinction was made between, on the one hand, artists and culture workers and, on the other hand, education (schools, adult education establishments) and cultural institutions (companies and centres). This decisive step represented a turning point as it launched a dialogue between governing bodies and artists and art mediators. As a way to decentralise the system and make it more democratic, different advisory and intermediate bodies were created.

The 1980s brought about an upsurge of large-scale events, numerous festivals and major exhibitions and a parallel cultural spending increase of approximately seven times the annual amount of the previous 25 years.[5] The LIKUS system (*Länder-Initiative Kultur-Statistik*) set up in 1996 constituted an effort towards transparency and comparability, insofar as it tracks the expenditures of the federal and regional administrations. By the end of the decade, right when a grand coalition between the ÖVP and SPÖ was crystallising, issues of cultural sponsorship and privatisation joined the public discussion about culture. These issues rapidly drew the attention of the majority of stakeholders in art forms such as musicals, popular operas and museums, which were perceived as being able to raise larger sums of funds from the market than more alternative and radical cultural expressions.

The coalition between the ÖVP and the FPÖ in 2000, re-elected in 2002, brought about a conservative shift that meant an emphasis on two cultural policy measures: outsourcing public cultural institutions and reducing the cultural budget. The collateral effects of this shift were a stronger focus on 'prestige culture', the creative industries and the promotion of economically oriented projects (such as festivals to increase tourism).

From 2007 to 2012, some key cultural institutions were reopened: there was support for the Austrian film industry, promotion of young artists and subsidies for federal theatres and museums; promotion of art and culture education in school intensified; and the international projection and mobility of Austrian creators was supported through public finance. Austrian creative workers have been reported as showing comparatively higher creative and innovative competences than those from other countries (Sostenuto Project, 2014). The country has indeed devoted substantial attention and resources to supporting the sector from the federal and regional levels, and ad hoc support was granted to the creative industries (e.g. the VINCI – Vouchers in Creative Industries of the Evolve initiative, and a number of studies).

Of particular importance to the present research was the focus on improving the labour conditions of cultural workers. Indeed, one of the current tasks of the Arts and Culture Division is to create suitable framework conditions for cultural workers. A study commissioned in 2008 to assess the social situation of artists showed dramatic poverty among artists and reached the conclusion that their precarious income had worsened in comparison to earlier years.[6]

An immediate response to this depiction was the creation of interministerial working groups (IMAGs) that gathered stakeholders from the public and private sectors and civil society, including trade union and social partnership representatives. The agendas of the IMAGs have included issues such as social security for artistic, cultural and media workers, employment law, unemployment insurance law, social security, gender diversity in the arts, support for the arts, copyright and taxation measures and mobility in order to improve the social situation of artists in Austria. It was at this point in time that the SMart model was presented to the Austrian audience (in May 2011).

In terms of specific measures, the following actions were taken:

- The opening of the Service Centre for Artists within the Social Insurance Authority (SVA) in 2011, gathering all the issues around social security and labour market services.
- The creation of the Artists' Social Security Fund (*Künstlersozialversicherung* –KSVF), which offered an opportunity to register an idle period in self-employment in order to improve compatibility of general social security with unemployment insurance.
- Other initiatives included a new actors' law, a mentoring programme for and by women for the improvement of the social situation of women artists and a guide on mobility for foreign artists and creators.

Unfortunately, these measures have not translated into any significant improvement for artists so far, as reported by interest groups and the *KulturratÖsterreich* (Austrian Cultural Council).[7] The main two sources of criticism related to the KSVF involved the inadequate insurance for artists in the case of unemployment and the preconditions for claiming benefit from the fund (a minimum income is required for artists to access the support mechanism). Moreover, KSVF's recognition of what constitutes 'artistic work' is very limited (e.g. it excludes teaching activities for artists, creators and cultural workers).

The typical work situation for the majority of artists in Austria is a combination of employment and self-employment. Since in Austria the type of working contract defines to which social insurance scheme workers have to contribute, artists end up contributing to two social security funds: the one for employees and for self-employed. Despite the high contributions to the social security system, they still do not qualify for the full benefit package from the insurance system. A 2008 study focusing on the status of artists concluded that 75% of the artists were considered ineligible for coverage by the unemployment system (Schelepa et al., 2008). According to this same study, 87% of the independent theatre sector works under a self-employed status although this status is not allowed by law (cinema industry actors are excluded from this regulation).

Theatre companies are supposed to employ their workers and so actors and related workers combine their work across several small companies, usually on a very short-term basis. A major problem for small size companies is that hiring actors represents an increase in terms of labour-related taxes. In turn, self-employed artists are obliged to subscribe to a health, accident and pension insurance through the Austrian Social Security Authority for Business (*Socialversicherungsanstalt* – SVA), if they earn more than 5,000€ through their self-employed activity in a year. In addition, umbrella employment is not permitted by Austrian law.

6.2.3 Main Conclusions from the Austrian Context Analysis

As we have seen, the context for social enterprises still shows certain barriers, such as an impressive set of benefits offered by the central state which decreases the collective entrepreneurial drive; the omnipresence of traditional NPOs and their interest groups, which act as lobby groups; and the set of well-established rules for financing, which prevent any flexibility for new collective initiatives or institutional arrangements. However, a number of untapped resources exist in Austria with relevance to potential development of CASE.

Firstly, an immediate result of this context for social enterprises is that they are likely to emerge in niches not exploited by hegemonic NPOs and to use resources that are not specifically earmarked for social service provision (Borzaga and Defourny, 2001). In this context, culture constitutes *a priori* one of these promising niches for social enterprise development with the potential of tapping a variety of resources and financing sources.

Secondly, the resources of Austrian foundations represent an untapped potential for social enterprise development and culture represents one of the interest fields for them. However, the law on foundations when this research was conducted may be seen as a barrier as it was not originally set up with a view to pursuing public benefit. Only about 200 (i.e. 7%) of the over 3,000 private foundations in Austria have a clear public benefit purpose, which is in sharp contrast with the German situation where over 95% of the 17,000 foundations have a public benefit purpose.

Thirdly, partnerships with existing successful third sector and social and solidarity organisations covering the whole territory constitute one of the possible, advantageous strategies toward the development of social enterprises. While Austrian NPOs may not be ready yet to team up with small-scale social enterprises, the model of transnational cooperation put forward by SMartat may provide an interesting ground for experimentation through Austrian social entrepreneurs with knowledge of interesting experiences in their field in other countries. Having said this, it should be mentioned that some large NPOs such as Caritas Vienna are offering inspiring examples on how to create these cross-sectoral partnerships.

Regarding cultural production, there is a long tradition of transnational cooperation in Austria that involves all kinds of cultural players (from federal institutions to grassroots initiatives). Given their geographic closeness, CEE countries represent a privileged area for collaboration in the cultural field in activities such as festivals (music, film, etc.), exhibitions (fine art, architecture, photography, etc.), conferences and workshops, and information and training programmes.

An illustration of the former points is found in the number of corporate and family foundations (e.g., ErsteStiftung, Generali Foundation, Bank Austria Kunstforum, Siemens Artlab) that are supporting initiatives to make culture and the arts more accessible to a broader public, particularly that of CEE countries. Keeping the required distance to ensure organisational and cultural content autonomy, these organisations represent an additional possible resource for CASE, as public administrations incorporate social enterprises into their support measures to contribute to culture and social development and sustainability.

Given the context described above, the arrival of SMartat can be considered very timely from the cultural standpoint, and despite the barriers facing social enterprise emergence, a supportive and vibrant context seems to be developing that includes a variety of mainly civil society and private actors with public administrators following at a distance.

6.3 A Focus on the Emergence of Social Enterprises and the Cultural Field in Spain

The recent history of Spain is marked by the transition to democracy from a dictatorial regime that followed a civil war, and the adaptation to a new economic and cultural rhythm imposed by joining the European Union and the effects of globalism. At the macroeconomic level, GDP rose from \$15,534 in 1998 to \$29,718 in 2014, with a peak of \$35,600 in 2008, right before the last global financial crisis (Council of Europe, 2015). Despite the many problems facing Spain's political institutions, the perception of control of corruption dropped from 1 (2012) to 0.5 (2014) point in only two years. However, this data hides the growing inequality in distribution of the newly created wealth; the emergence of new types of exclusion such as 'energy poor' or 'working poor'; and the diminishing purchasing power of an increasingly precarious group of workers.

Recently, as a result of an accumulated disenchantment with the consequences that the two abovementioned overarching forces had imposed upon citizens, a wave of social mobilisation, aiming to bring real political change, took over the majority of Spain (Calle, 2016). Even though Spain has been characterised by its social capital deficit and a poorly articulated civil society (Montagut, 2009), the fact that it has a long tradition of social movements and grassroots associationism articulated around concrete formal and informal arrangements can help explain the emergence of this wave. In this context, Spain has seen a series of political and social movement cycles take place in combination with a solid 'social push' (*empuje social*), which could have represented a true option for political transformation. However, unfortunately, this three-layered complimentary process (political cycle / social cycle / social push) has remained out of synchrony regarding their true transformational potential, as a result of the way in which the sociopolitical evolution of the country has unfolded over the last 30 years (Calle, 2016).

6.3.1 The Development of Civil Society, Third Sector and Social Enterprises

Through the nineteenth and most of the twentieth centuries, the responsibility for attending to social needs fluctuated between the Catholic Church and the public sector, except for the periods of democratic government (1904–1921, 1931–1936) when policies of social responsibility and social rights were implemented by the public administration (Sarasa and Moreno, 1995; Montagut, 2000). Spain began the construction of a modern welfare state with a significant delay if compared with its neighbouring countries. It did so while building its political system, which resulted in a subsequent series of reforms, even before it was completely constituted, as was the case in other European countries (Montagut, 2009).

NPOs (and the organised civil society that supports them) basically only came to policy prominence in the 1980s and 1990s. Social welfare and social services, along with the non-profit sector, came under the spotlight at a moment of consolidation of the welfare state (Montagut, 2009; Ruiz Olabuénaga et al., 1999). In the case of Spain, as in many other countries, there is a division of opinion about whether solidarity is achieved through economic democracy or through the organised action of civil society (Rodríguez Cabrero, 2005), depending on whether the sector is mainly market- or non-market-based (Marbán Gallego, 2007). Unlike the other Western European countries, Spain's third sector organisations ensured their income less through government grants and subsidies than through private fees and charges for services (Ruiz Olabuénaga et al., 1999). As for the social economy, they have a strong market dimension, and their level of institutionalisation is very high. In short, in Spain the use of commercial purposes to generate income to support organisations that ensure the welfare of citizens covers a wide spectrum of activities that are sometimes difficult to identify. Talking about social enterprises in Spain inevitably entails talking about the social economy and other NPOs in the third sector of the social and solidarity economy. Among the three, there is a broad spectrum in which Spanish social enterprises have been emerging.

As far as the Spanish social economy is concerned, it includes different types of organisations, such as cooperatives and foundations, as well as other NPOs that have nevertheless developed income-generating activities. Already in the nineteenth century, 'mutual relief societies' were the precursors of the current mutual society and laid the foundations of social security as we know it today. These societies sought to respond collectively to individual needs or risks, for example, by providing health insurance in the event of illness or by coping with situations of lack of protection in the event of unemployment. This collective dimension represents one of the main characteristics of the social and solidarity economy in Spain, which contrasts with the more individualistic perspective of the 'social entrepreneur', who continues to generate great interest in Europe.

The different economic contexts throughout our history have paved the way for the emergence of social entities in Spain. For example, the economic situation of the nineteenth and early twentieth centuries in rural areas led to the emergence of agrarian cooperatives and their credit sections and savings banks that favour the financial inclusion of their members.[8] Also, the industrial crisis of the 1970s (which coincided with the transition) resulted in high levels of unemployment and the first substantial cuts in public spending. Subsequently, civil society organisations that could be considered as 'proto-social enterprises' began to emerge; they tried to respond to unmet demands for social services by citizens as well as to high unemployment problems. It was only then that in Spain (as in the rest of Europe) institutional formulas appeared that would come together under the umbrella of the social economy, such as the socio-labour integration of groups at high risk of exclusion (e.g. drug addicts and long-term unemployed). The third social and economic crisis in Spain in recent years has led to the emergence of new models of companies that seek to meet the economic, social, environmental and cultural needs, among others, of their communities. It has been an important stimulus for emerging social enterprises, sometimes linked to legal innovations that allow a better development of these entities.

Social enterprises in Spain have been characterised by Kerlin (2013) as 'dependent focused', which means that the welfare partnership tradition of the Spanish civil society has determined the space where this new institutional arrangement can emerge. Indeed, there is a well-articulated relationship between government agencies and third sector/social and solidarity actors and a tradition of financing the sector largely via public funding. This relationship, however, is rapidly changing, and new forms of interaction are being defined such as public procurement and public–private partnerships.

Spain is considered to be in an innovation-driven stage of its economy, which supposedly produces the required resources to maintain the Mediterranean welfare state model and policies. Unfortunately, the recent crises and the subsequent reactions to them have resulted in a weakening of some of these traditional welfare institutions, although the robustness of the corporatist model of third sector and social economy may offer a safety net from where transformative proposals for other economies can be proposed and tested.

6.3.2 The Cultural Field in Spain

The advent of the political transition from a dictatorship to a democratic regime was marked by a number of compromises that reached the cultural sector as well. Culture in Spain cannot be understood without taking into account the dictatorship period that followed the Civil War (1936–1939). For almost four decades (1939–1975), cultural actors and institutions were tightly controlled. The first period (until 1960) saw a 'powerful press and propaganda machine' to emerge that erased regional and local cultural expressions and supported mass entertainment events known as 'evasion culture'; these were driven by a populist sense of traditional cultures and folklore aimed at producing political unawareness (Council of Europe, 2015). After 1960, and in parallel with the economic opening of the country, public funding was granted to modern events and expressions, such as the San Sebastian film festival.

After the Moncloa Pacts in 1977, a 'culture of the Transition' (Martínez, 2012) appeared: it would become the country's cultural framework up to the present. Indeed, the 1978 constitution was preceded by some blunt moves to end the hegemony over culture and media. The Ministry of Culture was established in 1977 and regional autonomy was granted via the new constitution, which brought about a gradual recognition of local cultural and linguistic heritage. City councils were instrumental in recovering what had been silenced under the dictatorial regime. The central government formally recognised the plurality of civil society as well as the principle of neutrality in cultural issues. The socialist party ruled the country for eight years and implemented some of the largest modernisation endeavours, including direct actions to preserve cultural heritage and develop cultural infrastructures. In 1985, the Ministry of Culture was reorganised so as to pass more competencies on to the regional authorities, and the decade that followed was one of authentic booming of the arts and culture in the public sphere. Major events, new cultural institutions and flagship artistic centres were created, and Spanish culture was projected worldwide via participation in international events and networks.

However, as some authors have pointed out, this culture of transition implied a total absence of critical stance or questioning of anything that was occurring at the time in the political or economic spheres. It was based on the consensus of the various parties involved with the aim of ensuring a political stability and a level of social cohesion (Serrano Vidal, 2012). In all, this cultural explosion did little service to the true situation of culture in Spain, as reading habits never caught up with those of European countries; phenomenal buildings were left empty due to lack of programming and/or vision; minorities and ordinary citizens did not participate actively and stayed within a 'spectator' role; and relevant cultural policy such as heritage was not co-created with local citizens.

Spain has a decentralised state model, and the largest part of its public financing of culture comes from autonomous communities and city councils. The main source of finance has traditionally been public funding through direct and discretionary grants, which create a culture of dependence on the state, which in turn creates an uncontested cultural control (Serrano Vidal, 2012). However, the trend of public expenditure on culture experienced a negative evolution between 2006 and 2012: in 2006 it accounted for 0.6% of GDP and represented 1.5% of public spending, while in 2012 it represented 0.46% of Spanish GDP and 0.9% of the total public expenditure. Beyond this, an additional level of concern is the reduction at every government level: autonomous communities had the highest decrease (42.6%), followed by the local governments (31.7%) and the central government (28.5%). In spite of what was just said about the increasing prominence of regional and local investment in culture, such data suggests that many of the current cultural institutions and programmes are at risk. According to the government, this reduction is based on the premise of ensuring 'the functioning of "core" institutions and cultural services' and on continuing 'the construction of complementary models of financing, with the greater participation of civil society' (Council of Europe, 2015).

Regarding how alternating governments have dealt with culture, the way in which the Ministry of Culture was reorganised with the arrival of every newly elected government illustrates how culture in Spain has not only been the target of political instrumentalisation for the past 40 years but has suffered from a lack of articulation of the sector, preventing it from having any kind of political negotiation power. Even in the most prosperous phases of the economy, cultural budgets only reached 0.11% of public expenditure from the central government.[9] Deregulation, opening to the private sector and identification of culture as a factor for economic development characterised this period of subsequent socialist and liberal-conservative party rule.

The creative and cultural industries became a political priority with the creation of the Directorate-General for Cultural Industries and Policy in 2008 by a re-elected socialist government. As a result, in Spain, 3.6% of GDP is related to the intellectual property rights of creative and cultural industries (ICC) that generate 488,700 jobs.[10] The brutal increase of VAT on culture (from 8% to 21%) implemented by the central conservative government in place in August 2012 brought the precarious situation of creative workers and artists, as well as the economic fragility of projects and cultural organisations, into the spotlight of the media and, therefore, public opinion. This measure not only placed Spain as the country with the second highest tax culture in the Euro zone, behind Portugal, but also represented an unaffordable tax for many citizens to absorb.

The response from employers in the cultural field, gathered under the Union of Business Associations of the Spanish Cultural Industry (which represents over 2,130 organisations and over 43,000 jobs), was immediate. They requested VAT to be reduced to 10% and energetically argued that, during the first year of full implementation of the VAT increase, the Spanish cultural sector suffered the biggest decline in recent years: 30% less public spending in culture, a 16.33% reduction in gross earnings and 22% decrease in net revenue. Social mobilisation, including hundreds of cultural associations from the sector, followed soon after, accompanied with slogans such as 'Culture is not a luxury' and 'We are all Culture'. However, despite these actions, industry professionals mostly self-employed or working 'under the table' (actors, craftsmen, technicians, screenwriters, writers, etc.) saw yet another obstacle appearing for them – the difficulty of making a decent living from their work. This dramatic VAT increase, coupled with the drastic cuts in public budgets for culture, has critically wounded the cultural and artistic sector in Spain. However, there are other challenges facing the sector, some of which are of an endemic nature, and some could be considered circumstantial.

Regarding the employment situation of cultural and creative workers, contracts are very rare, which creates an endemic precariousness that has come to be associated with the sector. Therefore project-based or work-for-hire contracts abound in the cultural sector: they overlook not only previous experience or training but also the preparation required to produce a high-quality cultural event or output, such as rehearsals or travel. An additional disadvantage is, of course, the lack of benefits and coverage offered to other workers. Moreover, in order to avoid illegal situations in terms of taxes, most artists with a minimum income (or the promise of one) are required to register under a self-employed status, which demands paying a fixed monthly payment into the social security system, whether one has made any money or not, and payment of the VAT regardless of whether the commissioning party has paid the invoice or not. Once they have registered as freelance workers, usually work-for-hire contracts (a type of civil non-employment contract) are signed. As these workers do not have permanent contracts, they do not enjoy rights such as training and occupational risk prevention courses. Moreover, work is very often contracted by oral agreement only and thus remains in the informal domain, forcing many of these activities to be hidden under the economic radar of the informal economy.

Particularly in the performing arts, artists usually sign agreements with, or are hired by, management companies that, in exchange for a fee, sign contracts with the employers and commissioning parties. These agencies are regulated in the Royal Decree 735/1995 of 5 May, aiming to contribute

Table 6.3 Cultural employment in Spain: Types of employment and economical activities (2015)

Sector	*Cinema, video, radio and television*	*Other design activities, creation, artistic and spectacles*	*Graphic arts, recording, instruments, music publishing, media production and applications*
Not salaried	56,2	21,1	11,8
Salaried	43,8	78,9	88,2
Salaried (permanent)	27,4	69,9	51
Salaried (temporary contract)	16,4	9	37,2
Total	100	100	100

Source: National Statistical Institute Active Population Survey 2015 (annual means).

to the creation of new employment using job placement agencies, also in the field of culture.[11] There is a tradition in the country, mostly among musicians, of creating employee-owned companies and, more recently, non-profit cooperatives. Traditionally, they have represented an emancipatory statement against the system rather than a real alternative to sustained employment alternative although this may be changing with the awareness increase brought about by community culture initiatives (REACC, 2021).

All in all, artists who have stable employment are a minority in the sector. Contracts can be open-ended or fixed term; however, the most widely used are work-for-hire contracts for the duration of a particular show or performance. In addition, cultural event organisers usually prefer to avoid paying the artists' social security contributions and therefore choose what has become the typical arrangement – employing artists who have previously registered as self-employed workers.

Even though there was not an 'artist' status in Spain by the end of this research period, some regulations existed aiming to facilitate access to benefits for artists 'in public entertainment events' so they can benefit from a 'regulatory specificity' which allows them to count some non-working periods as days contributed to, and covered by, the social security system. Table 6.3 provides an overview of the employment situation in the cultural sector.

6.3.3 Main Conclusions from the Spanish Context Analysis

The budgetary crisis in Spain has increased the tension between the central government and the regional authorities, and culture is one of the most conflictual policy areas. The investment of local authorities in cultural activities accounted for over 50% of all public spending on culture at all levels in 2012 (Council of Europe, 2015). An additional layer of complexity, often invisible, should also be considered: the growing divide between urban cultural centres and the periphery, mostly medium-sized towns, with high levels of depopulation rates. However, this rural–urban divide is reflected also in the way cities can finance culture: while the largest cities finance blockbuster festivals and exhibitions, smaller towns can only cover the basic library service provision and some strictly local events.

A second consequence of these budget cuts in the majority of European countries has been the equating of Spanish cultural and arts organisations to their peers in Europe, where most of them rely on a mixed funding model that combines public funding, private donations and sponsorship and box office and/or merchandise-generated revenue (Fuentes La Roche, 2009). However, path dependency dynamics are going to be complex to overcome: the almost exclusive dependence on public administrations will make it more complicated to find new financing and entrepreneurship formulas for professionals in the sector to continue producing and showing their work.

While this transformation of the financing model of culture could be a challenge to be tackled collectively, a shared consciousness among professionals of the arts and culture is almost non-existent, both in general (as a community or class) and discipline-wise (with the exception of some highly structured professional guilds). As a result, the sector remains atomised and lacks self-organising mechanisms (although this may have begun to change after the Covid-19 pandemic). This structural circumstance, paired with the solitude required for the conception and execution of the creative process, hinders formal associationism beyond collaborations for projects. Moreover, there is an absence of means and tools to develop and maintain formal exchanges and connections with other sectors and groups in society, such as universities, business associations and so on. The result is that artists and cultural professionals are absent from the public sphere and do not participate in debates on issues of social relevance beyond cultural themes.

From the administration standpoint, the lack of strategic vision when it comes to conceiving cultural policies perpetuates opportunism and clientelist relations between the sector and public administrations, as well as instability in the sector and the cultural impoverishment of the citizens. In this regard, despite the official effort to increase the participation of civil society in the creation of symbolic cultural goods and the participation in culture, Spanish citizens are far from being directly involved in the creation, implementation and evaluation of their cultural policies and programmes.[12]

These elements compose a picture that makes it challenging for culture to be a true vector of transformation. At the crossroads of these elements is where SMartib's contribution could be most significant – by advocating for the structuring of the professional culture sector through the removal of administrative and legal obstacles so that creators can concentrate on creating and cooperating at the local, national and European levels. This sustained practice and exchange among artists and culture professional could result in a process of self-reflection and awareness within the sector itself as a step towards reaching a level of articulation that places culture at the centre of the actions and discussions affecting it.

6.4 A Focus on the Emergence of Social Enterprises and the Cultural Field in Hungary

The modern borders of Hungary were set after World War I when the country became a part of the Austro-Hungarian Empire. During World War II, Hungary joined the sphere of the Soviet Union, and a communist dictatorship was imposed for the following four decades (1947–1989). Hungary's participation in the Revolution of 1956 and the opening of its borders with Austria in 1989 paved the way for the fall of the communist regime there as well as the entire Eastern Bloc.

Administratively, Hungary is divided into 19 counties (*megye*, plural *megyék*) plus the capital, Budapest, which is independent of the counties. Hungary has a multi-party system currently led by the conservative Hungarian Civic Union (*Fidesz*), the left-wing Hungarian Socialist Party (MSZP), the nationalist Movement for a Better Hungary (*Jobbik*) and the Christian Democratic People's Party (which was crucial for ensuring the two-thirds conservative majority in 2010). Since 1989, Hungarian politics have undergone radical shifts: following the first elections in 1990, a conservative coalition government came to power; it was followed by fifteen years of rule by the Hungarian Socialist Party with a coalition government of FIDESZ-MPP and FKGP from 1998 to 2002. The current prime minister since 2010, Viktor Orbán, occupied the position twice, previously from 1998 to 2002.

Negotiations to join the EU began in 1998, but the country would not effectively enter until May 2004. In 2010, the EU and the Council of Europe openly criticised the Orbán government for its new constitution and media law that were considered to lack human rights and democratic rule.[13] Orbán-led policy has become increasingly pro-Russian, and it is currently focused on neutralising dissident voices and stopping immigrants from entering the country.

After returning to a democratic parliamentary republic, the country underwent a serious fiscal austerity plan that included measures such as the elimination of numerous subsidies. This led to an initial crisis, but in a few years, Hungary's economic evolution was spectacular with its per capita GDP more than tripling in the period covered in this research ($4,735.3 in 1998 to $14,021.9 in 2014) with a peak in 2008 of $15,600 (see Graph 6.1). This growth is associated with other countries in the region undergoing a rapid transition from a communist-based economic system to a neoliberal type.

The 2008 global financial crisis caused a severe recession in Hungary, and the unemployment rate reached 11%, although it was cut down to

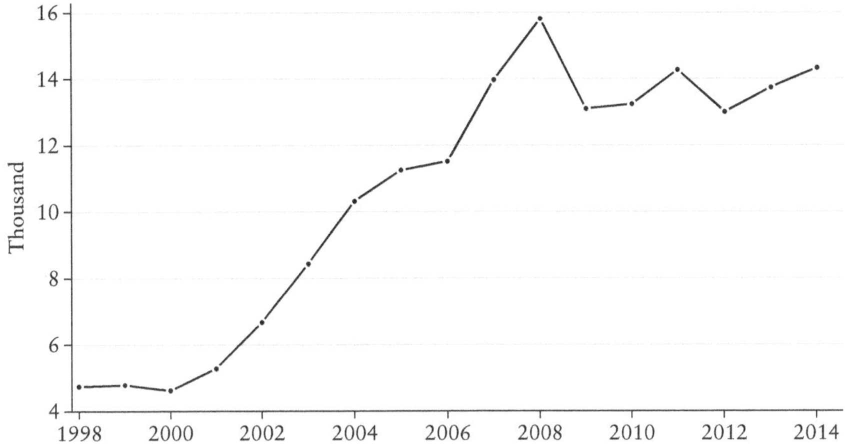

Graph 6.1 Hungary GDP per capita (current US$), 1998–2014.
Source: World Bank national accounts data and OECD National Accounts data files.

6% by 2015.[14] However, in July 2016, Hungary's National Association of Employers and Manufacturers (MGYOSZ) raised a red flag about the increasing labour shortage in the country, which could cause the economy to stagnate again.

6.4.1 *The Development of Civil Society, Third Sector and Social Enterprises*

The wider institutional landscape of socioeconomic entities working for the common good beyond the traditional for-profit or the public sector is primarily captured by the term non-profit sector (mainly in scientific documents), but civil society, social economy, third sector and community enterprises have also been used. Hungary and the Czech Republic have two of the better developed non-profit sectors in Central and Eastern Europe, and the attitude of their governments towards the sector was generally benign during the early 1990s (Sebestény et al., 1999). Table 6.4 gives an idea of size of the civil society sector in comparison to employed people and to other country (Spain) included in this analysis for which there was data available. Unfortunately, Austria was not included in the Salamon and Sokolowski (2014) study consulted.

Hungary is considered to have a 'deferred democracy' model of civil society, characterised by a constrained overall size of the civil society sector and a reduced number of volunteers involved in it. Moreover, expressive functions of civil society (voicing discontent, enhancing participation

Table 6.4 Civil society sector workforce as a percentage of the economically active population, Hungary and Spain (1995–2000)

Country[a]	*Paid staff*	*Volunteers*	*Total*
Hungary	0.94%	0.21%	1.15%
Spain	2.82%	1.48%	4.31%

Source: Salamon et al. (2004).

[a] Excludes religious organisations. Data not available for Austria.

in the public arena) are low (Sebestény et al., 1999). The main source of support for the non-profit sector, and more recently social enterprises, in Hungary has traditionally been international aid (Norwegian Civic Fund and the Swiss Fund), although an increasing withdrawal of international donors took place as countries joined the European Union (Kerlin, 2009). Moreover, the term 'social enterprises' was introduced in the country via international development organisations, namely Ashoka and NESsT.[15] Its use was rapidly adopted by a growing community of experts and development organisations, which resulted in the emergence of a consultancy-based market driving the original development of the sector. Social enterprises exist under different legal forms in the non-profit sector, such as foundations, non-profit companies, social cooperatives and cooperatives. The original form is the 'Integrated Community Service Space' (*Integrált Közösségi és Szolgáltató Tér* – IKSZT) which acts as a catalyst for community services in rural areas, although it is not independently run but depends on the public administration (mostly local).

The term 'social economy' is most widely used together with social cooperatives (which are a type of social enterprises), although not in any legislation or statistics. No government agency dedicated to the social economy exists right now either, so social economy and social enterprise were mainly used in EU-related documents. Indeed, the Hungarian Partnership Agreement for the 2014–2020 period explicitly uses the term 'social enterprises'. However, the level of awareness about social enterprises remains low in Hungary, although a growing number of practitioners, academics, public administrators and business representatives are becoming interested in it. Moreover, organisations from the social and solidarity economy that have been traditionally active in the field of culture and the arts in Hungary (mostly associations and foundations, albeit with restrictions on commercial activities and trading) are not economically viable (Fekete et al., 2017). Even though they are actively involved in the production of goods and services, their tradition of dependence on external funding jeopardises their sustainability.

According to the 'autonomous mutualism' model proposed by Kerlin (2013), social enterprises operate independently from and even in opposition to the government, which is confirmed in the case of Hungary. While the efficiency-driven stage of economic development and the growing GDP could represent an opportunity for developing Hungarian civil society and a social and solidarity economy via redistributive action by the government, the policies of the current president are unlikely to support this development. Confirming the attributes identified by Kerlin for this model, social enterprises are small- and medium-sized organisations that focus on making up for market and welfare state voids. Moreover, they are likely to be perceived as a type of social activism and even constitute a social movement given the tradition of civil society opposing and criticising the regime in a country like Hungary (Young and Kim, 2015).

Despite the traditional robustness of the Hungarian civil society sector, the relationship with the government has shown signs of rapid deterioration lately. A noteworthy anecdote describes events taking place in 2014 that show the relationship between the broad non-profit sector and the government: the central government accused an independent entity (*Ökotárs Foundation* in charge of distributing 15 million euros coming from the Norwegian Civic Fund among NPOs) of mismanagement, fraud, forgery of private documents and unauthorised financial activities. The case was reported in national media as well as in internet-based outlets for months and continues to be referred to as the 'Norwegian affair' with a negative connotation about the interference of government in the actions of civil society.

6.4.2 The Cultural Field in Hungary

The social structure of Hungary is similar to that of other East European countries, with a highly advanced and prosperous elite and the majority being economically held back, with no middle class. Cultural policy played a role in reconstructing the Hungarian identity and self-image after harsh political periods. In this sense, Hungarian culture has always had the social function of empowering the masses while also playing an aristocratic function by adding to the national pride through the creation of cultural expressions. Examples of this emerge right after the Ottoman and Austrian rules in the nineteenth century as well as after the two World Wars and the fall of communism. The Soviet rule can be considered a parenthesis that brought about a cultural dogmatism around a Bolshevik, centrally planned policy that supported access to culture, cultural consumption and an explicit political relevance of the arts. In that context, Hungarian artists showed a level of engagement with the political situation that was quite different from artists in the rest of the Eastern Bloc countries, who mainly engaged in discussions about the autonomy of arts ('politics of autonomy'). In Hungary, artists adopted a strategy of political autonomy more typical of contemporary art that openly criticised 'the Apparatus aimed at both its politics and ideology' (Piotrowski, 2012: 97).

After the political turn of 1989–1990, there were two main sources of inspiration for cultural policy: pre-communism national traditions and

Table 6.5 Civil society sector FTE workforce in culture, Hungary and Spain (1995–2000)

Country	*% of total civil society workforce*[a]	*Total (thousands)*
Hungary	36.8	54.8
Spain	15.2	728.8

Source: Salamon et al. (2004).

[a] Excludes religious organisations. Data not available for Austria.

modern western examples. The National Cultural Fund was created in 1993 to finance cultural projects following the 'arm's length principle' of the British and the Dutch. This type of arm's length agencies was born in response to the collapse of old structures, the need for reform, the desire for participation in decision-making, the increasing recognition of the civil sector and so on. Table 6.5[16] shows the percentage (and total figure) of civil society working in the field of culture in Hungary and Spain at this time. As shown by the comparison, the engagement of Hungarian civil society in culture doubled that of Spanish civil society.

The 16 years that followed saw a back-and-forth movement between conservative and progressive cultural policies. The two main aspects that changed during those shifts were the level of centralisation of cultural policy and the degree of emphasis put on national heritage and pride and on the connections with Hungarians abroad. Both increased during conservative governments. Culture was used by the first Orbán government (1998–2002) to consolidate its vision for Hungary based on five principles: 'national unification', a 'central arena of power', a change of elites, power politics and an era of 'revolutionary circumstances' (Bozoki, 2012).

The concentration of decision-making power that brought about the second victory of Orbán in 2010 found a fertile ground in the lack of formal articulation of cultural policy in Hungary in the form of official plans, strategies, documents and legal acts.[17] Indeed, the second Orbán mandate considered culture an unnecessary cost and source of potential criticism, so it focused on changing the elites. Some attempts to alter this in the 2010s have been rapidly interrupted, and only three exceptions were identified by the Council of Europe publication: the legislation enacted on the cultural domains of film and performing arts, the medium-term strategies disclosed in 2012 by all nine sub-boards of the National Cultural Fund (although their impact on the field was almost null) and the 2007–2013 National Strategic Reference Framework for the EU Structural Funds. The latter example included buzzwords for European cultural policy such as modernisation of libraries, museums and houses of culture or the development of culture in urban development and regeneration. In 2014, Orbán's Minister of Foreign Affairs and Trade, Tibor Navracsics, was appointed the Commissioner of Education, Culture, Youth and Sport of the European Commission.

In Hungary, no formal definition of culture has been enshrined in law. More recent terms such as 'cultural industries' and 'creative sector' have somewhat entered the public sphere but without having been enacted in any high-level document. However, an important institution supporting Hungarian amateur cultural activities, particularly folk culture, is the houses of culture (*művelődési házak*). In the 1970s they evolved into the grassroots 'dance houses' that are still popular today, particularly in small villages where they are synonymous with local culture and take up the majority of the cultural budget. They are considered local community centres or socio-cultural institutions, and they are well structured and networked across the country. Considered a multipurpose cultural institution, the houses of culture survived the communist appropriation and are currently undergoing a reappropriation process. This institution cuts across the social and cultural sectors and is considered a hybrid. Houses of culture have received substantial funding from the European Structural Funds in the framework of the New Hungary Development Plan 2007–2013 as they contribute to social cohesion and cultural development.

A second type of institution already mentioned – the Integrated Community Service Space, ICSS – was established in the frame of the rural development programme of the EU. By 2013, 400 IKSZT were created in villages of 5,000 inhabitants or less to act as a cultural and social hub for rural communities. They offer types of compulsory programmes such as youth and culture, library service, internet service for the community and information for local enterprises, giving places for rural development experts (Katona-Kovacs and Bóta-Horváth, 2012; Fekete, 2014).

The crisis that hit the country from 2006 to 2010 added an additional negative influence on cultural financing which, coupled with the interference of the government in culture, meant a clear backlash for culture in Hungary. Indeed, as part of the new constitution, the government was rearranged and the highest-level cultural administration (the Ministry of Education and Culture) became a state secretariat in the Ministry of Human Capacities. This continues to be the situation today. The National Cultural Fund of Hungary finances cultural and artistic projects with a yearly budget of 2.2–2.6 million euros, 90% of which comes from national lottery revenues. Forty per cent of this budget can be assigned discretionarily, whereas 60% is to be spent according to the guidelines of the main board of the cultural state secretariat; the average funding amount the lottery contributed in 2011 was around 5,300€ per project. As for the management of IPR in the music sector, the responsible organisation is Artisjus. In 2013, without prior consultation, the parliament decided to channel 25% of their 2012 revenues (over 40 million euros) to the National Cultural Fund of Hungary.[18] The message that seemed to be taking hold was that it was simply unimaginable to exist outside the 'system of national cooperation' (Bozoki, 2012).

During an interview with one of the staff members of SMarthu, she estimated that over 65% of actors, dancers, musicians, arts managers, technicians, designers and other cultural operators in the field do not have an employment relationship with their clients, many of them being self-employed. The official number of employees in the cultural sector was always relatively limited, but since 2010, critical artists began to find it increasingly hard to work in the country and many chose to emigrate. In parallel with the neoliberal economic policies in place that involved a cut of culture expenditure, a suffocating and authoritarian context seemed to be emerging for thinkers and creators with shrinking tolerance for the freedom of expression and critical attitudes. This general feeling was confirmed by the '2015 Cultural Climate Barometer', produced by the Budapest Observatory: over one-third (39%) of the eastern experts consulted complain about political influences in culture against only 19% in the west.[19] An immediate result is the lack of financing to make a living as an artist, but also the reduction of opportunities for artists to share their work with audiences.[20]

Within this framework, some present-day artists (Cseke, El-Hassan, KissPál, Kaszás) are engaged with the political situation, which connects them to the generation of critical artists criticising the Apparatus during the communist regime. Their criticism is done, as suggested by Rancière (2006), within the limits of their own artistic practice and discipline, which provides them with a reasonable level of relevance and legitimacy. By doing so they are likely to contribute to expanding the autonomy of the arts and the change in the order of reality (Hungarian reality) as sought by Rancière's heterogeneity principle.

The gender issue is also very important in Hungary, although after the fall of communism, it took a conservative turn. A scrutiny of the discourse of female emancipation shows that the conservative turn did thrive in part due to the absence of any ideological pressure and in part due to unemployment (Tatai, 2014). In addition to lower employment rates and uneven representation in public versus private domains of work, the reality is that only 8.8% of members of the parliament are women, which places Hungary next to the last in Europe. Tatai (2014) critically states that the fact that women outnumber men in higher art education does not reflect female emancipation, but a devaluation of the artistic career.

6.4.3 Main Conclusions from the Hungarian Context Analysis

The rich, modern history of Hungarian institutions, with a vast number of influences, has had an impact on this country despite the communist dictatorial interlude of 40 years. Despite the currently hostile contexts for co-construction processes that take into account the views of all stakeholders, there seem to be some paths leading to developments in the area of social enterprise within the field of culture and the arts.

ICSSs represent a double potential for cultural and creative workers: on the one hand, they could provide employment opportunities as animators of local groups, playing a crucial role as 'innovation brokers'; on the other hand, they can act as pools for future creators and artists who would be networked and mentored from early stages.

In line with Stokfiszewski's (2015) proposals on how culture can contribute to democracy in Central Europe, SMarthu could contribute to transformative social innovation in the country by creating community bonds among artists and creative workers, by empowering them to devise and implement changes they want to see happening around them and by reforming concepts of property and identifying areas of common good that are better managed collectively. The challenge is enormous as former communist countries undergo a 'profound reinterpretation of the historical foundations of collective identity' where traces of multicultural heritage are fading and progressive agendas are being delegitimised (Stokfiszewski, 2015: 210). Indeed, SMarthu is already building a technology-enabled platform that allows creative workers to play an active role in their own future and has the capacity to develop other services that makes it possible for them to interact among themselves and with other citizens (e.g. Agora in SMartbe, an online sales platform that is forthcoming in Spain, etc.). In this context, the ongoing connection with other European countries within the SMarteu network represents a unique source of inspiration for workers, supporters and members of SMarthu. Likewise, other European SMart country leadership should gain consciousness of the critical crossroads that Hungary (and the wider region) is currently facing.

By increasing opportunities for 'civic self-expression' based on the common good (understood as what we all share as well as what thrives from collective action and management) in Hungary, more and more open spaces for imagining and testing alternatives could emerge. A parallel process would be a pedagogical interaction with traditional art institutions (which are likely to be customers of the members of SMarthu) so they can welcome co-governance with workers and stakeholders as well as co-creation and participatory dynamics from the general public. The task ahead is substantial insofar as it involves the institutional and organisational reform that is being requested from critical thinkers and grassroots initiatives in order to ensure that culture contributes to real democracy processes.

Notes

1 This sub-section draws mainly from two sources: the ICSEM working paper on Austria by Anastasiadis and Lang (2016) and the study 'A map of social enterprises and their eco-systems in Europe' by EC (2014).

2 Austria was not included in the non-profit sector study by Johns Hopkins University (Bosma and Levie, 2010; Salamon, 2010) or the social entrepreneurial section of Global Entrepreneurship Monitor (GEM) in 2009.

3 Other terms connected to traditional legal forms are more prevalent such as *Sozialwirtschaft* (social economy), *Sozialintegrationsunternehmen* (social integration enterprises) *gemeinnützige organisationen* (public benefit organisations focused on work integration) and *Genossenschaften* (cooperatives).

4 This sub-section draws mainly from the chapters devoted to Austria of the *Cultural Policies and Trends in Europe: A Compendium of Basic Facts and Trends*, produced by the Council of Europe.

5 Public support for the arts was acknowledged by the Federal Arts Promotion Act in 1988. Unlike social policy, most cultural competences are assigned to the *Bundesländer* through the 'cultural sovereignty' principle. Each region (except Vienna) has its own Arts Promotion Laws defining culture according to regional specificities and highlighting the cultural activities to be promoted. Regarding the federal level, between 1998 and 2006 all cultural policy agendas were in the hands of the State Secretary for Art and Culture, who was part of the office of the federal chancellor. From 2007 to 2013, culture and the arts were again the responsibility on the Federal Ministry for Education, the Arts and Culture, and since 2014, they have been assigned to the agenda of the Federal Minister for Arts and Culture, Constitution and Media via the Arts and Culture Division, which is attached to the Federal Chancellery of Austria.

6 The study 'ZursozialenLage der Künstler und Künstlerinnen in Österreich' (On the social situation of artists in Austria) was commissioned by the former Ministry for Education, the Arts and Culture. Available in German at www.kunstkultur.bka.gv.at/Docs/kuku/medienpool/17401/studie_soz_lage_kuenstler_en.pdf.

7 The Council presents itself as 'a consortium of the associations representing the interests of art, cultural and media workers'. It includes among its demands that no repayments are requested from the Artists' Social Security Fund, an unconditional basic income for all. Source: http://kulturrat.at/organisation/mission_en (accessed 11 August 2016).

8 Interestingly, a century later, we can speak of a certain parallelism around the resurgence of the collective impulse in agrarian surroundings and rural areas under the umbrella of agroecology. However, these recent initiatives are infused with a grassroots and participatory dimension that had been diluted in their social economy predecessors. This is why they tend to adhere better to the term 'solidarity economy'.

9 División de Estadísticas Culturales, Ministerio de Cultura, *Anuario de Estadísticas Culturales 2011*, Madrid: Secretaría General Técnica, Subdirección General de Publicaciones, Información y Documentación, 2011, p. 31. Available at www.calameo.com/read/0000753352beb3dcf337a (accessed 4 October 2016).

10 Source (in Spanish): www.boe.es/diario_boe/txt.php?id=BOE-A-2013-3725.

11 Source (in Spanish): http://sid.usal.es/idocs/F3/3-4389/3-4389.PDF.

12 Indeed, a Pact for Culture co-created, endorsed, followed-up and evaluated by all parties active in culture and the arts (including citizens) would be one of the signs pointing to the level of maturity of all the parties involved that Spain seems to be lacking.

13 According to this law, journalists working in publicly owned media have to produce 'balanced articles which strengthen Hungary's national identity'. Source: www.dw.com/en/hungarys-thinkers-protest-cultural-suppression/a-15842557 (accessed 11 August 2016).

14 Hungarian Central Statistical Office, www.ksh.hu/gyorstajekoztatok/#/en/document/mun1601 (accessed 11 August 2016).

15 An international organisation offering business training and funding for startup social enterprises – NESsT – has been in operation in Hungary since 2001 (www.nesst.org/hungary). In addition to its core business, it produces a publication titled *The Social Enterprise Ecosystem in Hungary* in Hungarian and English, describing the general environment of social enterprises in the country, and puts it in a global perspective by providing best practices from around the world. NESsT has undoubtedly contributed to the visibility and recognitions of social enterprises in Hungary and the rest of the CEE area.

16 Budapest Observatory (2001), Arm's Length Financing in Culture: Why? Why Not? Available at www.budobs.org/papers/57-public-grants/294-arms-length-2001.html (accessed 11 August 2016).

17 The new leadership of Budapest's New Theater (*Új Színház*) was directly appointed in 2011, overruling the advice of a panel. Its ambition is that only Hungarian national drama should be performed and without any foreign influence. Another notable case was the substitution of Róbert Alföldy, after five successful years as director of the National Theatre in Budapest and after being the target of radical right-wing attacks mostly based on his open homosexuality.

18 Sources: English webpage of the National Cultural Fund of Hungary (*Nemzeti Kulturális Alap*; https://nka.hu/kategoria-nelkul/national-cultural-fund-of-hungary/) and interview with SMarthu representative.

19 Available at www.budobs.org/files/concisereport15.pdf (accessed 11 August 2016).

20 For instance, the case of the Hungarian author Akos Kertesz is very telling. In August 2011 he published a letter with a fierce criticism of his country fellows that created a nationwide scandal:

> The Hungarian is genetically subjugated. He happily wallows in the slurry of dictators, grunts, swallows the muck and disavows the fact that one would kill him. He will not learn, not work, he can only begrudge others, and when he is given the opportunity, he kills anyone who achieves anything through work, study or innovation.

Soon after he exiled to Canada. The government also launched an investigation on leading Hungarian philosophers on the basis of the accusation of fraudulent appropriation of state research funds. Although nothing could be proven, the accusing media campaign that followed lasted several months. Source: www.dw.com/en/hungarys-thinkers-protest-cultural-suppression/a-15842557 (accessed 11 August 2016).

References

Anastasiadis, M. (2006) The Future of Work and Its End? In A. Heimgartner (ed.), *Face of Research on European Social Development*, 199–213, Wien: Lit Verlag.

Anastasiadis, M. (2017) Work Integration Social Enterprises in Austria: Characteristics, Evolution and Perspectives, *Nonprofit Policy Forum*, Vol. 7 (4), pp. 541–564.

Anastasiadis, M. and Lang, R. (2016) Social Enterprise in Austria: A Contextual Approach to Understand an Ambiguous Concept, ICSEM Working Paper No. 26, Liege: The International Comparative Social Enterprise Models Project. Available at www.iap-socent.be/sites/default/files/Austria%20-%20Anastasiadis%20%26%20Lang.pdf [accessed 7 July 2016].

Borzaga, C. and Defourny, J. (eds) (2001) *The Emergence of Social Enterprise*, London: Routledge.

Bosma, N. and Levie, J. (2010) *Global Entrepreneurship Monitor, 2009*, Glasgow: Hunter Centre For Entrepreneurship.

Bozoki, A. (2012) The Crisis of Democracy in Hungary, Heinrich Böll Stuftung blog. Available at www.boell.de/de/node/276334 (accessed 14 August 2016).

Calle, A. (2013) *La transición inaplazable. Salir de la crisis desde los nuevos sujetos políticos*, Barcelona: Icaria.

CIRIEC (2007) *The Social Economy in the European Union*, Brussels: EESC.

Council of Europe (2015) Cultural Policies and Trends in Europe: A Compendium of Basic Facts and Trends. Available at www.culturalpolicies.net/web/austria.php?aid=1 [accessed 7 July 2016].

Defourny, J. and Nyssens, M. (2010) Social enterprise in Europe: At the crossroads of market, public policies and third sector, *Policy and Society*, Vol. 29 (2), pp. 231–242.

Defourny, J. and Nyssens, M. (2016) *Fundamentals for an International Typology of Social Enterprise Models*, ICSEM Working Paper No. 33, Liege: The International Comparative Social Enterprise Models Project. Available at www.iap-socent.be/sites/default/files/Typology%20-%20Defourny%20%26%20Nyssens_0.pdf. (accessed 3 February 2017).

Doherty, R., Haugh, H. and Lyon, F. (2014) Social Enterprises as Hybrid Organizations: A Review and Research Agenda, *Journal of Management Review*, Vol. 16, pp. 417–436.

Esping-Andersen, G. (1999) *Social Foundations of Postindustrial Economies*, Oxford: Oxford University Press.

European Commission (2014) *Mapping Study of Social Enterprises and Their Ecosystem in Europe*, Brussels: European Commission.

Fekete, É. (2014) Cross-Community Cooperation in Post-Socialist Hungarian Rural Space. In E. Kasabov (ed.), *Rural Cooperation in Europe*, 68–100, Basingstoke: Palgrave.

Fekete, É., Hubai, L., Kiss, J. and Mihály, M. (2017) Social Enterprise in Hungary, ICSEM Working Paper No. 47, Liege: The International Comparative Social Enterprise Models Project.

Fisac-García, R. (2015) *Modelo de análisis organizativo para la mejora del desempeño de empresas sociales*, doctoral thesis, Polytechnic University of Madrid. Available at http://oa.upm.es/33676 [accessed 15 November 2016].

Fisac-García, R., Moreno-Romero, A., Acevedo-Ruiz, M. and Juan-Ruiz, J. (2015) Identificación de los elementos organizativos clave en el desempeño de las empresas sociales. El caso de los telecentros en Latinoamérica [Identifying key organizational elements in the performance of social enterprises. The case of telecentres in Latin America], *Dirección y Organización*, Vol. 56 (2015), pp. 43–56.

Katona-Kovacs, J. and Bóta-Horváth, N. (2012) Rural Team-Entrepreneurs: An Answer to Innovative, Multi-Disciplinary Human Capital Education, *International Food and Agribusiness Management Review*, Vol. 15 (A), pp. 1–5.

Kerlin, J. (2009) *Social Enterprise: A Global Comparison*, Lebanon, NH: Tufts University Press.

Kerlin, J. (2010) A Comparative Analysis of the Global Emergence of Social Enterprise, *Voluntas: International Journal of Voluntary and Nonprofit Organizations*, Vol. 21 (2), pp. 162–179.

Kerlin, J. A. (2013) Defining Social Enterprise across Different Contexts: A Conceptual Framework Based on Institutional Factors, *Nonprofit and Voluntary Sector Quarterly*, Vol. 42 (1), pp. 84–108.

Lang, R. and Novy, A. (2014) Cooperative Housing and Social Cohesion: The Role of Linking Social Capital. *European Planning Studies*, Vol. 22 (8), pp. 1744–1764.

Lehner, O. (2011) The Phenomenon of Social Enterprise in Austria: A Triangulated Descriptive Study, *Journal of Social Entrepreneurship*, Vol. 2 (1), pp. 53–78.

Marbán Gallego, V. (2007) Tercer Sector, Estado de Bienestar y Política Social, *Revista Política y Sociedad*, Vol. 44 (2), pp. 153–169.

Montagut, T. (2000) *Política Social: una introducción*, Barcelona: Ariel.

Montagut, T. (2009) The Third Sector and the Policy Process in Spain: The Emergence of a New Policy Player. In J. Kendall (ed.), *Handbook on Third Sector Policy in Europe: Multi-Level Processes and Organized Civil Society*, 119–139, Cheltenham: Edward Elgar.

Neumayr, M., Schneider, U., Meyer, M. and Haider, A. (2007) The Non-Profit Sector in Austria: An Economic, Legal and Political Appraisal, Working Paper 01/2007, Vienna: WU Vienna University of Economics and Business.

Novy, A. and Hammer, E. (2007) Radical Innovation in the Era of Liberal Governance: The Case of Vienna, *European Urban and Regional Studies*, Vol. 14, pp. 210–222.

Piotrowski, P. (2012) *Art and Democracy in Post-Communist Europe*, London: Reaktion Books.

Rancière, J. (2006) Democracy, Republic, Representation, *Constellations*, Vol. 13 (3), pp. 297–307.

REACC (2021) Articular las artes y la cultura transformadoras desde la participación ciudadana y la justicia social: La germinación y proceso de consolidación de la Red de Entidades y Agentes de Cultura Comunitaria, REACC, Madrid: Ministry of Culture and Sports. Available at https://culturayciudadania.culturaydeporte.gob.es/dam/jcr:46253c41-1832-4476-9ddf-5fa6b7f21188/reacc.pdf [accessed 21 November 2021].

Rodríguez Cabrero, G. (2005) Los retos del tercer sector en España en el espacio social europeo. Especial referencia a las organizaciones de acción social, *Revista Española del Tercer Sector*, Vol. 1, pp. 63–94.

Ruiz Olabuénaga, J. I., Jiménez Lara, A., Anheier, H. K. and Salamon, L. M (1999) Spain. In L. M. Salamon and H. K. Anheier (eds), *Global Civil Society: Dimensions of the Nonprofit Sector*, 163–178, Baltimore, MD: Johns Hopkins Center for Civil Society Studies.

Salamon, L. M. (2010) Putting the Civil Society Sector on the Economic Map of the World, *Annals of Public and Cooperative Economics*, Vol. 81 (2), pp. 167–210.

Salamon, L. M. and Sokolowski, S. W. (2014) The Third Sector in Europe: Towards a Consensus Conceptualization, Working Paper No. 02/2014. Available at http://thirdsectorimpact.eu/site/assets/uploads/documentations/tsiworking-paper-no-2-third-sector-europe-towards-consensus-conceptualization/TSI-Wrkg-Ppr-2-Conceptualiza-fnl-2-17-15-.pdf [accessed 9 September 2016].

Salamon, L. M., Sokolowski, W. and Associates (2004) *Global civil society: Dimensions of the nonprofit sector*, Bloomfield, CT: Kumarian.

Sarasa, S. and L. Moreno, L. (1995) *El Estado del Bienestar en la Europa del Sur*, Madrid: CSIC.

Saunders, M., Lewis, P. and Thornhill, A. (2007) *Research Methods for Business Students*, London: Prentice Hall.

Schelepa, S., Wetzel, P. and Wohlfahrt, G. (2008) *Studie zur sozialen Lage der Künstlerinnen und Künstler In Österreich* (*On the Social Situation of Artists in Austria*), Vienna: Ministry for Education, the Arts and Culture.

Sebestény, I., Kuti, É, Toepler, S. and Salamon, L. M. (1999) Hungary. In L. M. Salamon, H. K. Anheier, R. List, S. Toepler and S. W. Sokolowski (eds), *Global Civil Society: Dimensions of the Nonprofit Sector*, 305–324. Baltimore, MD: Johns Hopkins Center for Civil Society Studies.

Serrano Vidal, A. (2012) Nuevos proyectos culturales en el entorno madrileño: una alternativa a la crisis actual (New Cultural Projects in Madrid: An Alternative to the Current Crisis), *Heritage & Museography*, Vol. 4 (3). Available at www.raco.cat/index.php/Hermus/article/view/313475/403594 [accessed 3 May 2016].

Sostenuto Project (2014) *Culture as a Factor for Economic and Social Innovation*, Valencia: Cultural Economics Research Unit (Econcult), University of Valencia.

Stokfiszewski, I. (2015) *New Municipalism, New Culture, New Democracy*, Amsterdam: European Cultural Foundation.

Tatai, E. (2015) Macaristanli Sanatci kadinlar neoliberal dunya duzeninde ne yapabilir? (What Can Hungarian Woman Artists Do in a Neoliberal World Order?), *Kadin/Woman* 2000, Vol. 16 (2), p. 45.

Yin, R. K. (2009) *Case Study Research: Design and Methodology*, London: Sage Publishing.

Young, D. R. and Kim, C. (2015) Can Social Enterprises Remain Sustainable and Mission-Focused? Applying Resiliency Theory, *Social Enterprise Journal*, Vol. 11 (3), 233–259.

7 SMart Arrives to Austria, Spain and Hungary

7.1 Scaling Up SMart in Austria: SMartat

Full name: Work SMartat *Legal structure:* Non-profit association *Legal address:* Gumpendorferstraße 63b, A-1060 Wien, Austria *Date of establishment:* 8 October 2012 *Start of operations:* February 2014 *Website:* www.smart-at.org *Social media:* www.facebook.com/SmartCoopAustria	*Full name:* SMartat e.Gen. *Legal structure*: Cooperative (for profit, with a social purpose) *Date of establishment:* 4 May 2015 *Start of operations:* November 2015

7.1.1 *Historical Perspective of SMartat*

The initial seed for a possible SMart in Austria was planted by a presentation delivered by Julek Jurowicz on 31 May 2011 as part of a panel organised by the interest group 'Free Theatre Work' (*Die Interessengemeinschaft Freie Theaterarbeit*, also known as IG Freie Theaterarbeit – IGFT).[1] For the first time, intensive discussions around the role of culture and the arts (and their professionals) were going on throughout the country under the auspices of the Ministry of Social Affairs and Labour. These initiatives were called 'Inter Ministerial Working Groups' (IMAG), described in Chapter 6, and such discussions acknowledged the crucial contributions that culture and the arts could make to Austrian society.[2]

Initially, discussions around the possibility of launching SMartat centred around the needs of the performing arts sector in Austria. Indeed, the aim was to promote employment opportunities in the independent theatre field. After this initial stage, the scope had been already broadened by October 2012, when SMartat took its first steps as an autonomous association named WorkSMartat. In 2013, SMartat opened its first office in Vienna, and the original team completed the Local Information Questionnaire (LIQ) in June 2013 with all the relevant contact information about the

DOI: 10.4324/9781003342144-8

main actors in the labour, social economy and cultural fields in Austria, plus some analytical reflections. In terms of market analysis, there were not any private employment agencies in the cultural and artistic sector in Austria, which meant that payroll agencies and tax advisors were the only possible competitors of SMartat. As for the management agency sector, it was not being well developed, except for the fields of classical music and opera. The strict labour regulations in Austria, however, represented a major obstacle for the development of SMartat. Particularly the employment of actors and musicians (who constitute a major target for SMart) is very complex. In short, the Theatre Employment Act (*Theaterarbeitsgesetz* – TAG) provides certain rules and juridical conditions for the treatment of actors and musicians by an organisation like SMartat. Likewise, the Austrian music trade law prevents employing musicians who work with agencies.

In January 2014, SMartat began its first operations. Its first campaign was launched during summer and autumn 2014, targeting musicians and designers. While these operations were running, the idea of setting up a cooperative was being explored: the perception was that this legal form would allow all the members to make their voices heard. This legal form was also perceived as ensuring that future profits would be reinvested fully back into the organisation with a view to expanding the services and facilitating the work of artists in all areas of their professional life.

On 4 May 2015, SMartat was founded as a 'registered cooperative society' (*eingetragene Genossenschaft* or 'e.Gen.') and publicly launched on 22 June 2015. International guests were invited to take part in the launch event, which attracted considerable media attention. Since then, the operations and staff members of SMartat were transferred from the association to the cooperative (although the association continued to exist).

7.1.2 SMartat Functioning and Services Offered

By December 2015, the services of SMartat could be divided into two general pillars, the main service, SMartProduction, and an additional service called SMartAdmin. The former constitutes an 'in-house' activity management service that takes full responsibility for any risk in production within the cooperative. Considered a 'SMart Production House', it focuses on providing employment to members at a fee of 7.5% of the invoiced amounts. The second pillar of the service is an 'out-house' service (called 'SMart Admin') to assist private individuals and groups (including formal associations) in administering, monitoring and controlling their projects. The risk and responsibility, however, remains with the user, who is charged a flat hourly rate of 30€, as opposed to a percentage. Given the strict labour regulations, and until alternative solutions are found, associations of creative and cultural workers represent a major potential for the out-house service of SMartat.

In addition to this core business, SMart launched a project in March 2017, financed by the Office of the Federal Chancellor (BKA) and the Federal Ministry of Culture, to create an online mobility information portal (similar to the personal help desk managed by SMartde; see www.touringartists.info). This project aims to collect and document specialised knowledge and expertise on social security, taxes, insurance options, labour law, copyright and types of organisations available to artists in Austria and beyond. SMartat is responsible for managing and updating this online platform. The ultimate goal is to provide advice on mobility to creative and culture professionals. Even though the official launch of this initiative fell outside the time period of this research, the fact that such a commitment (plus the source of finance and potential for impact) existed at an early stage of the adaptation process is a crucial factor in the consolidation of SMartat.

In terms of human resources, during the first year of its activity (2014), many tasks were fulfilled by internally employed staff: the strategic and executive management of SMartat, the development of its mobility website, the development of new services, providing advice to new members and accounting and communication tasks. Lastly, the regional development of the SMartat was fulfilled by employed workers although some tasks related to communication, development of new services, and the development of the mobility project platform were complemented with workers who were considered as internal but had a self-employed status. As of December 2015, the team included four employees – three part time with varying degrees of responsibility and one self-employed legal expert.[3] In addition, a communication consultant/project manager worked part time within SMartat, while a trainee and a project worker were associated with SMartat with the support of employment agencies. An accountant, a lawyer, an IT consultant and a tax advisor were also mobilised for external support.

In addition to the general assembly, SMartat has two organs: an executive board composed of Sabine Kock and Andrea Wälzl, who manage the cooperative, and an advisory board that monitors the operations, consisting of Prof. Oliver Fabel (from the Faculty of Business, Economics and Statistics of the University of Vienna), Julek Jurowicz (co-founder of SMartbe and initiator of the European development of SMart) and Sabine Mitterecker (an independent theatre director and producer).

So far, tasks have been managed via an ad hoc adaptation of Excel spreadsheets by a team member working on a part-time basis. Regarding the website, a fully English version was launched in January 2016. However, the limited administrator rights available to national partners represent a hurdle to site maintenance, as everything must go through the Belgian technical team.

SMartat combines a variety of financial sources that characterise social enterprises. As of 2015, it included the following sources of finance:

Table 7.1 SMartat turnover and surplus since year of establishment

2015		*2016**	
Turnover	*Surplus*	*Turnover*	*Surplus*
61,400€	8,000€	160,450€	–

*Projected.

1. Members' purchase of initial shares. Members were asked to buy at least one share each at 50€ per share, while other users could decide whether to buy shares or not. In addition, SMartbe also purchased some shares. The total amount collected from members was 3,000€ by 2015, while SMartbe invested 150,000€ in shares for the 2016 budget.
2. Collecting a 7.5% fee from SMartProduction and SMart Admin. The collective turnover was 61,400€ with a surplus of about €8,000 from SMart Admin and SMart Production in 2015.
3. Grants from public funding. For 2015, this included an agreement with BKA for the mobility portal project valued at 25,000€.
4. Investments made by SMartbe through the acquisition of capital shares and loans to cover operating costs (mostly users' salaries) until new resources come in. The total amount collected was 70,000€ in the 2015 budget (in addition to plans for buying more shares in 2016). Cash flow advancements to ensure that all salaries are paid at the end of the month have not been necessary yet.

Table 7.1 shows the evolution of turnover size and surplus generated by SMartat since 2015, including a projection for 2016.

Regarding users, they are mainly based in Vienna and about 20% in other Austrian regions. It is worth noting that a high number (20–25%) of users come from other countries or continents and/or have an international working background, which has been a surprise from the beginning and the percentage continues to rise. Clients are based all over Austria and also in other countries of Europe, including Switzerland, Germany, Italy, Belgium, Sweden, Norway and the UK. Despite the limited growth in membership, the wide diversity of artistic disciplines and cultural sectors represented is a promising factor for future increases in the number of creative workers who may be joining SMart. Table 7.2 lists the various cultural sectors in which SMartat users are active.

Within the cultural sector, SMartat was beginning to be perceived as an interest group (such as the *IG Freie Theaterarbeit*). This recognition was built not only by the validity and timeliness of the services offered but also by the strategic partnerships and collaborations that SMartat has created since its formation. Collaboration exists with national public administrations (BKA, the Federal Ministry of Culture and the Federal Ministry of Social

Table 7.2 Sectoral profile of SMartat users

Sectors	*2014*	*2015*		*2016*
	Real	*Exp*	*Real*	*Exp*
Performing arts (theatre and music)	8	40	33	65
Literature and language	–	–	–	–
Visual arts	–	5	8	10
Graphic design	–	4	1	5
Architecture, fashion, design, decoration	–	–	1	3
Artisanry	–	–	–	1
Audio-visual	–	5	5	10
Training and education	–	–	–	3
Art education and workshops	1	1	–	3
IT and web development	–	–	–	5
Events	–	–	–	5
Other (cultural management/non-artistic sectors)	3	5	2	10
	12	60	50	120

*Projected.

Source: Adapted from SMarteu.

Table 7.3 Implementation of SMart in Austria

Phase 1: Initial contact (3–6 months)	*Phase 2: Preliminary setup (1–2 years)*	*Phase 3: First operations (3–4 years)*
First contact: March 2011* Formal creation: 2014	*Completed by the end of 2016* *(including full repayment of the loan to SMartbe)*	*Full-fledged operations: 2017* *Break-even point ('point 0'): 2019*

*Effective dates vs. *planned dates* (in italics).

Affairs and Labour) and the national Chambers of Commerce and Labour. Recognition began to appear also from other cultural institutions such as the MICA (Music Information Center Austria), which has been supporting SMartat since its very beginning, and the Academy of Fine Arts (*Akademie der Bildenden Künste*). In addition, SMartat began networking with other social enterprises such as Otelo, which allowed for synergies and opportunities to emerge.

Given their cultural and geographic closeness, SMartde represents a source of inspiration for SMartat on how to move in the scaling-up process. Indeed, the Austrian team made a series of visits to the office of SMartde to learn about the online tool and their internal procedures, working documents and workflows. Regarding the technical resources, given the strict Austrian employment regulations, SMartat had to implement a new national bookkeeping system to be linked to the online tool.

Table 7.3 summarises the duration of scaling-up and adaptation (implementation) of SMart in Austria.

7.1.3 Take Away Points from the Implementation and Possible Future Developments

7.1.3.1 Scaling-Up Factor Analysis

A summary of the lessons learned during the initial steps of the scaling-up process begins with a brief reflection on the statistical data gathered from the surveys, which is included in Table 7.4.

The data gathered from the five different categories of stakeholders in Austria showed that the most important factor in the scaling-up process is the ability to meet social demands (5.23). Such weight is understandable considering the conditions of emergence of SMartat consisting of its embeddedness in the performing arts sector and in the middle of growing privatisation dynamics in the cultural sector. Factor 3, as shown in Table 7.4 concerning the replicability of the model, was not only valued the lowest (3.45) but also showed the least deviation from the mean, which suggests greater agreement among the respondents. Moreover, regarding factor 3, the Austrian team did not connect the failure of the scaling-up to issues of lack of network, finance or peer support.

Extreme values are rarely present in the aggregated Austrian data, as shown in Table 7.4. Moreover, of the 65 items observed, all except nine were assigned scores in the range of 3–5. However, the standard deviation was quite high for most of the items, which points to the diversity of perceptions in the Austrian team. The deviation seemed to large on the statement about the online tool (SD of item 3.2 = 3.0), whereas there was agreement on the capacity of the management team to mobilise support (SD of item 2.5 = 0.55).

Based on an analysis of survey results, the Austrian team seemed to be very certain about the validity of the model, as shown by the highest value assigned to the item (item 5.4 = 6). Interestingly, they assigned the lowest

Table 7.4 Factors of the scaling-up process in Austria (N = 5)

Scaling-up factor	*Minimum*	*Maximum*	*Mean*	*Standard deviation*
Commitment of individuals driving the scaling process	2.00	5.00	3.95	1.239
Competence of the management	3.00	5.50	4.46	1.035
Full or partial replicability of the operational model	2.42	4.58	3.45	0.796
Ability to meet social demands	3.83	6.33	5.23	0.961
Ability to obtain necessary resources	3.50	5.67	4.66	0.783
Potential effectiveness of scaling social impact in partnership	2.13	5.50	4.05	1.410
Adaptability	2.57	5.00	3.94	0.950

value to the item measuring the disruptiveness of the model (item 7.7 = 1.5), which is consistent with the maximum value described just before. Once it has been proven that the SMart model works and that it does so through an array of innovative services (item 4.3 = 5.8) clearly fulfilling a need (item 4.1 = 5.6), then its model should not be too disruptive to implement (not to be confused with innovative).

Some additional items (reaching a high score around 5.8) relate to the ease of replication of information and advice service (item 3.3), the importance of creating a financial stream that secures operations (item 5.2) and the relevance of partnerships in the implementation process (item 5.9).

The value assigned to the role of volunteers (item 1.5 = 4.33) is curious considering that volunteering is not formally recognised within SMartat (beyond, of course, the members of the council or board, who are volunteers). Such value may indicate either that there are people acting *de facto* as volunteers whose work is highly appreciated or point toward the wish that such a figure becomes a reality within SMartat.

7.1.3.2 Lessons Learned and Prospects

Beyond the data analysis, the Austrian team felt that a stronger variety in terms of profile of the initiators' team could have ensured that knowledge, experience and contacts in various cultural and artistic fields were present. Since most of the Austrian team of initiators were experts in the performing arts, the void in other artistic fields is being filled up via new users stemming from those sectors that become ambassadors and share their knowledge with the SMartat team. This expertise is also being brought into SMartat by its staff members, who also have accumulated and increased knowledge about many artistic sectors.

Delayed payments constituted a mayor issue (13% of invoices suffered delay in 2014 and 25% in 2015); indeed, national SMart offices are encouraged to put in place a system of invoice recovery. The situation of unpaid invoices is closely monitored in the annual reports submitted to SMartbe. Specifically, Annex 3 (monitoring and evaluation) requests that the national administrative system allows for assessing the invoiced amounts, the amounts paid and due, issuing and paying dates of invoices and amounts due by invoice, order and user.

Worth noting is the promising mobility platform currently under development in cooperation with the BKA and the Federal Ministry of Culture. In addition to the value that it is likely to create for the user, the crucial element for SMartat is the identification of a potential new market niche (mobility advice) that had not been well covered, despite the long-standing interest in artist mobility on the part of the Austrian federal administration. Moreover, there is potential for taking the lead within the SMarteu platform in collaboration with SMartde to develop a replicable version of this platform that could be taken up progressively by other SMart partners. Such evolution would be in sync with the SMart ambition of promoting the mobility of European artists.

In parallel with the development of this platform, the idea is to include full artistic projects into the 'SMart Production House', described above. Such a strategy implies attracting not only individual creators and workers but going a step further and negotiating directly with funding institutions. Depending on who these institutions are, support from advocates outside SMartat will have to be mobilised in order to obtain the necessary buy-in from different key policymakers and private decision-makers. This support may range from endorsement from public administrations (at all levels) of the services and model of SMart, to explicit recommendation from employers (the bodies financing the project), and to artists involved in the project to join SMartat. Handling this lobbying effort properly requires not only devoted staff hours but a clear understanding of the legal implications of managing public funds, as well as the repercussions for other intermediate bodies and finance recipients. Luckily, SMartat plans to address this challenge by working together with its members and users and with public administrations to gauge the organisational demands that such initiative would put forward and get ready to face them properly.

Regarding the formal process and the documents that new SMart country offices were requested to complete, it was understood that those related to research and background information (e.g. LIQ) could have been premature given the very early stage of the scaling-up process in which they were filled out. In this context, it was felt that having them completed (or updated) in a later phase - when services were already in place - could have helped gain deeper insight about the process.

In terms of growth expectations, SMartat is likely to undergo a slow growth process during the first three years of operation, mainly due to a non-supportive environment. The legal constrains in terms of employment laws (described in the previous chapter) represent serious hurdles to the growth of SMartat. However, it is acknowledged that, once a critical point in membership is reached (around 150), the level of acceptance and rate of joining will increase. The three indicators that have been used to compare performance among the country studies (speed of the implementation process, number of members, and turnover size and surplus) indicate that the goal of attracting 150 members in 2016 could be considered plausible (see Table 7.5).

However, the experience accumulated in the two last years shows that, even though the services offered seem to convince most of the potential users, the intermittency of their work represents a true obstacle for them to join SMartat. At the time, the assumption was that 150 users might join at the end of 2016, which would need to be activated and motivated in order for them to become ambassadors. Adding to the initial media interest created

Table 7.5 Evolution of members at SMartat (net figures and percentages)

	2014	*2015*	*2016**
Members/users	n/a	80	132
Growth compared to the previous year	0	80%	60%

*Projected.

with the launch of the cooperative, SMartat is engaged in the following process, generating promotional and commercial actions which, in combination with the new services and activities available to members described above, aim to attract new members in the coming years:

1. A follow-up strategy with the initial potential users convinced by the SMart model but who identify their lack of stable employment as an obstacle to joining the cooperative. The goal is to jointly explore how this situation can be overcome.
2. An awareness-raising campaign at art departments in universities and other targeted groups (e.g. small cultural organisations). After a successful presentation at the Academy of Fine Arts for students and alumni, information actions at higher education institutions and special initiatives are in the making in the field of music with the goal of attracting new users stemming from more informal and youth sectors.
3. A target group identification effort, focusing on untapped potential users (both individuals and larger groups) who could need their service (e.g. ushers, red noses, clown doctors).
4. An ongoing conversation with representatives of performing artists and musicians to identify and develop solutions to the labour restrictions applicable to them. For the first group, an awareness-raising effort to have public and private cultural project funders endorse SMartat for their project is under development. As for musicians, the idea of offering additional services that they need such as a label is also under way. At the time, SMartat was planning to submit a funding application to launch a 'SMartRecords'.
5. An effort to promote the out-house SMart Admin service among associations while it is not possible to run projects within the in-house SMart Production House service as a limitation imposed by the strict labour regulations and music trade law.
6. External financing via national sources as well as European ones. Indeed, SMartat has been part of the two Erasmus applications in 2014 and 2015 and has coordinated the submission of one in 2016 focused on best practices in mobility handling.[4] They are also interested in exploring the feasibility of future applications in the context of the European Social Fund (ESF).

7.2 Scaling Up SMart in Spain: SMartib

Full name: SMart Ibérica de Impulso Empresarial, S. COOP. AND. *Legal structure:* Cooperative *Legal address:* Caserón de la Virreina – Avda., Jane Bowles, s/n, 29014 – Málaga *Date of establishment*: April 2014 *Website:* www.smart-ib.coop *Social media:* www.facebook.com/SmartIberica and https://twitter.com/smart_iberica	*Full name:* Asociación para los trabajadores de la cultura SMartib *Legal structure:* Non-profit association *Legal address:* La Piconera, Carrer Sancho Marraco 6, 08004 Barcelona *Date of establishment*: April 2014

7.2.1 Historical Perspective of SMartib

The story of the arrival of SMart and its subsequent adaptation into Spain is very different from that of other countries. SMartib (*SMartIbérica*) was born through contacts with the dance scene in Catalonia, via an artistic partner based in Barcelona and a group of cooperatives based in Andalusia. These were informal contacts between the representatives of SMarteu and dance professionals installed in Barcelona well informed about the situation of creative and culture professional in Spain. In parallel, representatives of the cooperative Aura in Andalusia (founded in 1996) participated in the 'ESEmpleo' programme, launched by CEPES-Andalusia, wherein they learned first-hand some initiatives for job creation in the cooperative sector in Belgium, Italy and France.[5] There are many types of cooperatives (labour, credit, education, housing, social, etc.), but the selected type was a newly created legal form – the 'entrepreneurial impulse cooperative' (*cooperativa de impulso empresarial* in Spanish).

Also known as an 'umbrella cooperative', this type of cooperative has been recognised by only two autonomous communities in Spain – Andalusia and Cantabria – by December 2015.[6] In fact, the 'entrepreneurial support cooperative' (*cooperativa de impulso empresarial* in Spanish) adopted by SMartib was inspired by the French model of 'activity and employment cooperatives' (*cooperative d'activités et d'emploi*) which was created in 1995.[7] Through establishing direct contacts in 2011 between professionals from both countries coupled with the visits of Spanish initiators to SMartbe, phase 1 (initial contact) was set off, which included an assessment of the possibilities of adapting SMart to the Spanish context. Following the initial assessment, SMartib was formally constituted in May 2013 and phase 2 (preliminary setup) was entered into. The original agreement included the possibilities of access to expertise and funding provided by the SMarteu structure. The goal in business terms was to reach the 'zero point' with reference to losses – or profitability – in three years.

SMartib is composed of two types of partners: 'structure partners', who are responsible for all the administrative work and job counselling, and 'user partners', who are professionals in the field of culture working independently under the administrative umbrella of SMartib.[8] Joining the cooperative is required in order to avail of the services it offers: each member provides a share capital of 150€ (that can be distributed across three years) when joining, which can be returned during the following year in case s/he decides to leave the cooperative.

SMartib's legal headquarters are located in Malaga, its central services in Seville, and its regional offices are present throughout the country in various autonomous communities. Since the beginning, Aura's operating offices were used to launch SMartib, which reduced structure and personnel costs until SMartib's first employees were hired in Barcelona, Seville and Madrid. Following SMartib's vocation of territorial presence in all the Autonomous Communities, the headquarters of Barcelona was added to the network of six offices (Antequera, Cordoba, Granada, Jerez, Malaga, and Seville) of Aura. In a second step of consolidation at the national level, SMartib was installed in the Community of Madrid, thanks to the agreement reached with the Association of Cultural Managers of Madrid (AGETEC). The decision to establish a collaboration between SMartib and AGETEC was based on the objective of dignifying the employment of the cultural sector in Madrid while improving the qualification and professional knowledge of members. This willingness to collaborate with local actors, already existing in a given territory by SMartib, opened the doors to a structure and to networks that would have otherwise taken a long time to build.

The fact that a possible two-headed organisation form could have resulted from the various contacts of the Belgian team in the same country in two different regions (Andalusia and Catalonia) and the fact that these contacts stemmed from such different contexts were addressed at four levels. Firstly, the Barcelona team was formally included in the structure of the cooperative as 'structure partner'. Secondly, SMartbe's supra-project membership brought in a non-Spanish partner to look on the adaptation process. Indeed, two staff members from SMartbe – very committed to the consolidation of the European platform – acted as intermediaries during conflicts: they focused on ensuring adherence to the previously agreed upon objectives and therefore the ability to go beyond concrete and contextual situations. Thirdly, through the name of the cooperative itself. By avoiding use of the official name of the state (Spain) as had been done in all other eight European countries where SMart was present, the organisation indirectly recognised a certain equality of Catalonia vis-à-vis the central government, even though the discussion was really limited in terms of participation and no consultation beyond the founding team was conducted. Fourthly, continuous communication was held between teams, including formal and informal interactions, both face to face and through new technologies.

The connection of SMartib with the social economy is latent both in its values and through the story of its creation. As indicated above, SMartib was set up as a cooperative, one of the major families within the social economy but, in addition, it is based on the two principles that also characterise the Belgian experience: the absence of profit and the pooling of risks and benefits. These two principles are attached to the seven principles for the management of cooperatives that defend the International Cooperative Alliance (http://ica.coop/es): voluntary and open membership; democratic governance; economic participation of members and partners; autonomy and independence; education, training and information; cooperation among cooperatives; and commitment to the community.

7.2.2 SMartib's Functioning and Services Offered

SMartib is a cooperative that aims to provide cultural workers and artists a legal framework in which they can work and defend their rights. It offers artists, creative industry workers, technicians, managers and other cultural professionals mutualised services. It offers them the possibility of contributing during periods of active work and receiving benefits during periods of lost work opportunities. As stated in its motto – 'intermittency is not synonymous with precariousness' – artists and creators will be able to achieve their professional potential without feeling at a disadvantage compared to other categories of workers. To this end, SMartib has developed a series of mutual services, legal and administrative advice and access to common protections and insurance while allowing members to be registered in the general regime of Social Security for the number of days they work. One solidarity aspect of the project is the 'Guarantee Fund', which ensures that members will receive their fees (at least in part) by the end of the contract even if their clients have not made the payment, provided the amount to be collected does not exceed twice the interprofessional minimum wage and with a limit of three months for a single user for sustainability reasons. SMartib emphasises the advantages that joining the cooperative offers over the other most common form of creative and cultural workers formal status in Spain, namely self-employment (*estatuto del trabajo autónomos*). There is no payment for a specific period of contribution, and civil liability is also limited to the contribution to the social capital of the cooperative (150€). This benefit contrasts with the unlimited civic liability with present and future assets that must be faced by the self-employed workers (*autónomos*).

By the end of this research, the services offered by SMartib included contract management and activity management, with a number of forms a user is required to complete. These forms should have been made available online, but the delayed development of the online tool for Spain has prevented this from happening. SMartib undertakes all the administrative (all paperwork related to contracts, execution of payments, etc.) and accounting (taxes, social security contributions, etc.) tasks on behalf of its

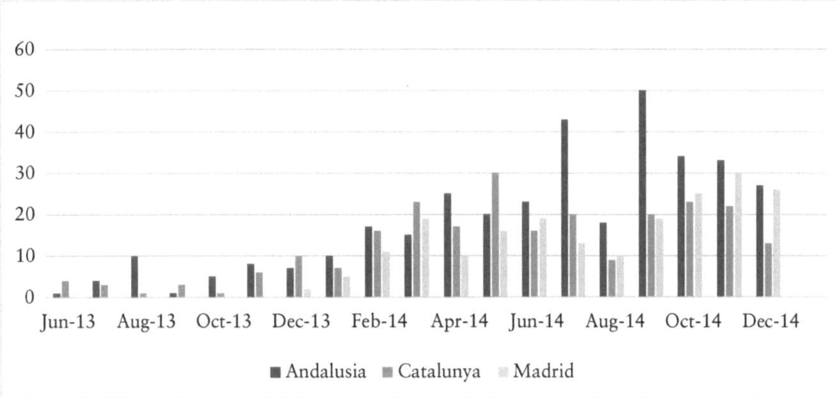

Graph 7.1 Evolution of SMartib members according to representation from autonomous communities (June 2013–December 2014).

Table 7.6 Evolution of members at SMartib (net figures and percentages)

	2013	*2014*	*2015*	*2016**
Members/users	64	800	1.439	2.871
Growth compared to the previous year	n/a	1250%	80%	100%

*Projected.

members through an increasingly automated back office and e-mail-based interaction with members. SMartib also manages insurance packages for its members and organises information sessions on the cooperative and the SMart model. In addition, legal support is offered in relation to copyright and intellectual property rights, e-commerce and new technologies as well as privacy and data protection issues.

In terms of its expansion, the consolidation of SMartib appears undeniable: in only 18 months, it reached 800 members and a turnover of 2,023,000€. Graph 7.1 and Table 7.6 illustrate this evolution.

As was the case in Austria and Hungary, SMartib has been able to mobilise a variety of financial sources between 2013 and 2015:

1. Revenue-making from the 7.5% fee for the members' invoices. For each contract or invoice, the cooperative receives 7.5%, which is intended to offer mutualised services, training, and advice for all aspects essential to the users for carrying out their activities (i.e. prevention of occupational risks, liability insurance, etc.). This constitutes the main self-generated source of income for the organisation and amounted to 469,919€.

2. Members' contribution to the capital of the cooperative (150€ at the moment of joining) which amounted to 55,057€.
3. Investment made by SMartbe in SMartib, which reached 143,750€ from 2013 to 2015 (43,750 in June 2013; 30,000 in August 2014, and 70,000 in April 2015). The first amount in 2013 helped SMartib take off while the other two were meant as liquidity injections and to be reimbursed.
4. Public aids and subsidies. Although there have been no direct grants or subsidies, the deep knowledge on the part of SMartib of the labour and tax laws at all administrative levels in Spain has allowed them to seize financing opportunities for the organisation. Indeed, an interesting provision in labour law in Spain called 'capitalisation of the unemployment allocation' (*capitalización de la prestación de desempleo*) allows workers to invest their unemployment subsidy (up to 33,000€) in the creation of a new individual or collective economic activity, including cooperatives. Two staff members in Barcelona and one in Andalusia provided this capitalisation to finance the operation of the branch. Moreover, also drawing from employment-related administrative advantages, the regional government granted a social security subsidy to hire two new staff members. Lastly, via one of the cooperatives in the group (Actúa), the Social Economy Department of the Andalusian Government provided a subsidy to hire a person to be responsible for communication across cooperatives.

Table 7.7 shows the evolution in terms of turnover size and surplus generated since 2013, including a projection for 2016.

In terms of workforce, Spain was able to incorporate workers gradually. By the end of 2015, a total of 15 staff members were working for SMartib with different levels of dedication. Of these, five worked dedicatedly for SMartib, namely one communication person in Seville, three advisors (one in Barcelona and two in Madrid) and one part-time administrator in Barcelona. The rest of them worked for SMartib on a shared basis with the other cooperatives, which included the president, the legal expert, the finance manager and the IT manager in the central headquarters and six advisors and administrative staff in offices at Antequera, Granada, Xerex, Málaga and Seville.

Table 7.7 SMartib turnover and surplus since year of establishment

2013		*2014*		*2015*		*2016**	
Turnover	*Surplus*	*Turnover*	*Surplus*	*Turnover*	*Surplus*	*Turnover*	*Surplus*
98,269€	1,808€	1.938.131€	5.631,01€	4.224.887€	4.736,25€	9,000,000€	137,300€

Table 7.8 Implementation of SMart in Spain

Phase 1: Initial contact (3–6 months)	*Phase 2: Preliminary setup (1–2 years)*	*Phase 3: First operations (3–4 years)*
First contact: January 2011* Formal creation: 2013	*Completed by the end of 2013 (including full repayment of the loan to SMartbe)*	*Full-fledged operations: 2013 Break-even point ('point 0'): 2017*

*Effective dates vs. *planned dates* (in italics).

Its future plans include offering professional training and workplaces (e.g. studios and co-working spaces), financial services (lending at zero rate of interest), an online sales platform, several European exchange programmes (e.g. studios and exhibition opportunities) and research at local, regional and national levels. A couple of interesting developments were underway during the period covered by this research. As we have seen, many artists and cultural workers are already registered as self-employed workers, but SMartib currently can only act as an employment agent of its own members. By creating an intermediate unit (most likely a different but related cooperative), SMartib will be able to apply VAT only to a part of the management fees and not for the whole amount of the invoice. In addition, it is aiming to be able to operate with self-employed artists as well and to launch an association in Barcelona that caters to the aims and needs of members (and other stakeholders) that are not directly linked to those related to the core services (labour and administrative paperwork).[9] There were also plans to prepare an Erasmus+ application to support the development of mobility information services. Lastly, a members-driven project called EIMUS (*Ecosistema de Impulso Musical SMartib* – SMartib Music Impulse Ecosystem) was approved by the general assembly held in December 2015. EIMUS aims to help SMartib's members to produce, distribute and manage their own music, thereby allowing for a better division of rights and income. The core idea is to eliminate intermediaries by creating two mutual guarantee funds: a general fund for investments covering general costs (web server, lawyers, etc.) and an emergency fund (like in traditional labels) to invest in rehearsals, concerts and so on. Table 7.8 summarises the duration of scaling-up and adaptation of SMart in Spain.

7.2.3 Take Away Points from the Implementation and Possible Future Developments

7.2.3.1 Scaling-Up Factor Analysis

Before we begin an overview of the lessons learned from the first steps of scaling-up in Spain, a brief reflection on the statistical data gathered from the Spanish surveys, shown in Table 7.9, follows.

Table 7.9 Factors of the scaling-up process in Spain (N = 5)

Scaling-up factor	*Minimum*	*Maximum*	*Mean*	*Standard deviation*
Commitment of individuals driving the scaling process	3.88	5.38	4.60	0.57
Competence of the management	3.25	5.25	4.30	0.81
Full or partial replicability of the operational model	4.50	6.08	5.43	0.60
Ability to meet social demands	4.50	6.33	5.40	0.67
Ability to obtain necessary resources	4.50	5.25	4.80	0.31
Potential effectiveness of scaling social impact in partnership	2.75	6.13	5.07	1.37
Adaptability	3.71	4.86	4.22	0.48

The responses of the stakeholders surveyed in Spain are quite measured in the sense that the two extreme values (1 and 7) are avoided. The range for the mean was 4.22 (factor 7) and 5.43 (factor 3), thus confirming the concentration of average observations around central values. Spanish respondents attributed the highest value to factor 3, namely the full or partial replicability of the operational model. This factor not only shows the highest mean but also a high minimum value (4.5) and a low level of deviation, which suggest little disagreement among respondents. Considering the swiftness with which the model has been implemented in Spain, having a replicable model seems to be the key to such a smooth process. Even though in Spain the online tool continues to be unavailable, the fact that the processes, ideas behind them, and the specific tools to implement them were readily available constitutes an important perceived benefit for the scaling-up process of SMart in Spain.

On the contrary, the lowest relevance was assigned to adaptability of the model which, although seemingly contradictory with the previous paragraph, actually is understood by looking closely at the various sub-factors (see Table 7.10). Indeed, the SMart model is perceived to be fully adaptable to Spain (6) and logically, its counter sub-factor (the disruptibility of the model) is perceived as being low (1.8). Interestingly, the replicability (factor 3) and adaptability (factor 7) of the model reflect the respondents' support of the need to expand services for maximising the social impact of SMartib (6.8) and the perception that doing so would not put the organisation at risk financially (2.4).

Going back to perception of the factors, respondents seem to agree on the relevance of factor 5 (ability to obtain necessary resources) as suggested by the low standard deviation (0.31). When looking at the aggregated data per sub-factor, this is indeed the case except for the sub-factor referring to the ability to get government agencies and officials to provide financial support for their efforts. Factor 6 (potential effectiveness of scaling social impact

Table 7.10 Adaptability of the scaling-up process in Spain (N = 5)

	Min.	*Max.*	*Mean*	*Standard deviation*
7.1. SMart is fully adaptable to the Spanish context.	3.0	7.0	6.00	1.73
7.2. Local regulations and policies in Spain require the SMart model to be substantially adapted.	2.0	6.0	4.40	2.19
7.3. The financial environment of Spain requires the SMart model to be substantially adapted.	2.0	6.0	3.80	1.79
7.4. SMart is way too disruptive for adaptation to Spain.	1.0	4.0	1.80	1.30
7.5. SMartib will maximise social impact by expanding the target groups we serve.	3.0	7.0	5.50	1.91
7.6. SMartib will maximise social impact by expanding the services we currently serve.	6.0	7.0	6.80	0.44
7.7. Expanding target groups and services is not sustainable financially in Spain.	1.0	6.0	2.40	2.07

with others) seems to cause the highest level of disagreement among Spanish respondents (SD = 1.37).

7.2.3.2 Lessons Learned and Prospects

Unpaid invoices represent a major hurdle for financial sustainability in SMartib. The process of debt collection involves contacting the client by telephone, e-mail or fax to request the payment. If the client fails to pay, a request is then made by a bureau fax with acknowledgement of receipt, which can be used as a proof in court. Small court claims can be presented for amounts up to 30,000€, but for amount less than 900€, the involvement of an attorney is not necessary. Internal debt collection procedures, however, were inefficient since a total of 74% of the invoices issued in 2014 and 2015 remained unpaid by October 2016 Therefore, SMartib hired a debt collection agency in 2015 hoping to cash in substantial amounts of funds that it had to advance to its members within the month of issuing the invoices but were never paid by the clients.

The existence of a consolidated group of cooperatives working in the field of employment creation in Spain (Aura, Actúa) offered a security net in terms of finance that has also been able to draw from financing possibilities stemming from Belgium. In this context, the economies of scale in terms of staff sharing as well as of financing (particularly cash flows for advancing payments) were created, thanks to the existing cooperative structure.

However, in terms of internal governance and possible mission drift, the existence of a pre-existing group of cooperatives represented a challenge to be overcome. Firstly, ensuring participatory decision-making across a group of cooperatives which are active in different activity fields is not an easy task. Indeed, after three years of operating under the same umbrella, plans are underway to split SMartib from the rest of cooperatives and make it more independent, under a SMart-specific Spanish group of cooperatives operating under the same mission and in the same field (culture and the arts). Secondly, sharing a commercial and administrative structure created situations whereby the resources at hand (mostly human capital) had to be prioritised toward one or another cooperative. Being the latest arrival within the group and operating with many small contracts (as opposed to fewer larger contracts in the other activity fields of the group), SMartib saw – particularly at the beginning – how its needs and specific requirements were put on hold as a result of a limited organisational capacity. However, the 'claim to fame' of SMartib within the group has been the rocketing growth in terms of members and turnover generated in a three-year period, as well as the increasing recognition by political actors, public administrations, and representatives of culture and the arts.

7.3 Scaling Up SMart in Hungary: SMarthu

Full name: SMarthu Non-profit Kft.
Legal structure: Non-profit limited liability company
Legal address: Lázár utca 16, 1065 Budapest, Hungary
Date of establishment: March 2014
Start of operations: November 2014
Website: www.smart-hu.org
Social media: www.facebook.com/smarthu.org (Last post: April 15th, 2020)

7.3.1 Historical Perspective of SMarthu

By the end of 2012, Dária Belinskaya, soon to be founder and manager of SMarthu, was introduced to Julek Jurowick, who managed the transnational scaling-up of SMart, by Simon Mundy, who was the main initiator of the scaling-up attempt in the UK. Belinskaya had a political science background and started her own company, focusing on design and architecture. She believed in SMart as she has been active in the creative and cultural scene in Budapest and had witnessed first-hand several hurdles in the field. With a couple of supporters at her side, she did most of the work related to setting up the association herself.

The reason for choosing a different legal form other than a cooperative was mainly due to the bureaucratic hurdles associated with the latter. It is likely that such legal hurdles will change in the near future to facilitate its transition towards a cooperative form, just like how other SMart countries are doing. According to Belinskaya, the fact of having a not-for-profit organisation makes the issue of ownership irrelevant: users consider it a 'co-used company' in the sense that they can use SMart for their own projects.

7.3.2 SMarthu Functioning and Services Offered

The process of establishing SMarthu was a long one: after an initial discussion by the end of 2012, the organisation was set up only in March 2014 but could not begin operations until nine months later, in November 2014. SMart in Hungary focuses on giving creative workers the possibility to work legally, avoiding the costs and obligations associated with the self-employed status (either as an employee or via a mandate contract[10]) and thus facilitating the workers to leave the grey labour market, where they are forced to work with no coverage or benefits. Therefore, the services offered until December 2015 included activity and contract management, legal counselling, information sessions and events and networking. The rest of the services (financing, insurances, online tools, research and professional training) were planned to begin in 2016. Particularly, two original services were in preparation – 'Brand Coaching' in collaboration with an external partner, and personalised media packages to help promote the work of members.

SMarthu focused its activity for now in the Budapest area, since the city held the highest number of creative and cultural workers in the country. While its services were accessible from across the country, it had only one office operating in Budapest for the time being. In terms of membership, there were 170 in 2015 and projections were to increase it by 120% by the end of 2016 (see Table 7.11).

As explained by Belinskaya, while the cultural workers were indeed the main target of the organisation, the boom in creative industries has created a new group of creative workers who mostly work under precarious labour arrangements or self-employed status. The members of SMarthu carry out activities mostly in the areas of design, graphic design, performing arts, artisanry, IT and web development, literature and languages, audiovisual and art education. It is also worth noting that no visual artists were represented in 2015, although there were plans to attract some in 2016. The clients of SMarthu focused on the following four areas in 2015: (1) performing arts; (2) architecture, fashion, design and graphic design; (3) IT and web development and (4) specialised services requiring the expertise of creative and cultural workers. Indeed, having so many sectors as potential

Table 7.11 Evolution of members at SMarthu (net figures and percentages)

	2015	*2016**
Members/users	170	380
Growth compared to the previous year	170%	120%

*Projected.

targets was perceived as a challenge, particularly in terms of communication, as specific messages and strategies were necessary to be appealing.

Unlike in Austria and Spain, there is no registration fee or contribution to social capital in Hungary. An administrative fee of 8.5% is charged to the net amount of each invoice. The advance payment feature was not available until January 2016, and therefore not included in this research.

With regard to the perception of SMarthu, its public communication via the website focuses on three pillars: activity management, knowledge sharing, and advocacy. The first one, activity management, emphasises the risk- and hassle-free nature of SMarthu's main service (activity management, billing, and legal counselling by December 2015) for creative and cultural workers. In addition, the notion of 'co-used company' where the users can use SMarthu's legal infrastructure to fully operate their projects is perceived as being an important added value. Secondly, sharing knowledge hinges on the power of joining forces with those in the same organisation and is achieved mainly through information and networking activities. The close service of advisors with the members is highlighted as part of the process since the first meeting and throughout the duration of the relationship with SMarthu. Moreover, SMarthu organises a number of networking events to strengthen the sense of belonging of SMart members and to build a community of freelancers in the creative sectors. Ultimately, the aim to is to prevent them from feeling isolated by creating a connection with their peers, sharing experience and good practices among them.

Lastly, the advocacy dimension underlines the value of the environment where creative and cultural workers develop their activity. As part of this area, the idea of defending professional interests (shared by a national and European community) is central. In this context, international mobility becomes an additional concrete added value, although it will not be offered until 2017. The term 'social dialogue' is specifically mentioned when describing this advocacy strategy, whereby SMarthu will become a main interlocutor in negotiations about the sector. The first step towards achieving this goal is to contribute to raising the awareness about the sector. The last strategy is the ongoing research effort as a way to collect information about members to strenghten the cultural field, as well as a way to feed information to all stakeholders about the activities of SMarthu.

Governance is understood in a way that is closer to participatory management, mainly through an active presence of stakeholder representatives in the formal decision-making organs of the association, but that does not really actively engage varied groups of stakeholders in decision-making processes. Members participate in the development of the organisation via regular consultations, mainly regular online and offline surveys, as well as face-to-face discussions. The goal is to guide some of the decision-making with this input as well as to make sure that the members' needs and challenges are taken into account from the strategic point of view. From this standpoint, SMarthu aims to stimulate a horizontal way of operating and making decisions, therefore emphasising the inclusion of both its employees and professional partners in strategic decisions and their concrete execution. In addition to users and professional partners, SMarthu also counts the formal involvement of SMartbe in the organisation, which aims to monitor the activities and provide feedback on the decision-making processes.

The Hungarian team of SMart aims to enhance communication and outreach to attain a twofold objective. Firstly, to connect with its target audience (mainly freelancers) and, secondly, to establish the image of SMarthu as social innovator and raise awareness about topics related to precariousness, alternative employment options, as well as sustainability of the cultural sector among stakeholders and the general public. Indeed, the first is achieved via their own specialised blog named 'Active Creative', featuring pieces of interest for freelancers and a biweekly newsletter. The second aim is to reinforce the public image of SMarthu as a social innovator in the sector, as well as to contribute to the public debate on issues of precariousness, new forms of solidarity-based and collaboration economy, social coverage for project-based workers, cultural mobility, etc. This second objective is achieved via the discussion of 'white papers' proposed to leaders of the cultural and creative sectors, so that they can share their views on a given topic. Lastly, round table discussions on various topics of interest will be organised with professionals from the creative industries. Two of these roundtables are planned for 2016.

Partnerships have been mobilised as an additional strategy for promoting SMarthu, although not primarily in order to attract financial resources, but rather to increase visibility and raise the profile of SMarthu among a design-driven and creative audience composed of professionals and the general public. In this context, SMarthu has established interesting partnerships with online platforms to obtain substantial coverage including monthly features in their web site and also on their social media channels (e.g. partnership with HG.hu).

Regarding its financial situation, unlike its counterparts in Austria and Spain, SMarthu had focused on two main sources of revenue-generating streams by the end of 2015:

1. Revenue-making from the 8.5% fee for the members' invoices.
2. Investment made by SMartbe in SMarthu, include monthly investments on the capital account for a total of 104,500€ in 2015. In addition, SMartbe contributed to the cash flow of the association for an amount of 2,000€ in 2015.

In fact, SMartbe was the only external financer of SMarthu in 2015. Untapped sources in SMarthu that are present in the other case studies are public funding and private donations from grant-making foundations. Table 7.12 shows the evolution of SMarthu in 2015 in terms of turnover

Table 7.12 SMarthu turnover and surplus since year of establishment

2015		*2016**	
Turnover	*Surplus*	*Turnover*	*Surplus*
5,000€	0€	42,500€	0€

*Projected.

Table 7.13 Implementation of SMart in Hungary

Phase 1: Initial contact (3–6 months)	*Phase 2: Preliminary setup (1–2 years)*	*Phase 3: First operations (3–4 years)*
First contact: December 2012* Formal creation: March 2014 (full operations: November 2014)	Completed by early 2016 (not including full repayment of the loan to SMartbe)	*Full-fledged operations: 2018* *Break-even point ('point 0'): 2020*

*Effective dates vs. *planned dates* (in italics).

and surplus size, including a projection for 2016 (the surplus column is empty as a break-even point was not expected until at least 2018).

The level of unpaid invoices was zero although, based on other countries' experiences, it is likely to increase substantially as the turnout grows. In this regard, the fact that the organisation is already working to set up a debt collection mechanism indicates that strategies are being put in place toward the sustainability of the organisation before problems identified in other countries arise in Hungary.

Table 7.13 summarises the duration of scaling-up and adaptation (implementation) of SMart in Hungary.

7.3.3 Take Away Points from the Implementation and Possible Future Developments

7.3.3.1 Scaling-Up Factor Analysis

As was the case for Austria and Spain, the statistical data gathered from Hungarian surveys is a way to throw light on lessons learned during the scaling-up of SMarthu (see Table 7.14). It is worth mentioning that this research covers only 18 months from the time of official founding of SMarthu, corroborating with the research timeframe. Moreover, the number of Hungarian surveys returned was low, despite a 60% response rate (three out of five). The limited human resource in the organisation (one full-time person and two additional part-time and external collaborators) made it challenging to find respondents from all the categories, namely board

Table 7.14 Factors of the scaling-up process in Hungary (N = 3)

Scaling-up factor	*Minimum*	*Maximum*	*Mean*	*Standard deviation*
Commitment of individuals driving the scaling process	5.75	6.25	5.95	0.26
Competence of the management	7.00	7.00	7.00	0.00
Full or partial replicability of the operational model	4.75	4.83	4.80	0.05
Ability to meet social demands	6.00	6.17	6.11	0.09
Ability to obtain necessary resources	5.42	5.58	5.50	0.08
Potential effectiveness of scaling social impact in partnership	5.88	6.00	5.95	0.07
Adaptability	4.57	4.86	4.71	0.14

members. This explains the narrow variation in responses as expressed by very low standard deviation scores.

Despite the methodological caveat, the analysis suggests that the competence of management obtained the absolute highest rating (7), also the highest compared to the other two countries, Austria and Spain, which were 2.54 and 2.7 points, respectively. Such results might point to the fact that two of the three surveys were answered by the person in charge of managing the scaling-up process, likely introducing a bias in terms of objectivity towards the action of the management.

The perception that SMarthu has addressed a specific social need comes in second place (6.11), consistent with the other two countries. The lowest ratings were given to two factors that are somewhat related (factor 7 – adaptability – with 4.71 points; and factor 3 – full or partial replicability of the operational model – with 4.8 points). This is consistent with the limited range of services that SMarthu has been able to implement by December 2015, which speaks of the limitations encountered in adapting the core SMart model. In comparison to the other two countries (see Annex), it is worth noting how Hungary attained the highest rates across all scaling-up factors, except for factor 3 (full or partial replicability of the operational model). Upon questioning the Hungarian key informant on this front, she stated that if the survey had been done following the introduction of the guarantee fund in November 2015, the scores would have been higher for factor 7 as well as for the ability to meet social demands (factor 4) and the full or partial replicability of the operational model (factor 3).

7.3.3.2 Lessons Learned and Prospects

The efforts put into in terms of promoting SMarthu and raising the awareness of key stakeholders have been phenomenal. Indeed, the number of institutional partners (including nine art and general higher education institutions), professional associations and cultural hubs is impressive. Their information sessions are held both in-house, usually with a monthly (group) or weekly (one-to-one) periodicity, but also at creative hubs in Budapest twice a month.

Lastly, 'Freelancer Fridays' are held monthly as networking and training event, while 'Creative Mornings' offer a unique lecture series for creative and cultural workers. Both are open and free to participants.

In terms of the documentation to track the scaling-up and adaptation process, SMarthu falls behind in terms of the depth of information provided. In this sense, tracking its development was more challenging than in the case of Spain or Austria. Therefore, monitoring has been completed via informal conversations and meetings.

Four action points worth following up were identified to ensure a correct evolution from the early stages of scaling-up to a solid consolidation:

1. The incorporation of workers with a freelance status into the services of SMarthu. While the focus is on providing the core SMarthu services to creative and cultural workers without a concrete labour status, self-employed professionals constitute a major portion of the workforce in the creative and cultural field in Hungary, so their voice should be heard as well.[11]
2. The diversification of financial sources, since most of the funds to cover the operating costs came from SMartbe. This represents a limitation insofar as local resources should be mobilised, ideally not only those stemming from the market. However, the Hungarian cultural sector (in general) is not prone to searching for external sources, since financial support is undergoing drastic changes and independent funding is undergoing restructuration.
3. The incremental development of additional services offered to members as a way of increasing membership and quality of services but also contributing to the financial sustainability of SMarthu. There is currently no similar organisation to SMarthu in Hungary, so it is important to leverage its advantageous position and scale up in terms of services as quickly as possible (the deadline for achieving the break-even point is the next two years).
4. The participation of members in the formal governance of the organisation (setting up a committed board of directors and a participative general assembly) in addition to the surveys and face-to-face discussions described below to ensure a horizontal decision-making structure.

That the membership base is still small makes it an ideal test-bed to experiment with participatory methodologies. In other words, the focus on communication could eventually translate into a weakness if it does not result in real participation from SMarthu members given the social innovator profile it is promoting for itself in the effort of contributing to the future of culture and the arts in Hungary.

Notes

1 IGFT was founded in 1989 as an advocacy and network of theatre and dance professionals. It included over 1,600 freelance theatre and dance professionals as well as other members supporting independent theatre.

2 In addition to a series of meetings and presentations, a survey on the sector was released in the fall of 2012.

3 In 2016, a plan was realised to have one full-time (a general manager for project development) and two half-time workers (an executive manager and advisor and an advisor for developing the SMartAdmin service).

4 None of these proposals were funded, but the proposal was to be submitted again in 2017 led either by SMartat or SMartde.

5 The main organisation supporting the creation of SMartib was Aura, a social interest cooperative by Andalusian law (*S. Coop. And. de interés social*) but also a temporary employment agency (*Empresa de Trabajo Temporal* in Spanish). This combination constitutes a real exception, both in the world of temporary employment agencies and in the world of non-profit maximization cooperatives pursuing a general social interest which is not limited to a specific group. As explained by Barco (2007), Aura is a cooperative with a long history of brokerage in the labour market in a region where success cases in the area do not abound. The core business of Aura is offering temporary staffing to businesses and companies but it does so with a radical novelty: as a cooperative, it offers workers not simply a contract but the possibility of becoming members of the cooperative, even if membership can be limited to the period of employment. From the activity and target group standpoint, Aura has specialised in the hospitality industry and 60% of workers come from groups at risk of exclusion. The publicly funded ESEmpleo project (www.cepes-andalucia.es/blog-esempleo) aimed to implement in Andalusia methods and knowledge derived from European experience of creating and promoting stable and quality employment through forms of social economy, with in order to apply to active employment policies in the region. The exchange study visit involved in this project was the seed of SMartib.

6 In Spain, the transfer of competences from cooperatives to the autonomous communities is regulated by the 1978 Constitution (Art. 129.2). In Andalusia, these exclusive competences related to cooperatives are regulated by Art. 58.1.4° of the 1981 Statute of Autonomy. Currently, Law 2/1999 of 31 March on Andalusian Cooperatives regulates the sector in addition to a state law to regulate the sector (Law 27/1999 of 16 July on Spanish Cooperatives). Generally, they offer frameworks concerning the legal recognition of cooperatives. The Ministry of Employment and Security maintains a list of existing autonomous laws in Spain, available here: www.empleo.gob.es/es/sec_trabajo/autonomos/economia-soc/EconomiaSocial/legislacion/leyesCoopAutonomicas.htm.

7 CAEs' projects have a success rate of 70% and they number about 100 across the country.

8 The structure partners of SMartIb were *Actúa Servicios S. Coop. And.*, *Aura ETT S. Coop. And. de interés social; Fondation SMartBe* and *Asociación para los trabajadores de la cultura SMartIb*.

9 The new cooperative will be called 'Self-Employed', which will operate exactly as SMartIb, except for the Social Security regime to which workers will contribute.

10 A special scheme allows self-employed artists to convert invoiced amounts into short-term employments, called 'creative mandate contracts'. This modality can

only be used when there is no relationship of subordination with the client and for artistic tasks only.

11 In preparing for this incorporation, training workshops were organized in 2016 presenting SMarthu as an 'umbrella service' for both SMarthu users and self-employed professionals, plus freelancers were included in feedback surveys as well.

References

Barco, S. (2007) From Corporativism to Soft-Governance Models: The Role of Internationalisation and Innovation – Andalusian Case Study. Available at http://socialeconomyhub.ca/sites/socialeconomyhub.ca/files/CIREIC/Papers/C4%20-%20Serrano.pdf [accessed 14 May 2015].

Weber, C., Kröger, A. and Demirtas, C. (2016) Scaling Social Impact in Europe: Quantitative Analysis of National and Transnational Scaling Strategies of 358 Social Enterprises, Berlin: Bertelsmann Stiftung. Available at www.bertelsmann-stiftung.de/fileadmin/files/userupload/BST_ScalingSocialImpactInEurope_final.pdf [accessed 12 December 2016].

Weber, C., Kröger, A. and Lambrich, K. (2012) Scaling Social Enterprises: A Theoretically Grounded Framework, Frontiers of Entrepreneurship Research, Vol. 32 (19), article 3. Available at http://digitalknowledge.babson.edu/fer/vol32/iss19/3 [accessed 12 December 2016].

8 Culture and the Arts as Companions in the Unpostponable Transitions

8.1 Cultural and Artistic Social Enterprises as Emerging Institutions Contributing to Unpostponable Transitions

The core of this research was to study whether a specific subset of social enterprises active in the field of culture and the arts – which I named 'Cultural and Artistic Social Enterprises' (CASE) – could contribute to the multiple and intricate 'unpostponable transitions' (economic, environmental, political, and cultural) at play in society, particularly by emerging as a new type of institution capable of providing transversal solutions.

Specifically, I asked: how could *social enterprises* in the field of *culture* bring about *social transformation*, thereby contributing to *social innovation*, and what is the supportive or hindering role of the larger *social and solidarity economy* in such process? To do so, I focused on how CASE emerges in a concrete setting and replicates across geographical borders. The selected case study was SMarteu, an informal European network of social enterprises active in the field of culture with presence in eight countries. The abovementioned overarching question was developed into research objectives and hypotheses, resulting in the following conclusions.

8.1.1 *Enlarging the Understanding of Social Transformation in Culture to Connect Transitions*

By exploring the meaning of *social transformation* in culture and the arts, in connection to a social enterprise active in those very fields, I wished to cast some light on the relationship between social enterprises (as concrete institutional arrangements that emerged in a specific socioeconomic context) and the effects its socioeconomic activity and interaction with other actors had in terms of social transformation.

It has been noted that the model analysed in this research, SMart, constitutes a special example of CASE insofar as it does not engage in the creation, mediation or circulation of cultural or artistic products as a primary goal, but rather focuses on clearing the administrative and legal barriers for creators so they can engage fully in their endeavour of producing,

DOI: 10.4324/9781003342144-9

mediating and diffusing culture. SMart also commissions artistic works for its members, participates in multi-level social dialogue discussions and plays an advocacy role for culture at the European and international levels. It does so by showing a strong commitment to the principles of the social and solidarity economy, formally recognising itself as a social enterprise.

Despite the indirect contribution of the SMart model to culture, it was selected in order to question and test new ways of creating social value for culture and society overall in the context of transitioning towards sustainability. As stated by one of the key informants at SMart, who originally came from the cultural sector, the main change in the field of culture in the next decade will be the increased precariousness of workers and public budgets, which has been accentuated by the Covid-19 pandemic (ENCC, 2021).

It is at this intersection that the meaning of social transformation in the field of culture emerges – to ensure that the best possible conditions are present for the development of culture and the arts. These 'best possible conditions' ought to be understood in an enlarged sense: they refer to actors, knowledge, practices and functions present in all spheres of social action, undergoing an unpostponable transition towards sustainability. Therefore, social transformation in the cultural sphere (namely creation, mediation and diffusion of cultural goods and services) will be fulfilled by working towards the improvement not only of cultural actors, knowledge, practices and functions but also of other social and environmental spheres undergoing transitions (such as the economy, energy, gender equality, health, food sovereignty, etc.). A precondition for this to happen would be the acknowledgement and internalisation of these other actors, knowledge, practices and functions as their own.

This acknowledgement and internalisation require, first, to establish connections among actors, knowledge, practices and functions from the various spheres. Networking in formal and informal settings and participation in transversal platforms (such as those devoted to the social and solidarity economy) are crucial to ensure this cross-fertilisation. Once acknowledgement is present, actors within the cultural sphere internalise them in two ways: firstly, by incorporating the needs and demands of other transition spheres (the economy, energy, gender equality, health, food sovereignty, etc.) via cultural production, mediation and consumption (e.g. theatrical productions, photographic exhibitions, film documentaries and literature); secondly, by appropriating the set of values and principles from those transition areas. It is worth noting that these values and principles have the potential of eventually transforming into concrete behaviours that contribute to achieving these transitions. Moreover, these two ways also represent powerful channels to raise awareness about the actors, knowledge, practices and functions of other spheres of transition among audiences and supporters of culture.

The logic beneath this understanding of social transformation is that there is reciprocity on the part of other spheres. The most pressing task in this mutual recognition and absorption of central demands and defining traits of the various spheres is making visible the needs, actors and demands that have remained silent across spheres. Some CASEs proudly show their 'social' dimension, or they use it strategically: for instance, professional theatres that work with special audiences or performing scripts addressing specific topics related to transitions can choose to promote some of these goals or continue acting as a regular theatre company. Therefore, the transformative potential of CASE stems from their potential to connect culture with other spheres of transition so that each other's values permeate the other spheres and become internalised by their agents.

What stems from this reflection is that combining artistic excellence with social value creation covers a broad spectrum: they are not mutually exclusive or antagonistic, but the main goal should be clearly stated. Even a CASE focused on artistic excellence (a photography centre, for instance) could bring about social transformation via participatory governance (e.g. co-creating programmes, inclusion of representatives from other CASEs, cultural institutions and extended audience groups in decision-making processes and organs). CASEs could also do so directly via their cultural output(s), that is, via photographic exhibitions, concerts, publications, training and so on, focusing on themes that incorporate other transition spheres' demands and concerns as well as indirectly by inviting actors from other transition spheres into their decision-making processes and organs. Moreover, a CASE could modify its organisational behaviour and set an example for its audiences (e.g. connecting with the energy transition by recycling paper tickets, saving energy with special lighting and joining a renewable energy cooperative).

Additionally, CASEs need to effectively deploy various levels of governance in order to achieve the kind of social transformation described above. Although the idea of multi-level governance is usually applicable to the public sector, this research has shown that it should also be applicable to social enterprises that have a presence at different geographic levels (local, regional and national). In addition, innovative approaches to the governance of CASEs continue to emerge, such as the rhizomatic model (Tanurovska-Kjulavkovski, 2021)

8.1.2 Social Innovation to Empower Communities through Social Creativity

By focusing on the evolution and various meanings of *social innovation* in the specific CASEs (particularly reflected in social transformation), my goal was to contribute to the understanding of the differences in meaning of social innovation in the context of culture and the arts.

Addressing this very issue is the object of the section titled 'The Complex Relationship between Culture and Social Transformation' and more specifically the sub-section titled '(Social) Innovation and Culture: Revealing the Implicit Connection' in Chapter 3. As stated therein, the relationship between culture and creativity and innovation is a complex one. Not only are these concepts polysemic, referring to multiple (even possibly contradictory) practices and values, but multiple logics are at work within each of them. In order to really understand these relationships, it is necessary to go beyond the commonplace idea that 'creativity and culture are the locus of social innovation' and clarify the connection. Creativity should be turned into 'social creativity' so as to go beyond the individual and empower communities to do things differently for the common good. Disentangling the relationship between, on the one hand, creativity and culture and, on the other hand, social innovation would also require a cultural artefact or expression to be considered innovative to make evident the artistic category to which it belongs, as well as its contexts and goals beyond the artistic, if any.

Going beyond the economisation of cultural practices when discussing innovation in culture (i.e. that an innovation needs a market) requires a social appropriation and dissemination of socially creative 'novelties'. Only when this is done can we speak of social innovation in culture. The question of how to ensure this collective intelligence is capitalised for the common good remains the central challenge.

8.1.3 A Solid Social and Solidarity Economy to Unleash the Transformative Potential of CASE

The main concerns of the research gathered in this volume were to review the connection between *social enterprise* and the larger *social and solidarity economy*, with a view to reframing the way in which they relate to each other, as well as to explore the contributions they can make to social transformation in the field of culture and the arts.

The research covered in this volume shows that socioeconomic, cultural and political contexts determine the emergence and institutionalisation processes of social enterprises across countries. In Spain, the social economy has reached a high level of corporatism among organisations and of collaboration with public administrations. The solidarity economy may lag behind but is rapidly confirming its presence in the public sphere and at the sub-national public administration levels. This consolidated institutionalisation of the social economy could nevertheless result in a reduced space for experimenting with new institutional forms, since they are clearly delimited by law. However, groups of citizens are setting up more and more initiatives framed within the social and solidarity economy with a socially transformative goal, many of them aiming to contribute to the transitions in whatever way possible.

Austria has some similarities to the Spanish situation, in the sense that the social economy is well developed and its level of corporatism is quite high as well. However, the evolution in Austria has been more focused on large service providers connected to the third sector, on the one hand, and the large cooperative movement, on the other. Therefore, the space left for transformative social enterprises to emerge in a context dominated by the institutional forms of social economy is currently quite reduced, although some vibrant examples exist (e.g. community-driven social enterprises working with refugees).

Hungary represents a radically different situation due to the legacy of communism and a political regime that is increasingly oppressive towards citizen-led initiatives, thus limiting the potential of the social and solidarity economy. Moreover, social entrepreneurship was introduced and financed in the country via international funders and organisations, so the model at work is less grassroots-oriented and more business- and entrepreneurs-oriented. The fact that grassroots initiatives could be interpreted as social activism by an unsympathetic government represents a risk in terms of sustainability for the organisations.

The variation in terms of levels of institutionalisation, corporatism and recognition of the social and solidarity economy across countries poses the question for social enterprises of how to move from a *corporatist* ecosystem based on having key political allies, achieving recognition from governments and political players and setting up formal coalitions and umbrella organisations (known as 'corporatism' or 'neo-corporatism') to a *post-corporatist* ecosystem where all actors show organisational empathy, behave unselfishly to achieve commonly defined goals and accept pluralism (Barco, 2011, 2016). Particularly in the case of SMart, the fact of counting on an international platform is tantamount to having the network and the message ready to mobilise decision-makers from within the sector as well as from outside.

The research conducted for this volume confirmed two important hypotheses.[1] Firstly, the higher the recognition by public administration of the social and solidarity economy (and the higher the tradition of collaboration among them), the higher the possibility of creating a supportive environment for adapting the CASE model of SMart. However, this possibility does not imply that a lack of recognition and/or collaboration with the public sector translates into the impossibility of adapting the operating model of SMart. The hypothesis refers to the creation of a supportive environment, which includes regulations, financial tools, fiscal incentives, capacity building and so on.

The main part of this hypothesis relates to two issues: namely, the level of recognition of the social and solidarity economy by the public administration, and the existence of a tradition of collaboration between them. The first issue is captured in the research through a qualitative analysis (contextual factor analysis in each of the three countries), while the second issue is captured by two survey factors, especially two specific items.[2]

Since in the countries analysed there is a tradition of collaboration between the public sector and the social and solidarity economy, SMart country offices show higher success rates (in terms of the speed of scaling-up, number of members and turnover size). The case of Spain confirms this hypothesis: the longstanding collaboration with the regional government (of the region where the headquarters of SMartib are located) resulted in a specific cooperative law that removed all barriers that SMartib could have run into. In addition to this ad hoc regulation, SMartib has been able to negotiate special fiscal treatment and some subsidies in the form of reduction in social security charges at the national level. Moreover, SMartib has been successful at entering into negotiations with local councils about agreements for specific professional communities (e.g. local band musicians) or the use of empty public spaces. In the case of SMartat, the main collaboration with public administrations takes the form of the Office of the Federal Chancellor (BKA) at the national level, while there is no significant cooperation between SMarthu and any level of the Hungarian government. In light of this analysis, it is worth noting that recognition by and collaboration with public administrations is desirable in the sense that it can remove barriers for development and speed up the consolidation process, but it is not essential for the development and success of the initiative.

The second hypothesis confirmed during this research is that the higher the level of collaboration of social enterprises as members of the social and solidarity economy, the higher the possibility of replicating a successful CASE model. This can be tested on the basis of the new dimension added to the Weber model which is named 'connection to the social economy' and distributed among four of the seven factors via five specific items (1.8; 2.11 and 2.12; 5.12; and 6.8).[3] This hypothesis relates to how the level of mutual recognition of social enterprises (and the wider social and solidarity economy context) in a given country can influence the scaling-up process. The initially predicted result was confirmed insofar as the scores assigned to the items above reflect that they were perceived to be between relevant and very relevant (item 1.8 = 4.93; 2.11 = 5.83 and 2.12 = 5.89; 5.12 = 4.83 and 6.8 = 5.97). Within factor 2, the ability of managers to position the national SMart within the social economy received the second highest score (5.83), while the highest score within this factor's items was given to the ability to nurture a feeling of membership and pride in belonging to the social economy (5.89).

The main point from the in-depth country analysis of relevance to this hypothesis relates to the embeddedness of SMartib in the social and solidarity economy and its recognition, not so much by other social enterprises but mostly by the public sector, as we have seen for the previous hypothesis. While this is not conclusive, it indicates a potentially interesting area for further inquiry.

8.1.4 The Relevance of Participatory Governance for Replication

By extracting lessons from the experience of SMart and analysing them, particularly relating to the geographic expansion in 2006, I aimed at questioning the innovation paradigm applied to culture and the arts and how new spaces for social transformation emerge in the cultural field. I wished to make a modest contribution to the field of social enterprise research, especially concerning organisational and business model scaling-up and replication as well as diffusion of social enterprise models.

Governance being so central to CASE, it seemed relevant to raise the question of whether it could be a factor coming into play in the cross-border replication of SMart. In this context, a third hypothesis was formulated. I suggested that the more participative the governance of CASE, the higher the possibility of adapting the social innovation to a specific context. The assumption was that if the national SMart office had implemented a participative governance model through the inclusion of various stakeholders, including internal ones, the success would be more solid. With regard to the statistical data, participative governance was captured by the survey through item 2.7, referring to the capacity of the management to mobilise the internal governance system (how members, staff, volunteers and directors participate in decision-making). Although the rating obtained was high (5.13), it does not represent enough ground to accept the hypothesis, so further study is required. Moreover, although participatory governance is in place in SMartat and SMartib through the regular cooperative organs (mainly the Council and the General Assembly), they do not actively engage external stakeholders in these organs. As for SMarthu, the current participatory management mechanism in place is impacting some of the strategies that aim to implement a horizontal structure. In any case, the conclusion is that a participatory governance system that goes beyond the mechanisms established by law does not represent a priority to any of the three SMart offices, something that can be understood in a context of resource scarcity and uncertainty that requires identifying and prioritising actions and objectives. While consolidating the core services and enlarging the membership base constitute a priority in phases 1 and 2, more effort needs to be invested in developing a participatory governance model in phase 3.

A fourth hypothesis was enunciated to suggest that two critical factors determine the success of a given social innovation in culture: the type of political regime and the adaptation to the local context. This hypothesis includes two elements that could be tracked from the in-depth contextual analysis: whether or not the political regime in a country (including at subnational levels) supports culture and recognises its value in a more cohesive and vibrant society, and the level of adaptation promoted by critical actors (in other words the initiators). I measured the level of involvement of critical local actors in the adaptation of SMart to the local context through factors

5 (ability to obtain necessary resources, not only financial, with a score of 4.74 over 7) and 6 (effectiveness of scaling up if done in partnership with others, with a rating of 4.87 over 7). In all, conclusions drawn from the qualitative analysis did not necessarily allow to accept this hypothesis, since none of the regimes particularly supported (politically) the transformative value of culture brought forward by CASE beyond the discourse level or beyond random initiatives. Although enough ground is lacking to accept the fourth hypothesis as conclusive, further statistical correlations among the items should be done. Notwithstanding this result, further research on the correlation between the type of political regime and the level of involvement of key local actors would cast light on how macro-contextual factors affect the predisposition to participate in the creation of CASE.

8.2 Lessons Learned about SMart

8.2.1 Lessons Learned from the Expansion Process and the Country Cases

This section includes an overview of the seven scaling-up factors included in the Weber model (Weber et al., 2012, 2016). From the factor analysis conducted, it seems that all seven are relevant with ratings over 4 on a scale of 1–7 and two of them being over 5 (the factors are discussed in detail in Chapter 5). Further research will be necessary to fine-tune the factors in terms of adapting them even more to the field of culture, but for now, the questionnaires yielded the following priorities in terms of factors that were perceived to be the most important:

1. *Ability to meet social demands* (factor 4 = 5.44): The ability to scale up the SMart model to create social value for cultural workers is rated as the most important factor in the replication and adaptation of SMart, confirming the true social enterprise dimension of SMart. Indeed, it is by being able to meet such needs that the transnational scaling-up of the model will be deemed successful.
2. *Competence of the management* (factor 2 = 5.23): Indeed, the role of leaders in ensuring that the social mission is well adapted in their countries is crucial. Beyond the technical dimension of the day-to-day operations, they are required to be able to think strategically, particularly in terms of allocation of (not only financial) resources. Despite the disparity in backgrounds and histories, all three case studies showed a reaction towards a strongly felt need that requires addressing (as confirmed by all interlocutors of this research and by the analysis on factor 4). In the Spanish case, the host cooperative (*Aura*) had been at work for over a decade, albeit not within the field of culture and the arts, whereas the Austrian and Hungarian teams had never worked in the provision of administrative and legal services to artists and creative workers.

3. *Effectiveness of scaling social impact through partnership* (factor 6 = 4.87): The relevance of teaming up and finding synergies with other local partners during the adaptation process was confirmed through the higher scores assigned to this factor. The most telling thing from the country case studies is the wide array of actors included in these alliances from within culture and the arts (e.g. professional organisations), related fields (e.g. research and education) and even organisations (mostly from the social and solidarity economy) committed to the transition movement (e.g. sustainable transition cooperatives hosting a local branch of SMartib).
4. *Ability to obtain necessary resources* (factor 5 = 4.74): The ability to generate the resources needed across the various phases of scaling-up constitutes a central and recurrent issue, but it comes fourth in the list of factors. A possible explanation for this could be the fact that SMartbe provides a financial safety net insofar as no major resource is required to access it. Thanks to this safety net, countries need to only focus on the previous three factors during the initial phases of the adaptation process.
5. *Commitment of individuals driving the scaling process* (factor 1 = 4.63): The level of personal involvement and commitment of the initiators appears fifth, but it is worth noting that sharp differences existed between internal and external key actors. While the commitment of internal actors (founders, SMartbe, management, staff and volunteers) was deemed as highly relevant for a successful scaling-up process, that of external actors (both local and national governments and social and solidarity organisations) was not.
6. *Full or partial replicability of the operational model* (factor 3 = 4.43): This factor addresses whether the SMart operational model is easy to replicate fully in other countries or whether intensive adaptation is needed. Therefore, this factor is connected to the factor 7 (adaptability of the model) and, therefore, it is not surprising that they appear together in the rating of factors, despite the fact that they do not appear subsequently in the survey.
7. *Adaptability of the model* (factor 7 = 4.12): The fact that this factor comes in last in terms of relevance could suggest that survey respondents have become very aware of the obstacles preventing this adaptability from happening fully, such as the delayed implementation of the online tool for the Activity Management core service. In all, since SMart hinges on processes related to one of the most country-specific areas (labour regulations and administration), it is understandable that its adaptability cannot be rated as easy and smooth. However, the fact that the need for this service is clearly present across countries (see the first factor listed above) bears witness to their willingness to devote as many resources as necessary (including time) to overcome the obstacles in model adaptability.

8.2.2 Issues and Challenges with the Scaling-Up Process

With its membership base doubling each year, increasing retrenchment of the welfare state through public funding cuts and the marketisation of culture and the lack of a unified voice to represent the cultural sector in Europe, SMart faces numerous challenges at different levels.

The main source of legitimacy in the scaling-up process is the translation function. Therefore, it is of paramount importance to understand the tasks that need to be performed in each phase of scaling-up as well as the relevance of various intermediaries and how they can hinder or support this intermediation.

From an organisational standpoint, process homogenisation across countries is required, as well as a certain level of coordinated 'organisational engineering' to achieve the turn towards the cooperative model. Paradoxically, ensuring the development of the associative culture (i.e. democratic member participation), while preserving an efficient performance, is vital in order to maintain the level of social value creation and fulfil the transformative potential SMart set out to achieve. An additional challenge that emerges from the research is the need to strike a balance between the essential proximity dimension of the services and the experience provided by SMart and its continuous technological innovation.

Related to the legitimacy of SMartbe, vis-à-vis its members and stakeholders, transnational scaling-up generates several internal tensions around how an organisation created to respond to specific local demands can absorb such burdensome requirements in terms of financial and human resources. A transitioning period already began in 2014 with the arrival of a new management, and several actions were put in place, mainly in 2015 and 2016, to address these internal tensions. Some of the concrete results included a restructuring of the EU expansion department, the re-evaluation of the amounts to be lent to country offices and renegotiation of the terms, and the increased formalisation of relationship via the signing of agreements.

The data included in the documents and the background information provided by each national partner could be used in an organic way to inform the process and provide some insights about the scaling-up efforts in the country. Particularly the comparative dimension would be very interesting as it will allow gauging what works best and identifying possible trends at the European level. In terms of supporting the European platform, gathering these experiences transversally could provide an added value both to SMart member countries but also for positioning SMarteu as a valid cultural representative across Europe. The *Bureau d'études* of SMartbe could certainly be an ideal starting point, but the goal would rather be to create an observatory or think tank to exchange, discuss and propose alternatives. Two concrete examples in terms of shareable experiences are the 'SMartib Interim' targeting freelancers, which was planned by the end of 2016, and the replication in Austria of SMartde's mobility portal to speed up the idea of pan-European mobility.

In terms of lessons learned, it emerged that some of the profiles within the leadership team should be adapted to the present challenges facing the organisation. Indeed, there is an impression that, in addition to establishing connections with mostly cultural networks, resources could also be tapped by making alliance with social and solidarity economy networks and by encouraging country offices to develop closer links with such networks and entities.

Slowing down further country developments seems to be not only a feeling widely shared, but also a reasonable strategy in view of the countries already involved and the very different stages of development completed. Concentrating on fewer cases could also allow SMarteu to contribute to identifying key funding sources and key partners, instead of financing the national initiatives directly.

In terms of lessons learned from the country cases, it appeared that the categories of actors leading the adaptation process in these countries were radically different. For instance, the leading person in Hungary had a connection with the creative industries there, while the Austrian team stemmed from the field of performing arts. In this sense, the Spanish case represented the only multi-category-actor-led process with two sub-groups within the initial leading team (one related to the cooperative sector having no previous connection to culture, and the other to dance and theatre). In all, the single-category-actor approach is deemed inappropriate both by country representatives and representatives of SMartbe, who all tend to value the diversity of actors within the core team.

However, other contingencies may alter the value of a diverse team of initiators such as key funding to launch the adaptation process, availability and willingness on the part of potentially promising actors, or a good contact in countries considered highly relevant for learning about the adaptation of the model to new contexts (such as new member states). In this sense, as in many other aspects of the transnational scaling-up process of SMart across Europe, there is no determinism ingrained in any strategy. Rather, each new constraint that appears causes new constellations of actors to form (or existing ones to reorganise themselves) which, in turn, has a direct impact on the direction of the organisation.

Delayed payments is a major issue for countries offering the guarantee fund (or advance salary payments), namely Austria and Spain (Hungary only began offering it in November 2015). This includes not only late payments in the current accounting year (e.g. 13% of invoices issues by SMartat suffered delay in payment in 2014, and 25% in 2015) but also a high percentage of invoices remaining overdue even several years after being issued (as an example, as of October 2016, 74% of invoices issued in 2014 and 2015 remained unpaid[4]). Since the beginning, national offices have been encouraged to put a system of invoice recovery in place, but the focus on implementing the core services and developing the membership base has placed invoice recovery in a rather secondary position within organisations. Particularly, Annex 3 of the scaling-up documents (monitoring and evaluation) looks into whether the system allows for assessing the invoiced amounts, the amounts paid and the amounts due, issuing and paying dates of the invoices and amounts due by invoice, order and user. When the amount of these overdue invoices becomes high within a given year, it affects liquidity, which can be solved in the form of liquidity injections from SMartbe. While this may endanger the 'mother' social enterprise if abused, it represents for now the only alternative apart from private banking methods (e.g. loans). Eventually, the strengthening of a European platform could result in the setting up of a European social fund to address liquidity problems across member countries.

8.3 Recommendations for Practitioners and Policymakers

By formulating specific recommendations for practitioners and their representative organisations as well as for policymakers at various levels, I aim to contribute modestly to bridging the divide between social innovation practice and research, bringing to light a more emancipatory approach to social innovation and emphasising the complex dimensions of science in its embeddedness with societies' challenges.

8.3.1 Recommendations for Practitioners

8.3.1.1 Recommendations for SMart

SMartbe expanded to nine European countries during 2013–2015, presenting new challenges on top of the organisational challenges existing already in such a vibrant and innovative entity. The way in which this process was implemented depended greatly on personal contacts and trust, with not so much resting on a predefined geographic expansion strategy (although an implementation plan was designed and tools were created to help partners along the way). While personal connections and trust certainly help communication, they are also complex to standardise, which has traditionally been the norm across scaling-up practices. SMartbe became the facilitator of a project dispersed among a myriad of national and regional cultures in a very short time, a daunting the task that required ensuring the timely implementation of crucial services and processes as well as their monitoring. Other challenges were avoiding mission drifts and safeguarding the SMart values across the nine countries, while guaranteeing as much as possible the participatory governance.

A certain transversal issue, however, was of paramount importance for the managers of SMartbe: the *affectio societatis*. Under French law, this term captures a key trait of any organisation: the feeling of belonging of its members. It can also be extended to a project. Thus, the core issue for the transnational expansion of SMart was how to ensure that a member in any of the countries felt a sense of belonging to the European project.

The way in which SMart has expanded has a lot to do with empowering the local level organisation; recognising its idiosyncrasies, dynamics, and relevant actors; promoting participation, exchange, and constructive criticism among members; allowing for failure; and giving itself enough time to make all of the above happen. In parallel, a vision for SMarteu has been in the making since 2010. When this research began it was clear that, while the initial impetus for crafting a vision for SMarteu had to come from SMartbe, it was only by decentralising its development process that the *affectio societatis* could take hold within the country members of the European platform. The objective was to combine the achievement of practical autonomy at the national level with a shared vision and solid sense of belonging across countries. Partners' meetings were considered the best way to do it, and so a total of seven partners' meetings were held until December 2015, plus two preparatory ones in 2010 and 2011 (see Table 5.4 for the full list with dates and places).

The way this European connection was presented in the 2015 Activity report highlighted the relevance of the SMart brand and the benefit to all members in the form of mobility across the continent,[5] plus the possibility of organised lobbying at various political levels and a wider support in the culture awareness-raising campaigns.

Based on this research, recommendations for the implementation of SMarteu include:

1. To encourage entrepreneurship within the SMarteu community by supporting a non-competitive 'leader' approach where one country can teach others about areas the former excels in, for example, the mobility portal led by Germany and Austria, or the development of a new law in Andalusia, Spain.
2. To create a 'knowledge hub' by identifying and featuring good practices, articulating stories and lessons learned and creating a working platform where this knowledge can be exchanged. In practical terms, it would be an internal 'Agora'. Even though language may represent a barrier, the knowledge generated should find its way to reach the entire platform.
3. To strengthen workflows and streamline processes. Teams seem to cluster based on cultural and administrative affinities (Austria–Germany or Belgium–France), so bilateral meetings and working teams could be taken as a way to generate new knowledge. The existing online communication tool for SMart staff members is mainly used as a 'reminder board' where events and meeting schedules are posted. In this sense, a tool that allows sharing of locally generated knowledge with other national members of SMarteu would be of much use.

4. Communication experts are needed to support the translation and facilitation role that SMartbe plays within the field of culture and the arts from a social economy perspective. Communication entails not only ensuring that messages are exchanged but understanding the process of engagement of a nascent community that shares needs and interests. The strategy should recognise the multi-stakeholder nature of SMart, which includes reaching out to opinion leaders and 'multiplicators', political as well as institutional partners, and the general public. Regarding the tone of the communication, it should be more persuasive than informative so as to provide sense for a new, transformative project. Moreover, it should focus on stressing the ability to address a shared need rather than on the specific services.
5. To engage in a collective reflection and joint strategic planning process at the European level. The 'SMart in progress' initiative conducted in Belgium in 2015 constitutes an excellent departing point.
6. The inclusion of representatives from the social and solidarity economy into the team of initiators. As shown by the survey data, the highest score (5.89 points out of 7) was received by item 12 within factor 2 – 'the ability to nurture a feeling of membership and pride in belonging to the social economy'. In terms of lessons learned for SMarteu, such ratings indicate that management teams composed of social and solidarity economy leaders have the greatest chance of success in leading scaling-up attempts in new countries.
7. Departing from the success factors proposed here and in other relevant literature, SMart should also engage in a reflection about which factors seem to be more relevant for each country. Eventually, there should be more in-depth research that looks at additional factors, analyses all countries, and considers latest developments so as to monitor the transnational scaling-up process. Most importantly, sharing the process with all the national partners would be crucial for reflecting upon past actions and improving future ones.
8. To continue reducing the complexity of the core operational model by making sure that processes are increasingly standardised and mechanised. This will enable local teams to enhance the proximity aspect of the services and identify key partners and supporters to ensure medium- and long-term sustainability.

8.3.2 Recommendations for Representatives and Umbrella Organisations

The two European communities relevant to this research (that of cultural actors and that of social and solidarity actors) usually have a presence in the EU policy ecosystem that can be considered as a strategy perceived to achieve more prominence in the political agenda. However, some recent studies suggest that this many not be the case (Zimmer and Hoemke, 2016). Or at least, such studies suggest this is not the only or most efficient strategy to raise the political profile of culture and social and solidarity actors.

8.3.2.1 Representatives in the Field of Culture and the Arts

Firstly, SMart clearly marks itself as an agent active in the field of culture, so its association with this diverse sector is explicit in all its communications and actions. All the interviews and focus groups conducted for this research as well as the document reviews confirm its strong association with this sector, crystallising the social mission of SMart. One of the concrete ways whereby this 'belonging' is confirmed is the high level of partnership and involvement in the cultural sector, mostly in Belgium but increasingly in the other SMart countries.

One of the factors analysed in the present study (factor 6, 'Potential effectiveness of scaling up social impact in partnerships') includes three items devoted to the perceived value of collaborating with other organisations (items 6.5 and 6.6) and with other supra-national networks (item 6.7). The ratings obtained by these items (6.5, 6.6 and 6.7) were relatively high in comparison to others (6.13, 6.30, and 5.77), with the highest rated being item 6.6 – the importance of belonging to networks for the social value creation of SMart. This was repeatedly sensed in the discussions held with SMart representatives during the course of this research.

In this context, a natural recommendation for umbrella organisations in the field of culture (in countries where SMart has a presence) is to establish alliances based on a win-win basis. Indeed, there seems to be a predisposition on the part of SMart country offices to team up with arts and cultural institutions not only in areas of production and diffusion but also education, training and research. For example, Austria and Spain had established partnerships with a large spectrum of actors (see Chapter 6).

Additionally, culture is core to the sustainability question under the label 'fourth pillar of sustainable development', closely interlinked with environmental responsibility, economic development and social equity (Hawkes, 2006). This view has been taken up by the UCLG Committee on Culture and its World Secretariat in its Agenda 21. Although this represents a promising way to put culture at the heart of multi-dimensional transitions that societies are undergoing, it focuses on the economic value of culture. There is a risk associated with putting the emphasis on the 'economic justifiers' for the arts community in general, especially for artists and artistic organisations, 'since serving the state as an economic generator is very different from taking risks artistically, or being innovative and creative generally' (Caust, 2003: 54).

8.3.2.1 Representatives in the Social and Solidarity Economy

The social economy has a relatively solid presence in the EU policy ecosystem as well as in some of the countries where SMart has a presence. However, the focus has a corporatist focus, that is, it relies on traditional social economy families (mainly associations, cooperatives, mutual societies and foundations). While this helps enlarge attention towards the agenda of the social economy, the startling variety and plurality of initiatives seeking the common good and led by citizens that exist around Europe may confuse some interlocutors. In this sense, the main recommendation for European national organisations would be to embrace the true plurality the term social and solidarity economy captures, in the sense defended by Hannah Arendt – to escape homogeneity and conformity and enable real transformative action (Arendt, 1958). Plurality is at the core of human action, but the sophism 'freedom is an individual dimension and therefore plurality reduces the chances to achieve it' has limited its relevance in modern societies.

Secondly, as can be seen from factor 6 in the survey, the teams behind the SMart national scaling-up effort perceive the fact of belonging to supra-national organisations (item 6.7 = 5.77) as very important, particularly to those of the social and solidarity economy (item 6.8 = 5.97). This constitutes a basis for us to encourage social and solidarity economy umbrella organisations to explicitly include culture and the arts as a leading action area and to position themselves more strongly within the cultural political agendas across Europe.

8.3.3 Recommendations for Policymakers

In the face of the commodification of common goods and services (including arts and culture), policies supporting the social and solidarity economy (including social enterprises) preserve and foster governance spaces that are amenable to social innovation (Fraisse, 2013). In general, we confirm the statement that promoting culture and the arts through policymaking within local development strategies may contribute to attuning social cohesion with economic competitiveness, but only if culture is conceived through a broad-based and participatory approach (André et al., 2013). Unfortunately, this is acknowledged to not be the norm since project-based public funding fails to fulfil the duties of care towards both artists and participating communities: this has been 'a moral failure of cultural policy' (Belfiore, 2022).

In this sense, it is worth noting that the key role of traditional institutions wishing to support social innovation, social enterprises and culture is to revise their assumptions about their own role and level of control of the processes that may produce virtuous circles of social transformation. It is no longer about (the large institutions) planning alone and implementing, but about facilitating, co-creating, ensuring the validity of the process in an ongoing dialogue with citizens and provisioning to ensure that artists and communities are covered. Public administrations should explore putting into practice multi-stakeholder dynamics and particularly encouraging the initiative of driven individuals among their public servants. In this regard, it is important to recognise the limited but 'transformative power' of pilot experiences.

Despite the inability of state-level bureaucracies to accommodate direct civil action, current social conditions have radically transformed and there exist some promising experiences both at national and local levels. A relevant experience was the first nationwide participatory budgeting project announced in Portugal in December 2016. Participatory budgeting, allowing citizens to have a direct say on how public budgets are to be spent, already counts 1,500 programmes worldwide, but the Portuguese were its pioneers.[6] Although seriously underfinanced (with only 3 million euros), it constitutes a 'transformative pilot' that can make strides in restoring trust and contact between citizens and their government and setting an example for other national, regional and local administrations.

This connects with the fact that 'social innovation needs a committed citizen and a civil and civic professionalism' (Montagut, 2014: 11). Indeed, the role of professions and the *ethos* of these professionals remain underestimated in the support of social innovations. This is particularly the case in the area of public services, given its mandate to ensure social well-being, but also in other areas of government directly involved in policymaking for social, economic, environmental, and cultural transitions. External citizen groups should be able to connect to good professionals within the body of public servants who already exist, but who usually keep a low profile. However, they have the potential of connecting with other colleagues beyond departmental or policy area silos to ally with citizens and to put their expertise and experience to work for equity, the public good, and social justice. In this context, public servant professional communities could embrace their transformative potential to co-create with their fellow citizens and other actors of society, particularly the traditional private sector and other social actors such as labour unions.[7]

8.3.3.1 Recommendations to Policymakers at the EU Level

While there are numerous initiatives to show that a road to real social transformation is the collaboration between the public and organised citizens, this collaboration seems to be too far removed when it takes place in Brussels. A recent report from a large European project (studying the impact of the third sector) has criticised the extent to which third sector organisations based in Brussels might help national and local third sector organisations to overcome the barriers and hurdles restricting their potentials (Zimmer and Hoemke, 2016). The findings are not optimistic insofar as the existing third sector policy community operating in Brussels has limited influence. Moreover, there is an under-representation of organisations from Eastern and Southern Europe compared with 'large member states' such as France, Germany or the UK.

At the level of social enterprises and the social and solidarity economy, several examples have been discussed in this research as having made great strides in the social and political agenda (e.g. the Social Economy Action Plan and the Social Business Initiative). However, much of this support and joint work is being done outside formal documents and under the leadership of specific civil servants, who act as *de facto intrapreneurs* within the European Commission. The high staff rotation and lack of transversal support joins the problem of coordinated action among Directorates General (employment and social affairs, research, growth and industry, enlargement, etc.); together they constitute major obstacles to transversal and coordinated action around social enterprises, causing a void in terms of sustained policies supporting the development of social enterprise, repetitious and even contradictory policy initiatives, and wasting of resources. The Commission in place when the research described in this book ended (December 2015) did not have any clear policy work plan or strategy aimed at the social and solidarity economy and/or social enterprises. However, this changed shortly after with the creation of an informal inter-departmental working group on the topic and in December 2021 with the approval of the European Social Economy Action Plan.

The three recommendations to the European Commission based on the findings of this research are:

1. To facilitate existing (temporary) networks of the social and solidarity economy to find ways to make themselves sustainable over time (and having a transparent governance), with the initial support of the European Commission. Some of these temporary networks are very efficient and committed, as a result of EU-funded projects such as the Cultural Base social platform, the Social Innovation Community, and the Third Sector Impact project. However, once project funding stops, so does the human capital gathered, causing an avoidable loss for the communities involved.
2. To ensure the representation of smaller countries and new member states in any kind of discussion, consultation, or action. This needs to be ensured at two levels: on the one hand, externally via a balanced geographic representation of actors and, on the other hand, internally with the Commission's own civil servants, including representatives from as many member states as possible.
3. To nurture committed civil servants, helping them connect with their fellows via formal or informal channels set up for such purpose. In this context, fora for public servants interested in social innovation could be created where they can exchange their experiences and views and eventually begin joint planning. In addition, they could incorporate some civil society representatives as observers.

8.3.3.2 Recommendations for Local Policymakers

The connection between social innovation and the local level has been already discussed, but there are few policies that directly address the creation of conditions for a supportive local environment. I will focus here on recommendations for policies targeting the social and solidarity economy and culture.

Some authors have emphasised that local social and solidarity policies could be considered an innovation in itself insofar as social enterprises and other social and solidarity organisations represent a pole of resistance towards 'new public management' methods that increase competition rules, austerity measures, involvement of citizens, transparency in all stages of the process, etc. (Fraisse, 2013). In addition to ensuring the participation of social and solidarity organisations, local authorities have a direct impact on the sustainability of these organisations (e.g. via public procurement and the inclusion of social or environmental clauses) as well as play a role in terms of connecting with research actors and universities (Nogales Muriel and Nyssens, 2023).

While European institutions are traditionally blamed for distancing from regular citizens, the risk of localism in policymaking for social innovation remains high (Fraisse, 2013). Localism represents, for the most part, an added value in terms of embeddedness of practices and nearness of the social value created, but it can also restrict the potential of social innovations not only geographically but also in terms of negative behaviours stemming from isomorphic pressures.

The abovementioned three recommendations aimed at European policymakers could also apply to local policymakers insofar as they guarantee sustainability of stakeholders' networks and platforms, high levels of stakeholders' representation, coordinated and transversal policy work and internal innovation from civil servants. An additional set of recommendations can be advanced, targeting local policymakers:

1. To join and actively participate in trans-territorial networks. By doing so, they are likely to mobilise diverse resources beyond the immediate geographic area. An example of this type of network is the 'Network of Municipalities for the Social and Solidarity Economy' launched in October 2015 in Catalonia that brought together 20 municipalities representing 40% of the Catalonian population.
2. To allow for shared and participatory testing of experiments on local governance (e.g. 'new municipalism' in cities) in addition to participating in multi-level governance systems that reinforce vertical governance across geographic levels. Some experiences at the municipal level (e.g. the city of Barcelona) have a solid track record, which reduces the risks involved and offers a good practice for others to test.

Certainly, support from the EU in implementing some of these recommendations would contribute to their chances of success.

8.4 Chartering Promising Research Avenues

8.4.1 Promising Conceptual and Theoretical Avenues

During the course of the present research, several concepts and theories have been identified that could strengthen further research in the area of CASE and social transformation.

The first one is the relevance of career paths in order to understand the evolution and current profiles of professionals within culture and creative industries. The motto 'activities turn dreams into reality, and artistic ambitions into professional career paths' (SMartbe, 2012) attaches a completely new sense to project-based work by combining it with a collective initiative. Research should be done on different career stages, motivations, barriers and conditions under which the subjectivities of current cultural and creative professionals are built.

A related issue has to do with the adaptive strategies that cultural and creative workers develop to cope with the resulting situation. Launching a CASE (collectively or individually) could be one of them, but not the only one.

With regard to governance, the multi-stakeholder logic has an impact on the way in which CASE is governed as well as on how the services and delivery processes are conceptualised and assessed. Little is known about how CASE strikes a balance in terms of representation and participation of various types of stakeholders. Indeed, although the terms 'customer' and 'beneficiary' are used in third sector literature (Pestoff, 2001), it remains unclear how responsibility and ownership are shared. In the specific case of SMart, cooperativism is the form most conducive for SMart's transformational vision. Indeed, even in countries that established SMart as different from a cooperative (Belgium, France and Austria), there is a clear move towards cooperativisation of the model. Such a move will bring about a set of issues and organisational challenges related to governance, participation and communication with stakeholders. An explicit challenge is directly connected to the issue of growth, which is at the heart of transformation which makes SMart to thrive, and its conflictual relationship with real participation in the organisation. The key challenge seems to be how to implement commitments, arrangements and initiatives that ensure sustainability and equality in socioeconomic development, not only of SMart members but ultimately of society overall.

A positive development stemming from this move towards cooperativisation is the potential of this new breed of social enterprises (gathered under the umbrella of social cooperatives) to support the general interest and truly democratic governance. Moreover, this new breed of social enterprises is generally committed to various transitions. By combining this new type of cooperativism with a powerful virtual platform active in nine countries, SMart can tackle the transformative power of 'platform cooperativism'.[8] Platform cooperativism 'is a term that describes technological, cultural, political, and social changes' and constitutes a mindset (Scholz, 2016: 14). Alternatives do not abound and are certainly not inevitable, so they have to be nurtured and supported by actors committed to a fair and sustainable transition. In addition to the potential of transforming into a 'criticism platform' that embodies resistance and imagines alternatives, SMart already represents a positive alternative that includes a new take on property, governance and solidarity issues (Scholz, 2016). Analysing the scaling-up process of SMart is tracing the development of its potential to be a real socioeconomic alternative rooted in platform cooperativism. Therefore, SMart as a concrete example of CASE offers two basic pillars that are basic for any transformation: a concrete platform for producing innovative services while generating participation. Indeed, as shown by the country studies and the evolution of SMartbe, the call-for-action and articulating discourse in the field of culture and the arts and the anti-precariousness and empowering practices counterbalance the gradual dispossession of rights that creative and cultural workers are enduring.

The deep local roots of SMart and its international presence give it a unique place in which to facilitate the social interactions of its members and stakeholders. In this context, crystallising the mission of SMart is tantamount to turning it into a 'critical network' – both at the European and national/local levels – that is able to articulate 'grammars of democracy' that counterbalance the mainstream technocratic and economic regime (Calle, 2013: 157). As the present research has illustrated, doing so requires not only that key contacts are established, that strategic partnerships are nurtured, that operational models are implemented and that bottom-up dynamics are brought into the process, but also ensuring that the sociopolitical contexts do not suffocate such an endeavour.

Having said that, critical readings of social enterprises will have to incorporate the internal tensions caused by their being located between the public and the private in the sense of Arendt and Habermas (Laville and Amaro, 2016; Eynaud et al., 2019). Indeed, they are private organisations dealing with the public interest and setting up public policy agendas, but they are privately managed, often with scarce resources (Eschweiler and Hulgård, 2011; Laville and Salmon, 2015; Laville and Amaro, 2016). Doing so may mean questioning the entrepreneurship mantra or the very fact that an enterprise is the best locus for collective actions. Moreover, some social enterprises are not focused on their transformative potential, but rather their market orientation and development, which has caused

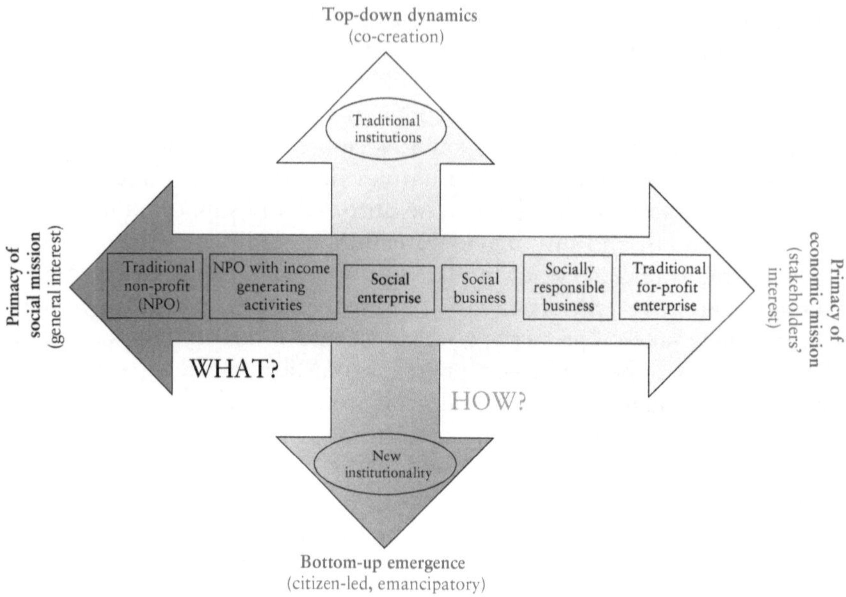

Figure 8.1 Social transformation in social enterprises: combining the *what* and the *how.*

a 'market of social well-being' to emerge (Montagut, 2014). Describing existing transformative social enterprises and advancing proposals for possible new breeds of social enterprises are beyond the scope of this work, but they will have to strike two critical balances: on the one hand, the social goal and the market orientation and, on the other hand, the combination of top-down and bottom-up dynamics at play within the organisation. In this sense, Figure 8.1 represents a crucial modification of Figure 2.1 (reproduced here again as Figure 8.2) that captures the unique, transversal dynamic that connects social enterprises to its social transformation potential: the way in which it delivers its social mission, WHAT. The HOW dimension, therefore, cuts across the 'social enterprise' square at the centre of the horizontal two-pointed arrow.[9]

In this context, terms traditionally associated with the self-organisation of citizens towards a common course of action, such as civil society, may not be appropriate in the context of emergent systems and new institutionality. Indeed, the study of its evolution over time has resulted in a rating of sorts across countries that is evaluated on the basis of a more or less organised and performing civil society. As already noted, invisibilised systems and actors exist, and a way to bring them to light is by defining and securing institutional spaces where they can participate. Moreover, the term civil

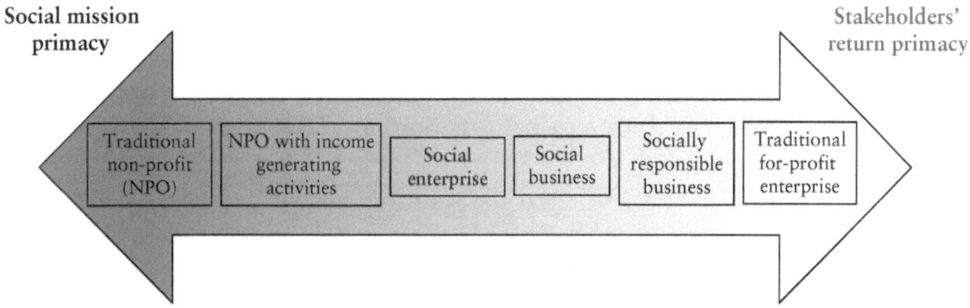

Figure 8.2 Social entrepreneurial activity spectrum.
Source: Adapted from Nicholls (2008) and Alter (2004).

society has traditionally been connected to specific institutions, and a discussion on their action may be limited to the institutional perimeter set within the boundaries of those organisations. In this sense, social enterprises stay once more at another crossroad, only this time at traditional and new institutionality. The vertical double-pointed arrow in Figure 8.1 captures this additional crossroad.

8.4.2 Critical Contribution of the New Institutionality Approach

Once Kerlin's macro-contextual factor analysis was conducted, several limitations were observed in relation to the ability of the model to capture tensions produced by newcomer agents and evolving patterns in such a changing environment. With a view to address this gap, the 'nueva institucionalidad' (new institutionality) approach developed by European and Latin American researchers offers an interesting framework to continue the inquiry. This approach has been nurtured mainly from urban experiences of trying to reconfigure institutional arrangements to face existing challenges at a time of the weakening of existing institutions. Contributions in this area have also looked at how public policies have been created to accompany such developments (Subirats and García, 2015).

New institutionality has already been operationalised and tested. One such model has been proposed by Laville and Sainsaulieu (1997), who set out to capture some of the tensions emerging from the oscillations between originality and normalisation within institutions. Indeed, focusing on the example of associations, they claim that the institutional dimension should be studied from a historical perspective capturing the moment of their creation, but also throughout their life course as they clash with the institutional order first and then engage in normalisation processes, which ultimately produce different effects from the originally intented ones.[10] Their analytical framework indeed aims to capture the 'retroactive loops between project and organisations ... by making explicit the iterations between the dynamics of the project and the organisation that carries it and which can result in its redirection or redefinition' (Laville and Sainsaulieu, 1997: 382). It includes five areas of study: (1) the identification of institutional logics; (2) the relationships within the institutional framework; (3) the breakdown of various resources; (4) the socio-professional analysis and (5) the strategic and cultural analysis.

Although SMart is not a formal association across the three countries studied (Austria, Hungary and Spain), the model fits the overall vision of SMart at the European level and is driven by the collective action of members who mobilise resources and aim at a larger project of political transformation.

8.4.3 Methodological Proposals for Future Research

8.4.3.1 Scaling-Up Model for Social Enterprises

By applying the only available model to measure the critical factors influencing the transnational scaling-up process of social enterprises (Weber et al., 2012, 2016), this study had its focus on the field of culture and the arts. The model was first proposed in 2012 and revised a few years later with a number of factors and prerequisites added. As already pointed out, the timing of the publication of its revision did not allow to incorporate it into the survey used in this research. However, the original model seemed to capture effectively the various dimensions and critical factors at play in the scaling-up process, as shown by the ratings of the factors, lesser number of items left unanswered and that the open-ended responses (in the form of 'comments') did not ask for major additions to the items covered under each factor. Analysing the revisions of the model *a posteriori*, it would have been interesting to refine some of the items, particularly those used to capture the interaction between the source organisation and the national partner, and those used to capture the cost of transfer costs, both internal and external (Weber et al., 2016).

When it comes to the external key stakeholders and interlocutors for the adaptation or implementation of the model, it is usually the public sector actors (local and national administrations). The importance of public administrators is explicit from factors 1 (items 1.6 and 1.7) and 5 (items 5.10 and 5.11); in both cases, the perceptions of survey respondents suggest a low involvement in, and support of, the project by public policymakers.

An interesting element still missing from the model is the traditional for-profit sector, whose ability to leverage some of the strengths associated with its market orientation have been tapped for decades now via partnerships and joint actions, both with cultural and social and solidarity actors. Such interaction is likely to be more intensive in countries with a longstanding philanthropic tradition and high levels of entrepreneurial culture or where the presence of the welfare state is reduced or non-existent.

The main contribution of the current research to strengthening the Weber model relates to highlighting the importance of connections within the social and solidarity economy. The focus was on this aspect and not on allegiance and connections to culture and the arts, due to the fact that the latter is most prominent in all communication and the positioning of SMart in each country. However, allegiance to the social and solidarity economy may pass unnoticed to potential and current users who are not familiar with the term. In this context, a stronger effort (beyond simple recognition of the selected legal form, usually a cooperative) has to be made to bring that trait forward and to connect the new organisation to the larger social and solidarity economy ecosystem. As we have seen, in those cases where the connection is explicit and stressed (e.g. Spain), the adaptation and membership increase rate seems to be faster. While this dimension could be captured in part by success factor 6 in the revised model, 'Legitimacy and reputation', Weber interprets this factor in terms of 'prizes, honours and media presence' (Weber et al., 2016: 21), and not in the way it was understood in this research.

8.4.3.2 Operationalising the New Institutionality Approach

As we have seen above, the analytical framework of the new institutionality approach includes five areas, each focusing on five distinct dimensions: the institutional logics, the relationships with the institutional framework, the various resources mobilised, the socio-professional situation and the strategic and cultural context in place. The research framework included recommended methods for gathering data in each of these areas.

The institutional logics (Laville and Sainsaulieu, 1997) include two different types of logics, namely *instituting logics* (those that stem from the domestic realm, are based on help or self-help, incorporate the aim of mobilising people and are multilateral) and *isomorphic logics* (those in which the actors set up the idea of the private or public realm as a reference for developing the institution). From a methodological perspective, the authors emphasise the danger of trusting only one view instead of comparing and confronting a multiplicity of discourses. This analysis has a merit of bringing to the surface the interaction between possible logics and whether there exists an opposition, juxtaposition or compromise among them.

Table 8.1 summarises the analytical framework of the new institutionality approach by including its four main areas and the central points to focus on.

Table 8.1 Analytical framework

Area number and title	*Main research foci*
1. Identifying the institutional logics at play (domestic, help, self-help, movement or multilateral)	Convergence (or divergence) between the discourses and implemented processes around • Shared conceptions: solidarity, social action, representations of relationship between public and private spaces, representations of production • Characteristic processes: relationship with the creators/staff, relationship between creators/staff and membership modalities • Defining traits: risks and opportunities
2. Relationships with the institutional framework	Resistance and redistribution of resources (production, co-production) Explicit strategies to impact the institutional framework (deconstruction, construction, co-construction)
3. Determining the various resources mobilised	Nature and origin of the resources (market vs. non-market and within the latter, stemming from reciprocity or redistribution)[a] Relationship with the public sector Political and social embeddedness
4. Understanding the socio-professional context	Structural configuration (simple, professional-bureaucratic, divisioned and adhocratic)
5. Conducting a strategic and cultural analysis	Sources of power (i.e. resources to tap in order to manage an incertitude or risk) mediating the relationships among groups (understanding, tacit collusion, negotiation and conflicting opposition) Unifying values, socialisation practices

a Since the original framework proposed by Laville applies to associations, the reciprocity logic is more common than in the case of SMart, which, following the author's own terminology, could be referred to as a 'quasi-enterprise'. This means that volunteers, for instance, are not formally foreseen even though de facto members of SMart could act as volunteers in organising events and initiatives to engage new members.

8.5 Closing Thoughts: On the Rough Sailing of Transitioning towards Dignity and Sustainability for All

As I hope to have illustrated in this volume, a vision of change stemming from emerging systems led by citizens is being articulated, and SMart has the potential of becoming one. Ultimately, what is a stake is the ability to overcome the current dissatisfaction with inequality in existing institutions, mainly political and economic systems, as well as transform them into emerging systems for change (Garcés, 2017).

The role of culture and the arts is so vital that no transition towards sustainability will be plausible without a profound transformation in how we relate to them and reposition them in the value system of our societies

(Nogales Muriel, 2019). Leaving aside the justification of culture by its weight in national GDP, it can be stated that the cultural and artistic sectors lack an articulated and solid discourse supporting their unique contribution to the European society. An 'emotional' starting point could be to ask ourselves: what would we be and do *without* culture? When a theatre or cinema house closes down, when a group of young dancers abandon their dream of setting up their company or when an artist cannot perform her work because of a lack of support structures or opportunity costs to do so would be too much to bear. It is not only the economy that suffers; it is mostly society and its potential to imagine alternatives that shrinks.

Despite the warning that 'the transition will not be smooth sailing', the alternative to not riding the boat may be too expensive for humankind and the planet to bear. The current challenge is to empower diverse economies and move from extractive capital to generative capital, and citizens have proven their potential as creators of this capital based on different dynamics. The mask of scarce resources under which capitalism used to hide has fallen: 'In the old days, capitalism was a way of allocating resources in a situation of scarcity, but now it is an engineered scarcity system' (Bauwens and de Grave, 2016: 306; Gibson-Graham and Dombroski, 2020; Kelly, 2012).

It is my hope that this research will generate some solar and wind impulse for our boat to continue the rough sailing towards the transitions still ahead of all of us.

Notes

1 Originally, the research included five research questions to be tackled through associated hypotheses that were to be rejected or accepted based on Yin's recommendations for exploratory and descriptive research (see the Annex).
2 They are item 1.6 in factor 1 (the local government is highly committed with the implementation of SMartX and 1.7 The national public administration is highly committed with the implementation of SMartX) and item 5.10 in factor 5 (SMartX has been fully successful at getting government agencies and officials to create laws, rules, and regulations that support our efforts and 5.11 SMartX has been able to raise our cause to a higher place on the political agenda).
3 The items that captured this construct are item 1.8 in factor 1 (Other social economy organisations are highly committed with the implementation of SMartX); items 2.11 and 2.12 in factor 2 (Our management is perfectly able to position SMartX within the social economy and Our management perfectly develops a feeling of membership and pride in belonging to the social economy, respectively); item 5.12 in factor 5 (SMartX has been fully successful at getting other social economy actors to provide support for our efforts) and item 6.8 in factor 6 (The connection to social economy federations and peer organisations always benefits the implementation process).
4 This situation was effectively addressed with the arrival of a new financial director in 2018.

5 Efforts in this direction have increased since the end of this research. For instance, SMart participated in the Task Force Cross-Border Culture (T4CBC) which, since 2014, has been working on the creation of a cultural network of border regions. Cultural actors from European border regions are working to reinforce their capacity to work with each other at the cross-border and European levels. SMart was one of the co-organisers of the conference on cultural actors' mobility in 2015 in Belgium.

6 https://apolitical.co/portugal-world-first-participatory-budget/.

7 A global example of the mobilisation and articulation of this potential is the online network of public servants at POLITICAL (www.politi cal.com), gathering professionals 'who care about effective government'. This platform constitutes an effective way to not only bring to light 'what is working' to make governments both closer to its citizens and more effective, but to raise the profile of internal innovators in terms of potential for change and innovation.

8 Scholz (2016) specifically refers to 'democratic ownership models for the internet' when talking about platform cooperativism. However, the 10 principles of platform cooperativism that he proposed can be considered as an update to the original cooperative principles, namely (1) shared ownership; (2) decent pay and income security; (3) transparency and data portability; (4) appreciation and acknowledgement; (5) co-determined work; (6) a protective legal framework; (7) portable worker protections and benefits; (8) protection against arbitrary behaviour; (9) rejection of excessive workplace surveillance and (10) the right to log off.

9 A third arrow (FOR WHOM?) could have been added to capture the multi-stakeholder dimension described in the literature (Nyssens, 2006). However, I preferred to focus on the less-developed 'HOW' dimension in contrast to the well-known 'WHAT' aspect of social enterprises.

10 They distinguish three in the case of associations: recuperation, banalisation and instrumentalisation.

References

André, I., Abreu, A. and Carmo, A. (2013) Social Innovation through the Arts in Rural Areas: The Case of Montemor-o-Novo. In F. Moulaert, D. MacCallum, A. Mehmood and A. Hamdocuch (eds), *The International Handbook of Social Innovation*, 242–255, Cheltenham: Edgar Elgar.

Arendt, H. (1958) *The Human Condition*, 2nd ed., Chicago: University of Chicago Press.

Barco, S. (2011) *Estudio de casos españoles. Las políticas públicas de Economía Social y el diálogo entre los poderes públicos y la sociedad civil*, Montreal: Chantier de l'économie sociale.

Barco, S. (2016) The Role of the Social Economy as a Partner in Policy Ecosystems, explanatory note for the conference, *Social Economy as a Key Player in Providing Effective Answers to the Current Societal Challenges in the EU and the World*, Bratislava. Available at www.sokio.coop/2016/12/bratislava-on-my-mind [accessed 22 May 2017].

Bauwens, M. and de Grave, A. (2015) The Transition Will Not Be Smooth Sailing. In *Build the City: Perspectives on Commons and Culture*, 305–321. Brussels: European Cultural Foundation.

Belfiore, E. (2022) Who Cares? At What Price? The Hidden Costs of Socially Engaged Arts Labour and the Moral Failure of Cultural Policy, *European Journal of Cultural Studies*, Vol. 25 (1), pp. 61–78.

Calle, A. (2013) *La transición inaplazable. Salir de la crisis desde los nuevos sujetos políticos*, Barcelona: Icaria.

Caust, J. (2003) Putting the 'Art' Back into Arts Policy Making: How Arts Policy Has Been 'Captured' by the Economists and the Marketers, *International Journal of Cultural Policy*, Vol. 9 (1), pp. 51–63.

Eschweiler, J. and Hulgård, L. (2012) Social Innovation and Deliberative Democracy, Working Paper No. 12/04, Liege: EMES International Research Network. Available at www.emes.net/site/wp-content/uploads/EMES-WP-12-04_Eschweiler-Hulgard_Final.pdf [accessed 2 September 2015].

European Network of Cultural Centres (2021) *Invisible Damage: Cultural Centres across Europe Warn against Severe Long-Term Effects on the Foundations of Socio-cultural Work*, Brussels: ENCC. Available at https://encc.eu/sites/default/files/2021-09/encc_report_invisible_damage.pdf [accessed 10 January 2022].

Eynaud, P., Laville, J. L., Dos Santos, L. L., Banerjee, S., Hulgård, H. and Avelino, F. (eds) (2019) *Theory of Social Enterprise and Pluralism: Social Movements, Solidarity Economy, and Global South*, London: Routledge.

Fraisse, L. (2013) The Social and Solidarity-Based Economy as a New Field of Public Action: A Policy and Method for Promoting Social Innovation. In F. Moulaert, D. MacCallum, A. Mehmood and A. Hamdouch (eds), *The International Handbook of Social Innovation*, 361–371, Cheltenham: Edward Elgar Publishing.

Garcés, M. (2017) *Nueva ilustración radical* (*New Radical Illustration*), Madrid: Anagrama.

Gibson-Graham, J. K. and Dombroski, K. (2020) *The Handbook of Diverse Economies*, Cheltenham: Edward Elgar Publishing.

Hawkes, J. (2006) The Fourth Pillar of Sustainability: Culture's Essential Role in Public Planning – Summary. Available at http://culturaldevelopment.net/downloads/FourthPillarSummary.pdf [accessed 27 June 2015].

Kelly, M. (2012) *Owning Our Future: The Emerging Ownership Revolution*, Oakland, CA: Berrett-Koehler Publishers.

Laville, J. L. and Amaro, R. (2016) Social Innovation in Europe: What Relation with Solidarity Economy? Towards a Plural European Vision of Social Innovation. Available at www.socioeco.org/bdf_fiche-document-4518_en.html [accessed 6 December 2016].

Laville, J. L. and Eynaud, P. (2019) A Cross-Disciplinary and International Perspective about Social Enterprise. In P. Eynaud, J. L. Laville, L. L. Dos Santos, S. Banerjee, H. Hulgård, and F. Avelino (eds), *Theory of Social Enterprise and Pluralism: Social Movements, Solidarity Economy, and Global South*, 44–66, London: Routledge.

Laville, J. L. and Sainsaulieu, R. (1997) *L'association. Sociologie et économie*, Paris: Desclée de Brouwer.

Laville, J. L. and Salmon, A. (2015) *Associations et action publique*, Paris: Desclée de Brouwer.

Montagut, T. (2014) De la innovación a la Innovacion Social, *Documentación Social*, Vol. 174, pp. 15–30.

Nogales Muriel, R. (2019) Comunes y nuevas institucionalidades en el arte y la cultura: ¿hacia una soberanía y democracia cultural? (The Commons and News Institutionality in the Arts and Culture: Towards a Cultural Sovereignty and Democracy?), RIESISE, *Revista Iberoamericana de Economía Solidaria e Innovación Socioecológica*, Vol. 2, pp. 77–102.

Nogales Muriel, R. and Nyssens, M. (2023) Empowering Knowledge and Training in Higher Education to Leverage Social Economy Action on Societal Challenges. In G. Krlev, G. Pasi, D. Wruk and M. Bernhard (eds), *Social Economy in Science: Transforming the Economy & Making Society More Resilient*, Oxford: Oxford University Press (forthcoming).

Nyssens, M. (ed.) (2006) *Social Enterprise: At the Crossroads of Market, Public Policies and Civil Society*, London: Routledge.

Scholz, T. (2016) *Platform Cooperativism, Challenging the Corporate Sharing Economy*, New York: Rosa Luxembug Foundation. Available at www.rosalux-nyc.org/platform-cooperativism-2 [accessed 3 February 2017].

SMartbe (2012) *Developing Your Artistic Projects. The Example of SMartbe Activities*, Brussels: SMartbe.

Subirats, J. and García, A. (eds) (2015) *Innovación social y políticas urbanas en España. Experiencias significativas en las grandes ciudades*, Barcelona: Icaria editorial.

Tanurovska-Kjulavkovski, B. (2021) *Modelling Cultural and Art Institutions*, Brussels: Peter Lang Verlag.

Weber, C., Kröger, A. and Demirtas, C. (2016) *Scaling Social Impact in Europe: Quantitative Analysis of National and Transnational Scaling Strategies of 358 Social Enterprises*, Berlin: Bertelsmann Stiftung. Available at www.bertelsmann-stiftung.de/fileadmin/files/user_upload/BST_ScalingSocialImpactInEurope_final.pdf [accessed 12 December 2016].

Weber, C., Kröger, A. and Lambrich, K. (2012) Scaling Social Enterprises: A Theoretically Grounded Framework, *Frontiers of Entrepreneurship Research*, Vol. 32 (19), article 3. Available at http://digitalknowledge.babson.edu/fer/vol32/iss19/3 [accessed 12 December 2016].

Zimmer, A. and Hoemke, P. (2016) Riders on the Storm, Working Paper No. 11. Available at http://thirdsectorimpact.eu/site/assets/uploads/documentations/tsi-working-paper-no-11-riders-on-the-storm/TSI-Working-Paper-No-11_Riders-on-the-storm.pdf [accessed 3 January 2017].

Afterword

Having worked and spent many happy hours with Rocío Nogales Muriel and having worked with SMartbe in different contexts in the cooperative world, I am happy to state that Rocío nails all the important stuff in this volume.

To me the readability of the thesis is a huge success. Very often good crime stories are described as being page-turners. This is certainly not a crime story, but still it is a solid piece of investigation. AND it certainly is a page-turner.

Very quickly we are dragged into the drama of how accomplished artists are often in a situation where their beautiful art is made impossible or their job situation precarious because of societal changes.

We got a deep and thorough look at the concepts of social enterprises and social innovation – setting the scene for diving into the SMart solutions. As a reader, you are in capable hands, and you will never feel left alone or in doubt about where the road is leading us.

The cooperative model has been a vehicle for change through more than a century. Its starting point has always been ordinary people's needs for solutions to everyday problems. And it still is. Today when we talk about social innovation, we need to remember – and recognise – that cooperatives have always been doing just that.

One of the most amazing things about the cooperative business model is that it is alive whenever and for whatever problems we must solve – across centuries, across cultures, across borders. It could be said that the model is 'the people's' way of social innovation. And as this volume illustrates, it is very much alive when we need answers to new questions, even in the super complex world of today.

But why do we need research? Is not more than a hundred years of cooperative practice and experience more-than-enough proof for the sustainability and game-changing ability of the model?

In this day and age, it has become imperative that you can document and prove everything. Especially if you want to talk to politicians and government officers about how our business model differs from other corporate forms, or if you want to showcase the sustainability of the model or the potential for change that is incorporated in a model where citizens own and drive businesses, for example, in connection to the green and digital transition, we need proof, we need academic literature. But it has to be research like this where the important things are the *why* and the *how* more than semantic quibbles.

A loud and huge thanks to Rocío for having made this effort – and congratulations on the publication of this important and inspiring work.

Susanne Westhausen
President of Cooperatives Europe and vice-president of the International Cooperative Alliance

Annex

Selection Criteria and Analytical Framework for Country Cases

For the research described in this volume, I used a combination of qualitative and quantitative research designs with emphasis on the former. Indeed, the current research is based on a revelatory case study, focusing on 'understanding the dynamics present within single settings' (Eisenhardt, 1989: 534), with an eye on the depth and novelty of these dynamics.

A.1 Criteria for Country Cases Selection

In order to use the Weber et al. model (2015) for scaling up social enterprises in the various countries, I made a selection of three countries (Austria, Hungary and Spain) out of the nine countries with a presence of SMart (leaving out Belgium, France, Germany, Italy, the Netherlands and Sweden). The country selection was made according to how they ranked in the following six categories:

1. Type of welfare model.
2. Type of model of civil society.
3. Type of model of social enterprise.
4. Variance in terms of the development of social and solidarity economy.
5. Variance in the evolution and shape of the cultural system.
6. New member state status (post original EU-15).

The present research did not produce an in-depth analysis of each of the different models and categorisations deployed within each of these sets of features, although some critical comments have been offered in Chapter 8. The idea was to underline some of the flaws observed during the analytical process in relation to the limitations of the explanatory power of these models and categorisations when dealing with the topic at hand.

A.1.1 Categorisation of Welfare Models

The comparative study and categorisation of welfare state models intensified in the 1980s in order to understand how they came to be and evolved into their current complexity (Flora and Heidenheimer, 1981). Two seminal contributions were considered to develop this first feature ('Categorisation of welfare models'), namely Esping-Andersen's and Ferrera's categorisations of welfare models. Esping-Andersen's initial categorisation into three types (social-democratic/Scandinavian regime, conservative/corporativist/Bismarckian regime and liberal/Beveridge regime) departed from the basic political movements that existed in Europe in the twentieth century. He would further refine his model by including new countries and categories, but was much criticised by other scholars; however, it remains a starting point for the analysis of welfare models (Esping-Andersen, 1990). The majority of countries where SMart is currently present are considered as corporativist regimes in Esping-Andersen's typology. The two countries that are considered as social-democratic (the Netherlands and Sweden) did not answer the survey and thus could not be included in this contextual analysis.

Austria and Germany have traditionally illustrated conservative/corporatist welfare states. In general, they feature social insurance whereby most of the benefits for unemployment or sickness are based on insurance contributions made in advance. Both the contributions made and the benefits received vary according to personal income.[1] In addition, 'the corporatist regimes are also typically shaped by the Church, and hence strongly committed to the preservation of the traditional family. Social insurance typically excludes non-working wives, and family benefits encourage motherhood' and 'the state will only interfere when the family's capacity to service its members is exhausted' (Esping-Andersen, 1990: 27). In Austria this need is fulfilled by strong third sector organisations supported by the state.

Departing from the insufficiency of this categorisation, particularly when analysing Mediterranean countries that had been excluded from the original 18 OECD countries analysis, Maurizio Ferrera (1996) studied health provision in depth to propose a fourth typology, a Mediterranean model, bringing into it Spain, Portugal and Greece.

A.1.2 Categorisation of Models of Civil Society

Salamon and Sokolowski (2002, 2010) identified five different models of civil society development from a social origins approach, which underlines the influence existing institutions exert on the emergence of civil society across the world (Monroe-White et al., 2015). The five models are liberal, welfare partnership, social-democratic, deferred democratisation and traditional. The first three are associated traditionally with advanced economies where the emphasis on the emergence of civil society is put on the welfare state more than on the action of the government. All countries where SMart has a presence, except Hungary, can be considered within this first classification set. Deferred democratisation and traditional civil society refer to countries where the action of the government is seen as critical to the development of their civil societies.

A.1.3 Categorisation of Models of Social Enterprises

Kerlin (2010, 2013) draws on the theory of historical institutionalism to connect civil society, government, market, international aid and social enterprise and to propose a framework that addresses the variety of models of social enterprises around the world. Her MISE framework identifies five types of models, each of them with specific attributes: autonomous mutualism, dependent focused, enmeshed focused, sustainable subsistence and autonomous diverse. Later on, Monroe-White et al. (2015) expanded and refined the geographic coverage of Kerlin's framework, particularly adding the option of 'transitional' for those countries still evolving into one of the five models.

Taking into account these three well-known categorisations (welfare state model, civil society model and social enterprise model), discussed at length in the literature, three countries (Austria, Spain and Hungary) were selected for the contextual analysis because they covered the widest possible combinations of categories included in points 1–6 above. The goal was to have countries as diverse as possible on the basis of those categories in order to have a varied set of cases. This three-country combination is presented in Table A.1, including the various categories that apply.

A.1.4 Variance in Terms of the Development of the Social and Solidarity Economy

As can be seen in the country descriptions, the way in which the notion of social and solidarity economy has emerged and evolved is very different in Austria, Hungary and Spain. While Spain enjoys a conducive environment for the development of organisations within the social and

Table A.1 Representation of three main categorisations in the selected countries

Categorisation	*AT*	*ES*	*HU*
Welfare state (Esping-Andersen, 1990; Ferrera, 1996)	Conservative/ corporatist welfare state	Mediterranean welfare state	Central and Eastern Europe
Civil society (Salamon and Sokolowski, 2010)	Social-democratic	Welfare partnership	Deferred democratisation (transitional)
Social enterprise (Kerlin, 2013; Monroe-White et al., 2015)	Enmeshed focused	Dependent focused	Autonomous mutualism

solidarity economy, the breadth of options is more limited in the case of Austria, due to the more restricted institutional forms and the predominance of traditional cooperatives and state-financed personal service providers. As for Hungary, the current political situation is de facto preventing the development of the social and solidarity economy, with strong control measures and little interaction between the central government and civil society.

A.1.5 Variance in the Evolution and Shape of the Cultural System

The nationally shaped evolution works well for the three countries studied, but it was important to bring together national contexts with different notions of culture and different developmental paths in terms of actors, institutions and practices present in the cultural sphere.

A.1.6 At Least One New Member State

Given the relevance of Central and Eastern European member states in European policymaking, and the weight in terms of populations they represent, they should be included in the analysis. The 10 new member states that joined the EU in 2004 plus two additional ones in 2007 and the last one in 2013 have income levels below the EU average and have greater income disparities at the sub-national level (European Commission, 2004; Sedelmeier, 2015). The only new member state where SMart is currently present is Hungary, although the initial process has already begun in Poland and initial contacts have been established in Estonia. Therefore, Hungary will be included in the country context analysis.

Based on these six criteria, the three selected countries are Austria, Spain and Hungary. An in-depth contextual study was conducted with these countries both at country level and also from the SMart standpoint.

The data obtained from the surveys was used to cast some light on the three countries selected. From a basic descriptive statistical analysis, six countries – Belgium (BE, source country), Austria (AT), Germany (DE), Spain (ES) and Italy (IT) – had 100% response rates (all five stakeholder categories replied), while Hungary (HU) had 60% (three out of five stakeholder categories replied). BE was not analysed in depth because it was the mother organisation where the SMart model originated; therefore, the relevance of the scaling-up factors was not critical for that country. Moreover, it would have represented an outlier in terms of years of operation (active since 1998) and many other values pertaining to the consolidated operating model of SMartbe (as a matter of fact, the survey questions related to the adaptation of the model were often left unanswered in Belgium).

Nevertheless, the survey was run in Belgium to test some of the assumptions underlying the study.

A look at the statistical data suggests that some heterogeneity existed among the three selected countries (Austria, Spain and Hungary). The following observations were made when analysing the data of six countries (excluding Belgium) shown in Table A.2:

- The first one refers to the data pertaining to the minimum and mean values: in almost all of them, Austria ranked the lowest, Spain more centred values, and Hungary extreme high values. For instance, in Hungary, the most important factor is the 'competence of management', which shows as the lowest scoring the highest value possible (7). This implies that the mean will be also 7 and that there is no deviation at all. In the minimum measurement, we observe that Austria has the lowest response (2.13) with reference to 'effectiveness of scaling social impact with others'.
- As for the value capturing the deviation, the situation was inverted: Austria shows the highest variance in terms of the relevance attributed to the various factors, while Hungary shows very little variance in its response (the limited number of responses may have likely influenced the result). Responses from the Spanish team remain again in the middle of the former two.
- The data showed an odd response pattern for Hungary, with very high responses and almost null standard deviation. This can be explained by the fact that in Hungary one respondent category (board member) did not exist, and the two corresponding to manager and founder were de facto merged into one single person. Needless to say, this limited number of respondents could represent a weakness insofar as the responses will be less varied, thus reducing the possibility of obtaining different ratings to the same questions.

According to the statistical analysis, Austria and Spain represented solid cases for further inquiry, but Hungary would have been rejected on grounds of low representation. However, since I did not use statistical variance and representativity as a formal criterion for selection, and since Hungary nicely meets most of the other qualitative criteria, I kept the choice. Having said that, interpretation of the Hungarian survey responses was done carefully to avoid wrong conclusions.

Table A.2 Results of scaling-up factors of all countries involved

Scaling-up factor	*Minimum*						*Maximum*				
	BE *(N=5)*	*AT* *(N=5)*	*DE* *(N=5)*	*ES* *(N=5)*	*HU* *(N=3)*	*IT* *(N=5)*	***BE*** *(N=5)*	*AT* *(N=5)*	*DE* *(N=5)*	*ES* *(N=5)*	*HU* *(N=3)*
Commitment of the individuals driving the scaling-up	3.50	2.00	4.38	3.88	5.75	2.88	5.38	5.00	6.38	5.38	6.25
Competence of the management	4.58	3.00	4.92	3.25	7.00	4.00	6.08	5.50	6.75	5.25	7.00
Entire or partial replicability of the operational model	5.33	2.42	2.67	4.50	4.75	3.75	6.17	4.58	3.92	6.08	4.83
Ability to meet social demands	3.83	3.83	3.67	4.50	6.00	4.67	6.67	6.33	5.83	6.33	6.17
Ability to obtain necessary resources	4.42	3.50	4.25	4.50	5.42	4.42	4.92	5.67	5.33	5.25	5.58
Effectiveness of scaling social impact with others	2.88	2.13	4.63	2.75	5.88	4.25	5.38	5.50	5.50	6.13	6.00
Adaptability	3.71	2.57	3.14	3.71	4.57	3.71	4.00	5.00	3.57	4.86	4.86

A.2 Analytical Framework for the Country Studies

Kerlin (2010, 2013) identifies five major areas that describe the national environment, as follows:

1. National culture, history and values.
2. Type of economy or stage of economic development.
3. Type of government and development of institutions.
4. Type of civil society sector.
5. International relations and influence.

A.2.1 History, Culture and Values

The history of a nation – including its historic events – influences the level of well-being and shape of its citizenry. Historic events also may explain the current socioeconomic situation, so they are crucial for understanding some of the societal challenges in a given country. An example of such influence

	Mean						*Standard deviation*					
IT (N=5)	***BE* (N=5)**	*AT (N =5)*	*DE (N=5)*	*ES (N=5)*	*HU (N=3)*	*IT (N=5)*	***BE* (N=5)**	*AT (N=5)*	*DE (N =5)*	*ES (N=5)*	*HU (N=3)*	*IT (N=5)*
4.63	4.72	3.95	5.10	4.60	5.95	4.07	0.74	1.24	0.77	0.57	0.26	0.72
5.58	5.43	4.46	6.03	4.30	7.00	5.02	0.56	1.03	0.68	0.81	0.00	0.62
5.25	5.86	3.45	3.27	5.43	4.80	4.38	0.46	0.79	0.47	0.59	0.05	0.57
6.17	5.63	5.23	4.97	5.40	6.11	5.50	1.06	0.96	0.89	0.67	0.09	0.54
5.50	4.63	4.66	4.65	4.80	5.50	4.75	0.20	0.78	0.43	0.31	0.08	0.44
5.38	4.72	4.05	4.90	5.07	5.95	4.80	1.07	1.41	0.35	1.37	0.07	0.48
4.57	3.81	3.94	3.31	4.22	4.71	4.29	0.16	0.95	0.19	0.48	0.14	0.33

of history would be a country that has been a physical ground for foreign wars and that has been an object of diplomatic repartitions among leading national powers.

Kerlin identifies two factors that may affect social enterprise: the level of in-group collectivism (vs. individualism) and the level of uncertainty avoidance in terms of what a society values (Kerlin, 2013). If the leverage of resources and generation of new ideas are crucial for economic success, then individualistic societies with a developed sense of personal autonomy would support the generation of variety through individually led innovation, whereas collectivist societies with a developed sense of belonging to communities and society would support the leveraging of resources internally and through external ties (Tiessen, 1997; Kerlin, 2013). As for tolerance to uncertainty, entrepreneurial activity is usually encouraged in risk-prone societies (Amorós and Bosma, 2013). A third interesting element is the social recognition of entrepreneurs and social entrepreneurs and the subsequent creation of role models to inspire new entrepreneurs (Amorós and Bosma, 2013).

Table A.3 Indicators for the analysis of national history, culture and values

Indicator	*Source*	*Influence on the characteristics of the social enterprise approach*
Episodes of a region's recent history	Civil wars, colonisation and independence processes, famines, revolutions	Type of activity and needs of beneficiaries
Values and preferences (individualism-collectivism, avoiding uncertainty in society)	Hofstede's study on national cultures (2001)	Outcome emphasis, legal form, main supportive actors
Characteristics and perceptions on business and social movements	Attention paid in media, recognition	Financial structure, profit distribution, main supportive actors
Societal values about what is desirable	Difficult to observe: deep-rooted assumptions, traditions	Type of activity and needs of beneficiaries

Source: Fisac and Moreno-Romero (2019).

Lastly, the societal values about what is desirable or needed, which serve as the basis for defining social objectives, are crucial for social enterprises, even though their observation and measurement are very complex (Cho, 2006; Fisac and Moreno-Romero, 2015). The issue at stake is legitimation: an action or organisation can be socially legitimate when it is perceived by the population in general that it is socially desirable, proper or appropriate within a socially constructed system of norms, values, beliefs and definitions (Suchman, 1995). This is very much the case of pragmatic cultural and artistic actions, which need to be recognised as being relevant for addressing the urgencies of the issues at stake, regardless of whether there is a long-term political plan behind it (BAVO, 2009). The main indicators for analysing the history, culture and values of a given country are summarised in Table A.3.

A.2.2 Type of Economy or Stage of Economic Development

One of the key factors in the development of social enterprises is the economic context and the level of economic development. Such influences can be both positive and negative depending on the economic development. For instance, a highly economically developed country creates synergies between social enterprises, the public sector and the traditional business sector (positive influence), but it could also suffocate the space for social enterprises by not providing a level-playing field for them to compete with traditional businesses (negative). Social enterprises indeed exist in all countries, regardless of the developmental level reached by their economies.

Table A.4 Indicators for the analysis of economic context

Indicator	*Source*	*Influence on the characteristics of the social enterprise approach*
Stage of economic development	Global Entrepreneurship Monitor (Amorós and Bosma, 2013), diverse macro-economic studies	Type of activity and needs of beneficiaries, financial structure, main supportive actors
Level of equality and societal problems derived from economy	GINI coefficient[a]	Type of activity and needs of beneficiaries
Characteristics of economy (level of competitiveness, productivity, etc.)	The Global Competitiveness Report (Sala-i-Martí et al., 2010)	Main supportive actors, financial structure

Source: Fisac and Moreno-Romero (2015).

[a] This coefficient is one of the most common measures of equality and reflects the statistical dispersion of income distribution of a nation's population. It varies between 1 (complete inequality) and 0 (total equality).

The economic development of a country is related to the development of social enterprises insofar as they can address the precarious situation of the population and the environment in transition or developing economies. In the latter, social enterprises have become developmental strategies for international cooperation to cover the basic needs in a given territory while empowering the citizens affected by societal issues in place. Such developmental focus is at play in developed economies where social enterprises are involved in social services provision and contribute to developing innovative plans to address market or state failures (Austin et al., 2006). Table A.4 summarises the main indicators for analysing the economy and stage of economic development in a given country.

A.2.3 *Type of Government and Development of Institutions*

Traditionally, the type of government in a country determines how institutions emerge and develop. The political regime (democratic, authoritarian, etc.), the level of civil rights and liberties, the presence of rule of law, the level of corruption and so on affect the way in which a society produces institutions in order to function. Kerlin follows a tradition of sociology and political science illustrating how micro- and meso-level institutions are highly influenced by state institutions and policies (Skocpol, 1979; Rueschemeyer et al., 1992). Social enterprises also depend highly on the norms and values the government chooses to institutionalise and those that are left outside (Kerlin, 2013).

Table A.5 Indicators for the analysis of the type of government and institutions

Indicator	*Source*	*Influence on the characteristics of the social enterprise approach*
Characteristics of political system (type of regime, stability)	Direct observation	Main supportive actors
Civil liberties and security, rule of law	Direct observation	Main supportive actors, governance
Implication of the state in citizens' well-being and coverage of social services	Normative texts	Type of activity and needs of beneficiaries, main supportive actors
Ideological influences from government or institutions	Direct observation	Type of activity and needs of beneficiaries, main supportive actors
Quality of public support: subsidies, legal protection, incentives	Normative texts	Financial structure, profit distribution, legal form, main supportive actors

Source: Fisac and Moreno-Romero (2015).

In developed countries, an essential element for social enterprise development is the level of development of their welfare system as they collaborate in various modalities to increase their citizens' well-being. Particularly, the activity of social enterprises is determined by the action of the state via the access to external resources (public procurement, subsidies, access to space, etc.) and the development of favouring or hindering public policies and schemes (Nyssens, 2006). The case of liberal states presents a different scenario for social enterprises that are often left to their own devices, and support for social enterprises may be understood as withdrawal of any action so as to leave them the space to act freely in the marketplace.

Other ways in which public bodies can influence the development of social enterprises include supporting their institutional recognition and visibility, providing support and training, supporting research and studies, supporting the networking at the national and international level, providing financial, human and physical resources and so on. Although less obvious to observe and measure, public bodies clearly have a strong influence on the government, the media and the church, which places them in a unique situation to effect ideological orientations (Salinas and Rubio, 2001).

The elements of the political and institutional contexts that affect social enterprises are summarised Table A.5.

A.2.4 Type of Civil Society Sector

Civil society is usually understood in different senses: a broad sense (a type of society) and an intermediate sense (markets and organisations). It is also

Table A.6 Indicators for the analysis of civil society

Indicator	*Source*	*Influence on the characteristics of the social enterprise approach*
Type of civil society	Salamon and Sokolowski (2010) framework	Main supportive actors, governance
Size of civil society sector (NGO, foundations, etc.)	National statistics	Main supportive actors, type of activity and needs of beneficiaries
Characteristics of civil sector (willingness to volunteer for activities, philanthropic support)	Difficult to observe: deep-rooted assumptions, traditions Direct observation, analysis	Main supportive actors
Presence of an articulated social economy	Level of articulation in representative bodies	

Source: Adapted from Fisac and Moreno-Romero (2015).

used with two restricted meanings: firstly, organisations and social networks of any kind; and secondly, a subset of organisations – typically associations – that convey a moral message connected with the value of civility (Pérez-Díaz, 2014). An important feature of civil society is that it is 'a fragile and superficial order of institutional and cultural conditions and other circumstances in which human agency might have some input' (Pérez-Díaz, 2014).

As we have seen, Salamon has done substantive work on the intermediate and restricted meanings of civil society. Civil society is a broad sector that comprises different types of organisations that can be studied through five elements: workforce size, volunteer share, government support, philanthropic support and expressive share (Salamon, 2010; Salamon and Sokolowski, 2010). According to the different levels of each of these elements, different types of civil society can be identified: liberal, welfare partnership, social-democratic, deferred democratisation and traditional. As explained in Chapter 3, the form an organised civil society takes varies according to regions and traditions, but it is referred to as either social and solidarity economy, non-profit sector or third sector.

Regarding support from external instances, civil society is usually supported by governments at all levels as well as by private sector entities (traditional firms and corporations, umbrella bodies, grant-making foundations, etc.).

Lastly, the presence (or absence) of a strong civil society (in Europe in the form of a robust social and solidarity economy) and the level of its internal organisation (e.g. via the existence of representative bodies or federations) are also critical to the development of social enterprises. Such levels of robustness and internal articulation illustrate the readiness of a society to assume collective responsibility following the ideal of civility as

Table A.7 Indicators for the analysis of international influences

Indicator	*Source*	*Influence on the characteristics of the social enterprise approach*
Existence of shared roots with neighbouring countries	Direct observation and documents	Outcome emphasis, legal form, governance
Characteristics of influences (existence of international umbrella organisations, degree of exchange and networked relationships)	Direct observation and documents	All
Level of international aid received	International statistics	Scope and focus, outcome emphasis, target audiences

Source: Adapted from Fisac and Moreno-Romero (2015).

the commitment to a good society and the ideal of a society of reflective individuals (Fisac and Moreno-Romero, 2015; Pérez-Díaz, 2014). In addition, such a vibrant sector serves to channel citizens' demands and define the amount of civil resources (economic, human, etc.) available for solving social problems (Fisac and Moreno-Romero, 2015).

Some elements related to civil society that most likely influence social enterprises are summarised in Table A.6.

A.2.5 International Relations and Influence

Kerlin's MISE framework considers that the cultural and historical roots of a country and its relation to neighbouring and far-away countries have a direct effect on the emergence and development of social enterprises. They might imply an exchange of practitioners, know-how and experiences, but also of finance, which will have a direct impact on shaping social enterprises. International influence can be channelled through specific representative bodies such as umbrella organisations that act as lobbying and advocacy units abroad.

Some elements related to the international influences that most likely influence social enterprises are summarised in Table A.7.

Note

1 This is known as the 'Bismarckian model' in opposition to the 'Beveridge model' in which all contributions and benefits were to be at a flat rate (Esping-Andersen, 1990). These two models refer to the modalities of access to the health system: the Beveridge model is universalist and seems to have long-term care integrated into healthcare systems, whereas the Bismarckian model has a low degree of

universalism and providers are often of private nature. However, as the socio-economic contexts are drastically changing (ageing populations, public budget cuts, precariousness and shorter professional lives, etc.), since these models and their boundaries were created, there are more often variations and innovations within and across models.

References

Amorós, J. E. and Bosma, N. (2013) *Global Entrepreneurship Monitor 2013 Global Report*, London: Global Entrepreneurship Research Association.

BAVO (2011) Artists, One More Effort To Be Really Political. In L. De Carter (De), R. Roo and K. Vanhaesebrouck (eds), *Art and Activism in the Age of Globalization*, 288–297, Rotterdam: NAi Publishers.

Cho, A. H. (2006) Politics, Values and Social Entrepreneurship: A Critical Appraisal. In J. Mair, J. Robinson and K. Hockerts (eds), *Social Entrepreneurship*, 34–56, London: Palgrave Macmillan.

Esping-Andersen, G. (1990) *Three Worlds of Welfare Capitalism*, Princeton, NJ: Princeton University Press.

European Commission (2004) *Catching-Up, Growth and Convergence of the Ten New Member States: The EU Economy 2004 Review*, Luxembourg: European Commission. Available at http://ec.europa.eu/economy_finance/publications/pages/publication7718_en.pdf [accessed 15 October 2016].

Ferrera, M. (1996) The 'Southern Model' of Welfare in Social Europe, *Journal of European Social Policy*, Vol. 6 (1), pp. 17–37.

Fisac, R. and Moreno-Romero, A. (2015) Understanding social enterprise country models: Spain, *Social Enterprise Journal*, Vol. 11 No. 2, pp. 156–177.

Flora, P. and Heidenheimer, A. J. (eds) (1981) *The Development of Welfare States in Europe and America*, New Brunswick: Transaction Books.

Eisenhardt, K.M. (1989) Building theories from case study research, *Academy of Management Review*, Vol. 14 (4), pp. 532–550.

Kerlin, J. A. (2010) A Comparative Analysis of the Global Emergence of Social Enterprise, *Voluntas: International Journal of Voluntary and Nonprofit Organizations*, Vol. 21 (2), pp. 162–179.

Kerlin, J. A. (2013) Defining Social Enterprise across Different Contexts: A Conceptual Framework Based on Institutional Factors, *Nonprofit and Voluntary Sector Quarterly*, Vol. 42 (1), pp. 84–108.

Monroe-White, T., Kerlin, J. and Zook, S. (2015) A Quantitative Critique of Kerlin's Macro-Institutional Social Enterprise Framework, *Social Enterprise Journal*, Vol. 11 (2), pp. 178–201.

Nyssens, M. (ed.) (2006) *Social Enterprise. At the Crossroads of Market, Public Policies and Civil Society*, London: Routledge.

Pérez-Díaz, V. (2014) Civil Society: A Multi-layered Concept, *Current Sociology Review*, Vol. 62 (6), pp. 812–830.

Rueschemeyer, D., Huber, E. H. and Stephens, J. D. (1992) Capitalist Development & Democracy, *Contemporary Sociology*, Vol. 72 (3), pp. 243–248.

Salamon, L. M. and Sokolowski, S. W. (2002) *Social Origins of Civil Society: Working Papers of the Johns Hopkins Comparative Nonprofit Sector Project*, Baltimore, MD: Johns Hopkins Center for Civil Society Studies.

Salamon, L. M. and Sokolowski, S. W. (2010), *Global Civil Society: Dimensions of the Nonprofit Sector*, 3rd ed., Greenwich: Kumarian Press.

Salinas, F. and Rubio, M. J. (2001), Tendencias en la evolución de las organizaciones no lucrativas hacia la empresa social. In *Revista de Economía Pública, Social y Cooperativa*, Vol. 37, 79–116, Valencia: CIRIEC España.

Sedelmeier, U. (2015) *Europe after the Eastern Enlargement of the European Union: 2004–2014*, Berlin: Heinrich Böll Stiftung. Available at http://eu.boell.org/sites/default/files/uploads/2014/06/eastern_enlargement.pdf [accessed 15 July 2016].

Skocpol, T. (1979) *States and Social Revolutions: A Comparative Analysis of France, Russia, and China*, Cambridge: Cambridge University Press.

Suchman, M. C. (1995) Managing Legitimacy: Strategic and Institutional Approaches, *Academy of Management Review*, Vol. 20 (3), pp. 571–610.

Tiessen, J. H. (1997) Individualism, Collectivism and Entrepreneurship: A Framework for International Comparative Research, *Journal of Business Venturing*, Vol. 12, pp. 367–384.

Index

Note: Endnotes are indicated by the page number followed by "n" and the note number